Ceph Cookbook

Over 100 effective recipes to help you design, implement, and manage the software-defined and massively scalable Ceph storage system

Karan Singh

PUBLISHING

BIRMINGHAM - MUMBAI

Ceph Cookbook

First published: February 2016

Production reference: 1250216

Published by Packt Publishing Ltd.
Livery Place
35 Livery Street
Birmingham B3 2PB, UK.

ISBN 978-1-78439-350-2

www.packtpub.com

Credits

Author
Karan Singh

Reviewers
Christian Eichelmann

Haruka Iwao

Commissioning Editor
Amarabha Banerjee

Acquisition Editor
Meeta Rajani

Content Development Editor
Kajal Thapar

Technical Editor
Menza Mathew

Copy Editor
Angad Singh

Project Coordinator
Shweta H Birwatkar

Proofreader
Safis Editing

Indexer
Rekha Nair

Production Coordinator
Melwyn Dsa

Cover Work
Melwyn Dsa

Foreword

One year ago, Karan published his first book, *Learning Ceph, Packt Publishing*, which has been a great success. It addressed a need that a lot of users had: an easy-to-understand introduction to Ceph and an overview of its architecture.

When an open source project has an enthusiastic community like Ceph does, the innovation and evolution of features happen at a rapid pace. Besides the core development team around Sage Weil at Red Hat, industry heavyweights such as Intel, SanDisk, Fujitsu, and Suse, as well as countless other individuals, have made substantial contributions. As a result, the project continues to mature both in capability and stability; the latter playing a key role in enterprise deployments. Many features and components that are now a part of Ceph were only in their infancy when *Learning Ceph, Packt Publishing*, came out; erasure encoding, optimized performance for SSDs, and the Virtual Storage Manager (VSM) are just a couple of examples. All of these are covered in great detail in this new book that you are holding in your hands right now.

The other day, I read a blog where the author likened the significance of Ceph to the storage industry to the impact that Linux had on operating systems. While it is still too early to make that call, its adoption in the industry speaks for itself, with multi-petabyte-sized deployments becoming more and more common. Large-scale users such as CERN and Yahoo are regularly sharing their experiences with the community.

The wealth of capabilities and the enormous flexibility to adapt to a wide range of use cases can sometimes make it difficult to approach this new technology, and it can leave new users wondering where to start their learning journeys. Not everybody has access to massive data centers with thousands of servers and disks to experiment and build their own experiences. Karan's new book, *Ceph Cookbook, Packt Publishing*, is meant to help by providing practical, hands-on advice for the many challenges you will encounter.

As a long-time Ceph enthusiast, I have worked with Karan for several years and congratulate him on his passion and initiative to compile a comprehensive guide for first-time users of Ceph. It will be a useful guide to those embarking on deploying the open source community version of Ceph.

This book complements the more technical documentation and collateral developed by members of the Ceph community, filling in the gaps with useful commentary and advice for new users.

If you are downloading the Ceph community version, kicking its tires, and trying it out at home or on your non-mission-critical workloads in the enterprise, this book is for you. Expect to learn to deploy and manage Ceph step by step along with tips and use cases for deploying Ceph's features and functionality on certain storage workloads.

Now, it's time to begin reading about the ingredients you'll need to cook up your own Ceph software-defined storage deployment. But hurry— the new exciting features, such as production-ready CephFS and support for containers, are already in the pipeline, and I am looking forward to seeing Karan's next book in another year from now.

Dr. Wolfgang Schulze

Director of Global Storage Consulting, Red Hat

About the Author

Karan Singh is an IT expert and tech evangelist, living with his beautiful wife, Monika, in Finland. He holds a bachelor's degree, with honors, in computer science, and a master's degree in system engineering from BITS, Pilani. Apart from this, he is a certified professional for technologies such as OpenStack, NetApp, Oracle Solaris, and Linux.

Karan is currently working as a System Specialist of Storage and Cloud, for CSC – IT Center for Science Ltd., focusing all his energies on developing IaaS cloud solutions based on OpenStack and Ceph, and building economic multi-petabyte storage systems using Ceph.

Karan possesses a rich skill set and has strong work experience in a variety of storage solutions, cloud technologies, automation tools and Unix systems. He is also the author of the very first book on Ceph, titled *Learning Ceph*, published in 2015.

Karan devotes a part of his time to R&D and learning new technologies. When not working on Ceph and OpenStack, Karan can be found working with emerging technologies or automating stuffs. He loves writing about technologies and is an avid blogger at `www.ksingh.co.in`. You can reach him on Twitter `@karansingh010`, or by e-mail at `karan_singh1@live.com`.

I'd like to thank my wife, Monika, for preparing delicious food while I was writing this book. Kiitos MJ, you are a great chef, *Minä rakastan sinua*.

I would like to take this opportunity to thank my company, CSC – IT Center for Science Ltd., and all my colleagues with whom I have worked and made memories. CSC, you are an amazing place to work, kiitos.

I'd also like to express my thanks to the vibrant Ceph community and its ecosystem for developing, improving, and supporting Ceph.

Finally, my sincere thanks to the entire Packt Publishing team, and also to the technical reviewers, for their state-of-the-art work during the course of this project.

About the Reviewers

Christian Eichelmann has worked as a System Engineer and an IT architect in Germany for several years, in a lot of different companies. He has been using Ceph since its early alpha releases and is currently running several Petabyte-scale clusters. He also developed `ceph-dash`: a popular monitoring dashboard for Ceph.

Haruka Iwao is an ads solutions engineer with Google. She worked as a storage solutions architect at Red Hat and has contributed to the Ceph community, especially in Japan. She also has work experience as a site reliability engineer at a few start-ups in Tokyo, and she is interested in site reliability engineering and large-scale computing. She studied distributed filesystems in her master's course at the University of Tsukuba.

www.PacktPub.com

eBooks, discount offers, and more

Did you know that Packt offers eBook versions of every book published, with PDF and ePub files available? You can upgrade to the eBook version at `www.PacktPub.com` and as a print book customer, you are entitled to a discount on the eBook copy. Get in touch with us at `customercare@packtpub.com` for more details.

At `www.PacktPub.com`, you can also read a collection of free technical articles, sign up for a range of free newsletters and receive exclusive discounts and offers on Packt books and eBooks.

`https://www2.packtpub.com/books/subscription/packtlib`

Do you need instant solutions to your IT questions? PacktLib is Packt's online digital book library. Here, you can search, access, and read Packt's entire library of books.

Why Subscribe?

- Fully searchable across every book published by Packt
- Copy and paste, print, and bookmark content
- On demand and accessible via a web browser

Table of Contents

Preface

We are a part of a digital world that is producing an enormous amount of data each second. The data growth is unimaginable and it's predicted that humankind will possess 40 Zettabytes of data by 2020. Well that's not too much, but how about 2050? Should we guesstimate a Yottabyte? The obvious question arises: do we have any way to store this gigantic data, or are we prepared for the future? To me, Ceph is the ray of hope and the technology that can be a possible answer to the data storage needs of the next decade. Ceph is the future of storage.

It's a great saying that "Software is eating the world". Well that's true. However, from another angle, software is the feasible way to go for various computing needs, such as computing weather, networking, storage, datacenters, and burgers, ummm...well, not burgers currently. As you already know, the idea behind a software-defined solution is to build all the intelligence in software itself and use commodity hardware to solve your greatest problem. And I think, this software-defined approach should be the answer to the future's computing problems.

Ceph is a true open source, software-defined storage solution, purposely built to handle unprecedented data growth with linear performance improvement. It provides a unified storage experience for file, object, and block storage interfaces from the same system. The beauty of Ceph is its distributed, scalable nature, and performance; reliability and robustness come along with these attributes. And furthermore, it is pocket friendly, that is, economical, providing you more value for each dollar you spent.

Ceph is the next big thing that has happened to the storage industry. Its enterprise class features such as scalability, reliability, erasure coding, cache tiering and counting, has led to its maturity that has improved significantly in the last few years. To name a few, there are organizations such as CERN, Yahoo, and DreamHost where multi-PB Ceph cluster is being deployed and is running successfully.

It's been a while since block and object interfaces of Ceph have been introduced and they are now fully developed. Until last year, CephFS was the only component that was lacking production readiness. This year, my bet is on CephFS as it's going to be production-ready in Ceph Jewel. I can't wait to see CephFS production adoption stories. There are a few more areas where Ceph is gaining popularity, such as AFA (All Flash Array), database workloads, storage for containers, and Hyper Converge Infrastructure. Well, Ceph has just begun; the best is yet to come.

In this book, we will take a deep dive to understand Ceph—covering components and architecture including its working. The Ceph Cookbook focuses on hands-on knowledge by providing you with step-by-step guidance with the help of recipes. Right from the first chapter, you will gain practical experience of Ceph by following the recipes. With each chapter, you will learn and play around with interesting concepts of Ceph. I hope, by the end of this book, you will feel competent regarding Ceph, both conceptually as well as practically, and you will be able to operate your Ceph storage infrastructure with confidence and success.

Happy Learning

Karan Singh

What this book covers

Chapter 1, Ceph – Introduction and Beyond, covers an introduction to Ceph, gradually moving towards RAID and its challenges, and Ceph architectural overview. Finally, we will go through Ceph installation and configuration.

Chapter 2, Working with Ceph Block Device, covers an introduction to Ceph Block Device and provisioning of the Ceph block device. We will also go through RBD snapshots, clones, as well as storage options for OpenStack cinder, glance, and nova.

Chapter 3, Working with Ceph Object Storage, deep dives into Ceph object storage including RGW standard and federated setup, S3, and OpenStack Swift access. Finally, we will set up file sync and service using ownCloud.

Chapter 4, Working with the Ceph Filesystem, covers an introduction to CephFS, deploying and accessing MDS and CephFS via kernel, Fuse, and NFS-Ganesha. You will also learn how to access CephFS via Ceph-Dokan Windows client.

Chapter 5, Monitoring Ceph Clusters using Calamari, includes Ceph monitoring via CLI, an introduction to Calamari, and setting up of Calamari server and clients. We will also cover monitoring of Ceph cluster via Calamari GUI as well as troubleshooting Calamari.

Chapter 6, Operating and Managing a Ceph Cluster, covers Ceph service management and scaling up and scaling down a Ceph cluster. This chapter also includes failed disk replacement and upgrading Ceph infrastructure.

Chapter 7, Ceph under the Hood, explores Ceph CRUSH map, understanding the internals of CRUSH map, followed by Ceph authentication and authorization. This chapter also covers dynamic cluster management and the understanding of Ceph PG. Finally, we created the specifics required for specific hardware.

Chapter 8, Production Planning and Performance Tuning for Ceph, covers the planning of Cluster production deployment and HW and SW planning for Ceph. This chapter also includes Ceph recommendation and performance tuning. Finally, this chapter covers erasure coding and cache tiering.

Chapter 9, The Virtual Storage Manager for Ceph, is dedicated to Virtual Storage Manager (VSM), covering its introduction and architecture. We will also go through the deployment of VSM and then the creation of a Ceph cluster using VSM and manage it.

Chapter 10, More on Ceph, the final chapter of the book, covers Ceph benchmarking, Ceph troubleshooting using admin socket, API, and the ceph-objectstore tool. This chapter also covers the deployment of Ceph using Ansible and Ceph memory profiling.

What you need for this book

The various software components required to follow the instructions in the chapters are as follows:

- VirtualBox 4.0 or higher (`https://www.virtualbox.org/wiki/Downloads`)
- GIT (`http://www.git-scm.com/downloads`)
- Vagrant 1.5.0 or higher (`https://www.vagrantup.com/downloads.html`)
- CentOS operating system 7.0 or higher (`http://wiki.centos.org/Download`)
- Ceph software packages Version 0.87.0 or higher (`http://ceph.com/resources/downloads/`)
- S3 Client, typically S3cmd (`http://s3tools.org/download`)
- Python-swift client
- ownCloud 7.0.5 or higher (`https://download.owncloud.org/download/repositories/stable/owncloud/`)
- NFS Ganesha
- Ceph Fuse
- Ceph-Dokan
- Ceph-Calamari (`https://github.com/ceph/calamari.git`)
- Diamond (`https://github.com/ceph/Diamond.git`)
- Ceph Calamari Client, romana (`https://github.com/ceph/romana`)

- ▶ Virtual Storage Manager 2.0 or higher (`https://github.com/01org/virtual-storagemanager/releases/tag/v2.1.0`)
- ▶ Ansible 1.9 or higher (`http://docs.ansible.com/ansible/intro_installation.html`)
- ▶ OpenStack RDO (`http://rdo.fedorapeople.org/rdo-release.rpm`)

Who this book is for

This book is aimed at storage and cloud system engineers, system administrators, and technical architects and consultants who are interested in building software-defined storage solutions around Ceph to power their cloud and virtual infrastructure. If you have a basic knowledge of GNU/Linux and storage systems, with no experience of software-defined storage solutions and Ceph, but are eager to learn, this book is for you.

Sections

In this book, you will find several headings that appear frequently (Getting ready, How to do it, How it works, There's more, and See also).

To give clear instructions on how to complete a recipe, we use these sections as follows:

Getting ready

This section tells you what to expect in the recipe, and describes how to set up any software or any preliminary settings required for the recipe.

How to do it...

This section contains the steps required to follow the recipe.

How it works...

This section usually consists of a detailed explanation of what happened in the previous section.

There's more...

This section consists of additional information about the recipe in order to make the reader more knowledgeable about the recipe.

See also

This section provides helpful links to other useful information for the recipe.

Conventions

In this book, you will find a number of text styles that distinguish between different kinds of information. Here are some examples of these styles and an explanation of their meaning.

Code words in text, database table names, folder names, filenames, file extensions, pathnames, dummy URLs, user input, and Twitter handles are shown as follows: "To do this, we need to edit `/etc/nova/nova.conf` on the OpenStack node and add the following perform the steps that are given in the following section."

A block of code is set as follows:

```
inject_partition=-2
images_type=rbd
images_rbd_pool=vms
images_rbd_ceph_conf=/etc/ceph/ceph.conf
```

When we wish to draw your attention to a particular part of a code block, the relevant lines or items are set in bold:

```
inject_partition=-2
images_type=rbd
images_rbd_pool=vms
images_rbd_ceph_conf=/etc/ceph/ceph.conf
```

Any command-line input or output is written as follows:

```
# rados -p cache-pool ls
```

New terms and **important words** are shown in bold. Words that you see on the screen, for example, in menus or dialog boxes, appear in the text like this: "Navigate to the **Options defined in nova.virt.libvirt.volume** section and add the following lines of code:"

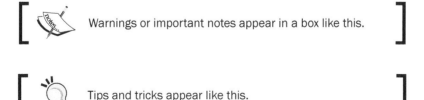

Warnings or important notes appear in a box like this.

Tips and tricks appear like this.

Reader feedback

Feedback from our readers is always welcome. Let us know what you think about this book—what you liked or disliked. Reader feedback is important for us as it helps us develop titles that you will really get the most out of.

To send us general feedback, simply e-mail `feedback@packtpub.com`, and mention the book's title in the subject of your message.

If there is a topic that you have expertise in and you are interested in either writing or contributing to a book, see our author guide at `www.packtpub.com/authors`.

Customer support

Now that you are the proud owner of a Packt book, we have a number of things to help you to get the most from your purchase.

Downloading the example code

You can download the example code files from your account at `http://www.packtpub.com` for all the Packt Publishing books you have purchased. If you purchased this book elsewhere, you can visit `http://www.packtpub.com/support` and register to have the files e-mailed directly to you.

Errata

Although we have taken every care to ensure the accuracy of our content, mistakes do happen. If you find a mistake in one of our books—maybe a mistake in the text or the code—we would be grateful if you could report this to us. By doing so, you can save other readers from frustration and help us improve subsequent versions of this book. If you find any errata, please report them by visiting `http://www.packtpub.com/submit-errata`, selecting your book, clicking on the **Errata Submission Form** link, and entering the details of your errata. Once your errata are verified, your submission will be accepted and the errata will be uploaded to our website or added to any list of existing errata under the Errata section of that title.

To view the previously submitted errata, go to `https://www.packtpub.com/books/content/support` and enter the name of the book in the search field. The required information will appear under the **Errata** section.

Piracy

Piracy of copyrighted material on the Internet is an ongoing problem across all media. At Packt, we take the protection of our copyright and licenses very seriously. If you come across any illegal copies of our works in any form on the Internet, please provide us with the location address or website name immediately so that we can pursue a remedy.

Please contact us at `copyright@packtpub.com` with a link to the suspected pirated material.

We appreciate your help in protecting our authors and our ability to bring you valuable content.

Questions

If you have a problem with any aspect of this book, you can contact us at `questions@packtpub.com`, and we will do our best to address the problem.

1
Ceph – Introduction and Beyond

In this chapter, we will cover the following recipes:

- ▸ Ceph – the beginning of a new era
- ▸ RAID – the end of an era
- ▸ Ceph – the architectural overview
- ▸ Planning the Ceph deployment
- ▸ Setting up a virtual infrastructure
- ▸ Installing and configuring Ceph
- ▸ Scaling up your Ceph cluster
- ▸ Using Ceph clusters with a hands-on approach

Introduction

Ceph is currently the hottest **Software Defined Storage** (**SDS**) technology that is shaking up the entire storage industry. It is an open source project that provides unified software defined solutions for **Block**, **File**, and **Object** storage. The core idea of Ceph is to provide a distributed storage system that is massively scalable and high performing with no single point of failure. From the roots, it has been designed to be highly scalable (up to the exabyte level and beyond) while running on general-purpose commodity hardware.

Ceph is acquiring most of the traction in the storage industry due to its open, scalable, and reliable nature. This is the era of cloud computing and software defined infrastructure, where we need a storage backend that is purely software defined, and more importantly, cloud ready. Ceph fits in here very well, regardless of whether you are running a public, private, or hybrid cloud.

Today's software systems are very smart and make the best use of commodity hardware to run gigantic scale infrastructure. Ceph is one of them; it intelligently uses commodity hardware to provide enterprise-grade robust and highly reliable storage systems.

Ceph has been raised and nourished with an architectural philosophy that includes the following:

- Every component must scale linearly
- There should not be any single point of failure
- The solution must be software-based, open source, and adaptable
- Ceph software should run on readily available commodity hardware
- Every component must be self-managing and self-healing wherever possible

The foundation of Ceph lies in the objects, which are its building blocks, and object storage like Ceph is the perfect provision for the current and future needs for unstructured data storage. Object storage has its advantages over traditional storage solutions; we can achieve platform and hardware independence using object storage. Ceph plays meticulously with objects and replicates them across the cluster to avail reliability; in Ceph, objects are not tied to a physical path, making object location independent. Such flexibility enables Ceph to scale linearly from the petabyte to exabyte level.

Ceph provides great performance, enormous scalability, power, and flexibility to organizations. It helps them get rid of expensive proprietary storage silos. Ceph is indeed an enterprise class storage solution that runs on commodity hardware; it is a low-cost yet feature rich storage system. The Ceph universal storage system provides Block, File, and Object storage under one hood, enabling customers to use storage as they want.

Ceph Releases

Ceph is being developed and improved at a rapid pace. On July 3, 2012, Sage announced the first LTS release of Ceph with the code name, Argonaut. Since then, we have seen seven new releases come up. Ceph releases are categorized as **LTS** (**Long Term Support**), and development releases and every alternate Ceph release is an LTS release. For more information, please visit `https://Ceph.com/category/releases/`.

Ceph release name	Ceph release version	Released On
Argonaut	V0.48 (LTS)	July 3, 2012
Bobtail	V0.56 (LTS)	January 1, 2013
Cuttlefish	V0.61	May 7, 2013
Dumpling	V0.67 (LTS)	August 14, 2013
Emperor	V0.72	November 9, 2013
Firefly	V0.80 (LTS)	May 7, 2014

Ceph release name	Ceph release version	Released On
Giant	V0.87.1	Feb 26, 2015
Hammer	V0.94 (LTS)	April 7, 2015
Infernalis	V9.0.0	May 5, 2015
Jewel	V10.0.0	Nov, 2015

Here is a fact: Ceph release names follow alphabetic order; the next one will be a "K" release.

The term "Ceph" is a common nickname given to pet octopuses and is considered a short form of "Cephalopod", which is a class of marine animals that belong to the mollusk phylum. Ceph has octopuses as its mascot, which represents Ceph's highly parallel behavior, similar to octopuses.

Ceph – the beginning of a new era

Data storage requirements have grown explosively over the last few years. Research shows that data in large organizations is growing at a rate of 40 to 60 percent annually, and many companies are doubling their data footprint each year. IDC analysts estimated that worldwide, there were 54.4 exabytes of total digital data in the year 2000. By 2007, this reached 295 exabytes, and by 2020, it's expected to reach 44 zettabytes worldwide. Such data growth cannot be managed by traditional storage systems; we need a system like Ceph, which is distributed, scalable and most importantly, economically viable. Ceph has been designed especially to handle today's as well as the future's data storage needs.

Software Defined Storage (SDS)

SDS is what is needed to reduce TCO for your storage infrastructure. In addition to reduced storage cost, an SDS can offer flexibility, scalability, and reliability. Ceph is a true SDS solution; it runs on commodity hardware with no vendor lock-in and provides low cost per GB. Unlike traditional storage systems where hardware gets married to software, in SDS, you are free to choose commodity hardware from any manufacturer and are free to design a heterogeneous hardware solution for your own needs. Ceph's software-defined storage on top of this hardware provides all the intelligence you need and will take care of everything, providing all the enterprise storage features right from the software layer.

Cloud storage

One of the drawbacks of a cloud infrastructure is the storage. Every cloud infrastructure needs a storage system that is reliable, low-cost, and scalable with a tighter integration than its other cloud components. There are many traditional storage solutions out there in the market that claim to be cloud ready, but today we not only need cloud readiness, but a lot more beyond that. We need a storage system that should be fully integrated with cloud systems and can provide lower TCO without any compromise to reliability and scalability. The cloud systems are software defined and are built on top of commodity hardware; similarly, it needs a storage system that follows the same methodology, that is, being software defined on top of commodity hardware, and Ceph is the best choice available for cloud use cases.

Ceph has been rapidly evolving and bridging the gap of a true cloud storage backend. It is grabbing center stage with every major open source cloud platform, namely OpenStack, CloudStack, and OpenNebula. Moreover, Ceph has succeeded in building up beneficial partnerships with cloud vendors such as Red Hat, Canonical, Mirantis, SUSE, and many more. These companies are favoring Ceph big time and including it as an official storage backend for their cloud OpenStack distributions, thus making Ceph a red hot technology in cloud storage space.

The OpenStack project is one of the finest examples of open source software powering public and private clouds. It has proven itself as an end-to-end open source cloud solution. OpenStack is a collection of programs, such as cinder, glance, and swift, which provide storage capabilities to OpenStack. These OpenStack components required a reliable, scalable, and all in one storage backend like Ceph. For this reason, Openstack and Ceph communities have been working together for many years to develop a fully compatible Ceph storage backend for the OpenStack.

Cloud infrastructure based on Ceph provides much needed flexibility to service providers to build Storage-as-a-Service and Infrastructure-as-a-Service solutions, which they cannot achieve from other traditional enterprise storage solutions as they are not designed to fulfill cloud needs. By using Ceph, service providers can offer low-cost, reliable cloud storage to their customers.

Unified next generation storage architecture

The definition of unified storage has changed lately. A few years ago, the term "unified storage" referred to providing file and block storage from a single system. Now, because of recent technological advancements, such as cloud computing, big data, and Internet of Things, a new kind of storage has been evolving, that is, object storage. Thus, all the storage systems that do not support object storage are not really unified storage solutions. A true unified storage is like Ceph; it supports blocks, files, and object storage from a single system.

In Ceph, the term "unified storage" is more meaningful than what existing storage vendors claim to provide. Ceph has been designed from the ground up to be future ready, and it's constructed such that it can handle enormous amounts of data. When we call Ceph "future ready", we mean to focus on its object storage capabilities, which is a better fit for today's mix of unstructured data rather than blocks or files. Everything in Ceph relies on intelligent objects, whether it's block storage or file storage. Rather than managing blocks and files underneath, Ceph manages objects and supports block-and-file-based storage on top of it. Objects provide enormous scaling with increased performance by eliminating metadata operations. Ceph uses an algorithm to dynamically compute where the object should be stored and retrieved from.

The traditional storage architecture of a SAN and NAS system is very limited. Basically, they follow the tradition of controller high availability, that is, if one storage controller fails it serves data from the second controller. But, what if the second controller fails at the same time, or even worse, if the entire disk shelf fails? In most cases, you will end up losing your data. This kind of storage architecture, which cannot sustain multiple failures, is definitely what we do not want today. Another drawback of traditional storage systems is its data storage and access mechanism. It maintains a central lookup table to keep track of metadata, which means that every time a client sends a request for a read or write operation, the storage system first performs a lookup in the huge metadata table, and after receiving the real data location, it performs client operation. For a smaller storage system, you might not notice performance hits, but think of a large storage cluster—you would definitely be bound by performance limits with this approach. This would even restrict your scalability.

Ceph does not follow such traditional storage architecture; in fact, the architecture has been completely reinvented. Rather than storing and manipulating metadata, Ceph introduces a newer way: the CRUSH algorithm. CRUSH stands for **Controlled Replication Under Scalable Hashing**. Instead of performing lookup in the metadata table for every client request, the CRUSH algorithm computes on demand where the data should be written to or read from. By computing metadata, the need to manage a centralized table for metadata is no longer there. The modern computers are amazingly fast and can perform a CRUSH lookup very quickly; moreover, this computing load, which is generally not too much, can be distributed across cluster nodes, leveraging the power of distributed storage. In addition to this, CRUSH has a unique property, which is infrastructure awareness. It understands the relationship between various components of your infrastructure and stores your data in a unique failure zone, such as a disk, node, rack, row, and datacenter room, among others. CRUSH stores all the copies of your data such that it is available even if a few components fail in a failure zone. It is due to CRUSH that Ceph can handle multiple component failures and provide reliability and durability.

The CRUSH algorithm makes Ceph self-managing and self-healing. In an event of component failure in a failure zone, CRUSH senses which component has failed and determines the effect on the cluster. Without any administrative intervention, CRUSH self-manages and self-heals by performing a recovering operation for the data lost due to failure. CRUSH regenerates the data from the replica copies that the cluster maintains. If you have configured the Ceph CRUSH map in the correct order, it makes sure that at least one copy of your data is always accessible. Using CRUSH, we can design a highly reliable storage infrastructure with no single point of failure. It makes Ceph a highly scalable and reliable storage system that is future ready.

RAID – the end of an era

RAID technology has been the fundamental building block for storage systems for years. It has proven successful for almost every kind of data that has been generated in the last 3 decades. But all eras must come to an end, and this time, it's RAID's turn. These systems have started showing limitations and are incapable of delivering to future storage needs. In the course of the last few years, cloud infrastructures have gained a strong momentum and are imposing new requirements on storage and challenging traditional RAID systems. In this section, we will uncover the limitations imposed by RAID systems.

RAID rebuilds are painful

The most painful thing in RAID technology is its super-lengthy rebuild process. Disk manufacturers are packing lots of storage capacity per disk. They are now producing an extra-large capacity of disk drives at a fraction of the price. We no longer talk about 450 GB, 600 GB, or even 1 TB disks, as there are larger capacity of disks available today. The newer enterprise disks specification offers disks up to 4 TB, 6 TB, and even 10 TB disk drives, and the capacities keep increasing year by year.

Think of an enterprise RAID-based storage system that is made up of numerous 4 or 6 TB disk drives. Unfortunately, when such a disk drive fails, RAID will take several hours and even up to days to repair a single failed disk. Meanwhile, if another drive fails from the same RAID group then it would become a chaotic situation. Repairing multiple large disk drives using RAID is a cumbersome process.

RAID spare disks increases TCO

The RAID system requires a few disks as hot spare disks. These are just free disks that will be used only when a disk fails, else they will not be used for data storage. This adds extra cost to the system and increases TCO. Moreover, if you're running short of spare disks and immediately a disk fails in the RAID group, then you will face a severe problem.

RAID can be expensive and hardware dependent

RAID requires a set of identical disk drivers in a single RAID group; you would face penalties if you change the disk size, rpm, or disk type. Doing so would adversely affect the capacity and performance of your storage system. This makes RAID highly choosy on hardware.

Also, enterprise RAID-based systems often require expensive hardware components, such as RAID controllers, which significantly increases the system cost. These RAID controllers will become the single points of failure if you do not have many of them.

The growing RAID group is a challenge

RAID can hit a dead end when it's not possible to grow the RAID group size, which means that there is no scale out support. After a point, you cannot grow your RAID-based system, even though you have money. Some systems allow the addition of disk shelves, but up to a very limited capacity; however, these new disk shelves put a load on the existing storage controller. So, you can gain some capacity, but with a performance tradeoff.

The RAID reliability model is no longer promising

RAID can be configured with a variety of different types; the most common types are RAID5 and RAID6, which can survive the failure of one and two disks respectively. RAID cannot ensure data reliability after a two-disk failure. This is one of the biggest drawbacks with RAID systems.

Moreover, at the time of a RAID rebuild operation, client requests are most likely to starve for IO until the rebuild completes. Another limiting factor with RAID is that it only protects against disk failure; it cannot protect against a failure of the network, server hardware, OS, power, or other datacenter disasters.

After discussing RAID's drawbacks, we can come to the conclusion that we now need a system that can overcome all these drawbacks in a performance and cost effective way. The Ceph storage system is one of the best solutions available today to address these problems. Let's see how.

For reliability, Ceph makes use of the data replication method, which means it does not use RAID, thus overcoming all the problems that can be found in a RAID-based enterprise system. Ceph is a software-defined storage, so we do not require any specialized hardware for data replication; moreover, the replication level is highly customized by means of commands, which means that the Ceph storage administrator can manage the replication factor of a minimum of one and maximum of a higher number, totally depending on the underlying infrastructure.

In an event of one or more disk failures, Ceph's replication is a better process than RAID. When a disk drive fails, all the data that was residing on that disk at that point of time starts recovering from its peer disks. Since Ceph is a distributed system, all the data copies are scattered on the entire cluster of disks in the form of objects, such that no two object's copies should reside on the same disk and must reside in a different failure zone defined by the CRUSH map. The good part is all the cluster disks participate in data recovery. This makes the recovery operation amazingly fast with the least performance problems. Further to this, the recovery operation does not require any spare disks; the data is simply replicated to other Ceph disks in the cluster. Ceph uses a weighting mechanism for its disks, thus different disk sizes is not a problem.

In addition to the replication method, Ceph also supports another advanced way of data reliability: using the erasure-coding technique. Erasure coded pools require less storage space as compared to replicated pools. In erasure coding, data is recovered or regenerated algorithmically by erasure code calculation. You can use both the techniques of data availability, that is, replication as well as erasure coding, in the same Ceph cluster but over different storage pools. We will learn more about the erasure coding technique in the coming chapters.

Ceph – the architectural overview

The Ceph internal architecture is pretty straight forward, and we will learn it with the help of the following diagram:

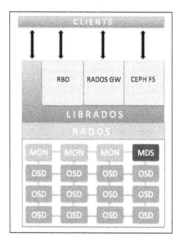

- ▶ **Ceph Monitors** (**MON**): Ceph monitors track the health of the entire cluster by keeping a map of the cluster state. It maintains a separate map of information for each component, which includes an OSD map, MON map, PG map (discussed in later chapters), and CRUSH map. All the cluster nodes report to Monitor nodes and share information about every change in their state. The monitor does not store actual data; this is the job of the OSD.

- ► **Ceph Object Storage Device** (**OSD**): As soon as your application issues a writes operation to the Ceph cluster, data gets stored in the OSD in the form of objects. This is the only component of the Ceph cluster where actual user data is stored, and the same data is retrieved when the client issues a read operation. Usually, one OSD daemon is tied to one physical disk in your cluster. So, in general, the total number of physical disks in your Ceph cluster is the same as the number of OSD daemons working underneath to store user data on each physical disk.

- ► **Ceph Metadata Server** (**MDS**): The MDS keeps track of file hierarchy and stores metadata only for the CephFS filesystem. The Ceph block device and RADOS gateway does not require metadata, hence they do not need the Ceph MDS daemon. The MDS does not serve data directly to clients, thus removing the single point of failure from the system.

- ► **RADOS**: The **Reliable Autonomic Distributed Object Store** (**RADOS**) is the foundation of the Ceph storage cluster. Everything in Ceph is stored in the form of objects, and the RADOS object store is responsible for storing these objects irrespective of their data types. The RADOS layer makes sure that data always remains consistent. To do this, it performs data replication, failure detection and recovery, as well as data migration and rebalancing across cluster nodes.

- ► **librados**: The librados library is a convenient way to gain access to RADOS with support to the PHP, Ruby, Java, Python, C, and C++ programming languages. It provides a native interface for the Ceph storage cluster (RADOS), as well as a base for other services such as RBD, RGW, and CephFS, which are built on top of librados. Librados also supports direct access to RADOS from applications with no HTTP overhead.

- ► **RADOS Block Devices** (**RBDs**): RBDs which are now known as the Ceph block device, provides persistent block storage, which is thin-provisioned, resizable, and stores data striped over multiple OSDs. The RBD service has been built as a native interface on top of librados.

- ► **RADOS Gateway interface** (**RGW**): RGW provides object storage service. It uses librgw (the Rados Gateway Library) and librados, allowing applications to establish connections with the Ceph object storage. The RGW provides RESTful APIs with interfaces that are compatible with Amazon S3 and OpenStack Swift.

- ► **CephFS**: The Ceph File system provides a POSIX-compliant file system that uses the Ceph storage cluster to store user data on a filesystem. Like RBD and RGW, the CephFS service is also implemented as a native interface to librados.

Planning the Ceph deployment

A Ceph storage cluster is created on top of the commodity hardware. This commodity hardware includes industry standard servers loaded with physical disk drives that provide storage capacity and some standard networking infrastructure. These servers run standard Linux distributions and Ceph software on top of them. The following diagram helps you understand a basic view of a Ceph cluster:

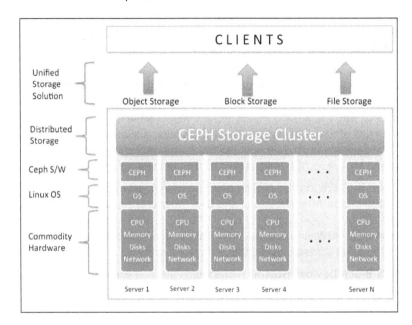

As explained earlier, Ceph does not have a very specific hardware requirement. For the purpose of testing and learning, we can deploy a Ceph cluster on top of virtual machines. In this section and in the later chapters of this book, we will be working on a Ceph cluster which is built on top of virtual machines. It's very convenient to use a virtual environment to test Ceph, as it's fairly easy to set up and can be destroyed and recreated any time. It's good to know that a virtual infrastructure for the Ceph cluster should not be used for a production environment, and you might face serious problems with this.

Setting up a virtual infrastructure

To set up a virtual infrastructure, you will require open source software such as Oracle VirtualBox and Vagrant to automate virtual machine creation for you. Make sure you have the following software installed and working correctly on your host machine. The installation processes of the software are beyond the scope of this book; you can follow their respective documentation in order to get them installed and working correctly.

Getting ready

You will need the following software to get started:

- **Oracle VirtualBox**: This is an open source virtualization software package for host machines based on x86 and AMD64/Intel64. It supports Microsoft Windows, Linux, and Apple MAC OSX host operating systems. Make sure it's installed and working correctly. More information can be found at `https://www.virtualbox.org`. Once you have installed VirtualBox, run the following command to ensure the installation:

  `# VBoxManage --version`

  ```
  HOST:~ ksingh$
  HOST:~ ksingh$ VBoxManage --version
  4.3.22r98236
  HOST:~ ksingh$
  ```

- **Vagrant**: This is software meant for creating virtual development environments. It works as a wrapper around virtualization software such as VirtualBox, VMware, KVM, and so on. It supports the Microsoft Windows, Linux, and Apple MAC OSX host operating systems. Make sure it's installed and working correctly. More information can be found at `https://www.vagrantup.com/`. Once you have installed Vagrant, run the following command to ensure the installation:

  `# vagrant --version`

  ```
  HOST:~ ksingh$
  HOST:~ ksingh$ vagrant --version
  Vagrant 1.7.2
  HOST:~ ksingh$
  ```

- **Git**: This is a distributed revision control system and the most popular and widely adopted version control system for software development. It supports Microsoft Windows, Linux, and Apple MAC OSX operating systems. Make sure it's installed and working correctly. More information can be found at `http://git-scm.com/`. Once you have installed Git, run the following command to ensure the installation:

  `# git --version`

  ```
  HOST:~ ksingh$
  HOST:~ ksingh$ git --version
  git version 1.9.3 (Apple Git-50)
  HOST:~ ksingh$
  ```

How to do it...

Once you have installed the mentioned software, we will then proceed with virtual machine creation:

1. Git clone `ceph-cookbook` repositories to your VirtualBox host machine:

    $ git clone https://github.com/ksingh7/ceph-cookbook.git

    ```
    HOST:~ ksingh$
    HOST:~ ksingh$ git clone https://github.com/ksingh7/ceph-cookbook.git
    Cloning into 'ceph-cookbook'...
    remote: Counting objects: 18, done.
    remote: Compressing objects: 100% (11/11), done.
    remote: Total 18 (delta 5), reused 14 (delta 1), pack-reused 0
    Unpacking objects: 100% (18/18), done.
    Checking connectivity... done.
    HOST:~ ksingh$
    ```

2. Under the cloned directory, you will find `Vagrantfile`, which is our Vagrant configuration file that basically instructs VirtualBox to launch the VMs that we require at different stages of this book. Vagrant will automate the VM's creation, installation, and configuration for you; it makes the initial environment easy to set up:

    $ cd ceph-cookbook ; ls -l

3. Next, we will launch three VMs using Vagrant; they are required throughout this chapter:

    $ vagrant up ceph-node1 ceph-node2 ceph-node3

    ```
    HOST:ceph-cookbook ksingh$
    HOST:ceph-cookbook ksingh$ vagrant up ceph-node1 ceph-node2 ceph-node3
    Bringing machine 'ceph-node1' up with 'virtualbox' provider...
    Bringing machine 'ceph-node2' up with 'virtualbox' provider...
    Bringing machine 'ceph-node3' up with 'virtualbox' provider...
    ==> ceph-node1: Box 'centos7-standard' could not be found. Attempting to find and install...
        ceph-node1: Box Provider: virtualbox
        ceph-node1: Box Version: >= 0
    ```

4. Check the status of your virtual machines:

    $ vagrant status ceph-node1 ceph-node2 ceph-node3

    ```
    HOST:ceph-cookbook ksingh$ vagrant status ceph-node1 ceph-node2 ceph-node3
    Current machine states:

    ceph-node1                running (virtualbox)
    ceph-node2                running (virtualbox)
    ceph-node3                running (virtualbox)

    This environment represents multiple VMs. The VMs are all listed
    above with their current state. For more information about a specific
    VM, run `vagrant status NAME`.
    HOST:ceph-cookbook ksingh$
    ```

The username and password that Vagrant uses to configure virtual machine are `vagrant` and Vagrant has `sudo` rights. The default password for root user is `vagrant`.

5. Vagrant will, by default, set up hostnames as `ceph-node<node_number>`, IP address subnet as `192.168.1.X`, and will create three additional disks that will be used as OSDs by the Ceph cluster. Log in to each of these machines one by one and check if the hostname, networking, and additional disks have been set up correctly by Vagrant:

```
$ vagrant ssh ceph-node1
$ ip addr show
$ sudo fdisk -l
$ exit
```

6. Vagrant is configured to update hosts file on the VMs. For convenience, update the `/etc/hosts` file on your host machine with the following content.

```
192.168.1.101 ceph-node1
192.168.1.102 ceph-node2
192.168.1.103 ceph-node3
```

```
HOST:ceph-cookbook ksingh$
HOST:ceph-cookbook ksingh$ cat /etc/hosts | grep -i ceph-node
192.168.1.101 ceph-node1
192.168.1.102 ceph-node2
192.168.1.103 ceph-node3
HOST:ceph-cookbook ksingh$
```

7. Generate root SSH keys for `ceph-node1` and copy the keys to `ceph-node2` and `ceph-node3`. The password for `root` user on these VMs is `vagrant`. Enter the root user password when it's asked by the `ssh-copy-id` command and proceed with the default settings:

```
$ vagrant ssh ceph-node1
$ sudo su -
# ssh-keygen
# ssh-copy-id root@ceph-node2
# ssh-copy-id root@ceph-node3
```

```
[root@ceph-node1 ~]# ssh-copy-id root@ceph-node2
The authenticity of host 'ceph-node2 (192.168.1.102)' can't be established.
ECDSA key fingerprint is af:2a:a5:74:a7:0b:f5:5b:ef:c5:4b:2a:fe:1d:30:8e.
Are you sure you want to continue connecting (yes/no)? yes
/bin/ssh-copy-id: INFO: attempting to log in with the new key(s), to filter out any that are already installed
/bin/ssh-copy-id: INFO: 1 key(s) remain to be installed -- if you are prompted now it is to install the new keys
root@ceph-node2's password:

Number of key(s) added: 1

Now try logging into the machine, with:   "ssh 'root@ceph-node2'"
and check to make sure that only the key(s) you wanted were added.

[root@ceph-node1 ~]#
```

8. Once the ssh keys are copied to `ceph-node2` and `ceph-node3`, the root user from `ceph-node1` can do an ssh login to VMs without entering the password:

   ```
   # ssh ceph-node2 hostname
   ```

   ```
   # ssh ceph-node3 hostname
   ```

   ```
   [root@ceph-node1 ~]# ssh ceph-node2 hostname
   ceph-node2
   [root@ceph-node1 ~]#
   [root@ceph-node1 ~]# ssh ceph-node3 hostname
   ceph-node3
   [root@ceph-node1 ~]#
   ```

9. Enable ports that are required by the Ceph MON, OSD, and MDS on the operating system's firewall. Execute the following commands on all VMs:

   ```
   # firewall-cmd --zone=public --add-port=6789/tcp --permanent
   ```

   ```
   # firewall-cmd --zone=public --add-port=6800-7100/tcp --permanent
   ```

   ```
   # firewall-cmd --reload
   ```

   ```
   # firewall-cmd --zone=public --list-all
   ```

   ```
   [root@ceph-node1 ~]# firewall-cmd --zone=public --add-port=6789/tcp --permanent
   success
   [root@ceph-node1 ~]# firewall-cmd --zone=public --add-port=6800-7100/tcp --permanent
   success
   [root@ceph-node1 ~]# firewall-cmd --reload
   success
   [root@ceph-node1 ~]#
   [root@ceph-node1 ~]# firewall-cmd --zone=public --list-all
   public (default, active)
     interfaces: enp0s3 enp0s8
     sources:
     services: dhcpv6-client ssh
     ports: 6789/tcp 6800-7100/tcp
     masquerade: no
     forward-ports:
     icmp-blocks:
     rich rules:

   [root@ceph-node1 ~]#
   ```

10. Disable SELINUX on all the VMs:

    ```
    # setenforce 0
    ```

    ```
    # sed -i  s'/SELINUX.*=.*enforcing/SELINUX=disabled'/g /etc/selinux/config
    ```

```
[root@ceph-node1 ~]# setenforce 0
[root@ceph-node1 ~]# sed -i  s'/SELINUX.*=.*enforcing/SELINUX=disabled'/g /etc/selinux/config
[root@ceph-node1 ~]# cat /etc/selinux/config  | grep -i =disabled
SELINUX=disabled
[root@ceph-node1 ~]#
```

11. Install and configure `ntp` on all VMs:

    ```
    # yum install ntp ntpdate -y
    ```

    ```
    # ntpdate pool.ntp.org
    ```

    ```
    # systemctl restart ntpdate.service
    ```

    ```
    # systemctl restart ntpd.service
    ```

    ```
    # systemctl enable ntpd.service
    ```

    ```
    # systemctl enable ntpdate.service
    ```

12. Add repositories on all nodes for the Ceph giant version and update yum:

    ```
    # rpm -Uhv http://ceph.com/rpm-giant/el7/noarch/ceph-release-1-0.
    el7.noarch.rpm
    ```

    ```
    # yum update -y
    ```

```
[root@ceph-node1 ~]# rpm -Uhv http://ceph.com/rpm-giant/el7/noarch/ceph-release-1-0.el7.noarch.rpm
Retrieving http://ceph.com/rpm-giant/el7/noarch/ceph-release-1-0.el7.noarch.rpm
warning: /var/tmp/rpm-tmp.y9SGTx: Header V4 RSA/SHA1 Signature, key ID 17ed316d: NOKEY
Preparing...                          ############################### [100%]
Updating / installing...
   1:ceph-release-1-0.el7             ############################### [100%]
[root@ceph-node1 ~]#
```

Installing and configuring Ceph

To deploy our first Ceph cluster, we will use the `ceph-deploy` tool to install and configure Ceph on all three virtual machines. The `ceph-deploy` tool is a part of the Ceph software-defined storage, which is used for easier deployment and management of your Ceph storage cluster. In the previous section, we created three virtual machines with CentOS7, which have connectivity with the Internet over NAT, as well as private host-only networks.

We will configure these machines as Ceph storage clusters, as mentioned in the following diagram:

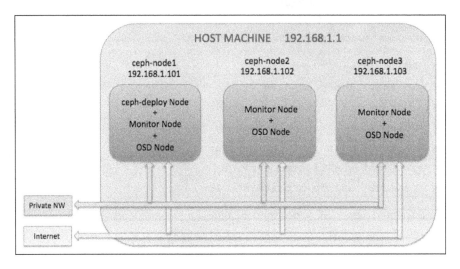

Creating Ceph cluster on ceph-node1

We will first install Ceph and configure `ceph-node1` as the Ceph monitor and the Ceph OSD node. Later recipes in this chapter will introduce `ceph-node2` and `ceph-node3`.

How to do it...

1. Install `ceph-deploy` on `ceph-node1`:

    ```
    # yum install ceph-deploy -y
    ```

2. Next, we will create a Ceph cluster using `ceph-deploy` by executing the following command from `ceph-node1`:

    ```
    # mkdir /etc/ceph ; cd /etc/ceph
    # ceph-deploy new ceph-node1
    ```

    The `new` subcommand in `ceph-deploy` deploys a new cluster with `ceph` as the cluster name, which is by default; it generates a cluster configuration and keying files. List the present working directory; you will find the `ceph.conf` and `ceph.mon.keyring` files:

```
[root@ceph-node1 ceph]# ceph-deploy new ceph-node1
[ceph_deploy.conf][DEBUG ] found configuration file at: /root/.cephdeploy.conf
[ceph_deploy.cli][INFO  ] Invoked (1.5.22): /usr/bin/ceph-deploy new ceph-node1
[ceph_deploy.new][DEBUG ] Creating new cluster named ceph
[ceph_deploy.new][INFO  ] making sure passwordless SSH succeeds
[ceph-node1][DEBUG ] connected to host: ceph-node1
[ceph-node1][DEBUG ] detect platform information from remote host
[ceph-node1][DEBUG ] detect machine type
[ceph-node1][DEBUG ] find the location of an executable
[ceph-node1][INFO  ] Running command: /usr/sbin/ip link show
[ceph-node1][INFO  ] Running command: /usr/sbin/ip addr show
[ceph-node1][DEBUG ] IP addresses found: ['192.168.1.101', '10.0.2.15']
[ceph_deploy.new][DEBUG ] Resolving host ceph-node1
[ceph_deploy.new][DEBUG ] Monitor ceph-node1 at 192.168.1.101
[ceph_deploy.new][DEBUG ] Monitor initial members are ['ceph-node1']
[ceph_deploy.new][DEBUG ] Monitor addrs are ['192.168.1.101']
[ceph_deploy.new][DEBUG ] Creating a random mon key...
[ceph_deploy.new][DEBUG ] Writing monitor keyring to ceph.mon.keyring...
[ceph_deploy.new][DEBUG ] Writing initial config to ceph.conf...
[root@ceph-node1 ceph]#
```

3. To install Ceph software binaries on all the machines using `ceph-deploy`, execute the following command from `ceph-node1`:

   ```
   # ceph-deploy install ceph-node1 ceph-node2 ceph-node3
   ```

   The `ceph-deploy` tool will first install all the dependencies followed by the Ceph Giant binaries. Once the command completes successfully, check the Ceph version and Ceph health on all the nodes, as shown as follows:

   ```
   # ceph -v
   ```

4. Create first the Ceph monitor in `ceph-node1`:

   ```
   # ceph-deploy mon create-initial
   ```

   Once the monitor creation is successful, check your cluster status. Your cluster will not be healthy at this stage:

   ```
   # ceph -s
   ```

```
[root@ceph-node1 ceph]# ceph -s
    cluster 975efaaa-387e-4528-9285-3fcc664c117e
     health HEALTH_ERR 64 pgs stuck inactive; 64 pgs stuck unclean; no osds
     monmap e1: 1 mons at {ceph-node1=192.168.1.101:6789/0}, election epoch 2, quorum 0 ceph-node1
     osdmap e1: 0 osds: 0 up, 0 in
      pgmap v2: 64 pgs, 1 pools, 0 bytes data, 0 objects
            0 kB used, 0 kB / 0 kB avail
                  64 creating
[root@ceph-node1 ceph]#
```

5. Create OSDs on `ceph-node1`:

    1. List the available disks on `ceph-node1`:

        ```
        # ceph-deploy disk list ceph-node1
        ```

        From the output, carefully select the disks (other than the OS partition) on which we should create the Ceph OSD. In our case, the disk names are `sdb`, `sdc`, and `sdd`.

    2. The `disk zap` subcommand would destroy the existing partition table and content from the disk. Before running this command, make sure that you are using the correct disk device name:

        ```
        # ceph-deploy disk zap ceph-node1:sdb ceph-node1:sdc ceph-node1:sdd
        ```

    3. The `osd create` subcommand will first prepare the disk, that is, erase the disk with a filesystem that is xfs by default, and then it will activate the disk's first partition as data partition and its second partition as journal:

        ```
        # ceph-deploy osd create ceph-node1:sdb ceph-node1:sdc ceph-node1:sdd
        ```

    4. Check the Ceph status and notice the OSD count. At this stage, your cluster would not be healthy; we need to add a few more nodes to the Ceph cluster so that it can replicate objects three times (by default) across cluster and attain healthy status. You will find more information on this in the next recipe:

        ```
        # ceph -s
        ```

```
[root@ceph-node1 ceph]# ceph -s
    cluster aade8340-a44b-45f5-9b79-39442daea18d
     health HEALTH_WARN 64 pgs incomplete; 64 pgs stuck inactive; 64 pgs stuck unclean
     monmap e1: 1 mons at {ceph-node1=192.168.1.101:6789/0}, election epoch 2, quorum 0 ceph-node1
     osdmap e11: 3 osds: 3 up, 3 in
      pgmap v17: 64 pgs, 1 pools, 0 bytes data, 0 objects
            67344 kB used, 10152 MB / 10217 MB avail
                  64 incomplete
[root@ceph-node1 ceph]#
```

Scaling up your Ceph cluster

At this point, we have a running Ceph cluster with one MON and three OSDs configured on `ceph-node1`. Now, we will scale up the cluster by adding `ceph-node2` and `ceph-node3` as MON and OSD nodes.

How to do it...

A Ceph storage cluster requires at least one monitor to run. For high availability, a Ceph storage cluster relies on an odd number of monitors and more than one, for example, 3 or 5, to form a quorum. It uses the Paxos algorithm to maintain quorum majority. Since we already have one monitor running on `ceph-node1`, let's create two more monitors for our Ceph cluster:

1. Add a public network address to the `/etc/ceph/ceph.conf` file on `ceph-node1`:

   public network = 192.168.1.0/24

2. From `ceph-node1`, use `ceph-deploy` to create a monitor on `ceph-node2`:

   # ceph-deploy mon create ceph-node2

3. Repeat this step to create a monitor on `ceph-node3`:

   # ceph-deploy mon create ceph-node3

4. Check the status of your Ceph cluster; it should show three monitors in the MON section:

   # ceph -s

   # ceph mon stat

```
[root@ceph-node1 ceph]# ceph -s
    cluster aade8340-a44b-45f5-9b79-39442daea18d
     health HEALTH_WARN 64 pgs incomplete; 64 pgs stuck inactive; 64 pgs stuck unclean
     monmap e3: 3 mons at {ceph-node1=192.168.1.101:6789/0,ceph-node2=192.168.1.102:6789/0,
ceph-node3=192.168.1.103:6789/0}, election epoch 10, quorum 0,1,2 ceph-node1,ceph-node2,cep
h-node3
     osdmap e11: 3 osds: 3 up, 3 in
      pgmap v21: 64 pgs, 1 pools, 0 bytes data, 0 objects
            100792 kB used, 15228 MB / 15326 MB avail
                  64 incomplete
[root@ceph-node1 ceph]#
[root@ceph-node1 ceph]#
[root@ceph-node1 ceph]# ceph mon stat
e3: 3 mons at {ceph-node1=192.168.1.101:6789/0,ceph-node2=192.168.1.102:6789/0,ceph-node3=1
92.168.1.103:6789/0}, election epoch 10, quorum 0,1,2 ceph-node1,ceph-node2,ceph-node3
[root@ceph-node1 ceph]#
```

You will notice that your Ceph cluster is currently showing `HEALTH_WARN`; this is because we have not configured any OSDs other than `ceph-node1`. By default, the date in a Ceph cluster is replicated three times, that too on three different OSDs hosted on three different nodes. Now, we will configure OSDs on `ceph-node2` and `ceph-node3`:

5. Use `ceph-deploy` from `ceph-node1` to perform a disk list, disk zap, and OSD creation on `ceph-node2` and `ceph-node3`:

   ```
   # ceph-deploy disk list ceph-node2 ceph-node3
   ```

   ```
   # ceph-deploy disk zap ceph-node2:sdb ceph-node2:sdc ceph-node2:sdd
   ```

   ```
   # ceph-deploy disk zap ceph-node3:sdb ceph-node3:sdc ceph-node3:sdd
   ```

   ```
   # ceph-deploy osd create ceph-node2:sdb ceph-node2:sdc ceph-node2:sdd
   ```

   ```
   # ceph-deploy osd create ceph-node3:sdb ceph-node3:sdc ceph-node3:sdd
   ```

6. Since we have added more OSDs, we should tune `pg_num` and the `pgp_num` values for the `rbd` pool to achieve a `HEALTH_OK` status for our Ceph cluster:

   ```
   # ceph osd pool set rbd pg_num 256
   ```

   ```
   # ceph osd pool set rbd pgp_num 256
   ```

 Starting the Ceph Hammer release, `rbd` is the only default pool that gets created. Ceph versions before Hammer creates three default pools: `data`, `metadata`, and `rbd`.

7. Check the status of your Ceph cluster; at this stage, your cluster will be healthy.

```
[root@ceph-node1 ceph]# ceph -s
    cluster aade8340-a44b-45f5-9b79-39442daea18d
     health HEALTH_OK
     monmap e3: 3 mons at {ceph-node1=192.168.1.101:6789/0,ceph-node2=192.168.1.102:6789/0
,ceph-node3=192.168.1.103:6789/0}, election epoch 10, quorum 0,1,2 ceph-node1,ceph-node2,c
eph-node3
     osdmap e64: 9 osds: 9 up, 9 in
      pgmap v189: 256 pgs, 1 pools, 0 bytes data, 0 objects
            317 MB used, 45663 MB / 45980 MB avail
                 256 active+clean
[root@ceph-node1 ceph]#
```

Using Ceph cluster with a hands-on approach

Now that we have a running Ceph cluster, we will perform some hands-on practice to gain experience with Ceph, using some basic commands.

How to do it...

1. Check the status of your Ceph installation:

   ```
   # ceph -s  or # ceph status
   ```

2. Watch the cluster health:

   ```
   # ceph -w
   ```

3. Check the Ceph monitor quorum status:

   ```
   # ceph quorum_status --format json-pretty
   ```

4. Dump the Ceph monitor information:

   ```
   # ceph mon dump
   ```

5. Check the cluster usage status:

   ```
   # ceph df
   ```

6. Check the Ceph monitor, OSD, and placement group stats:

   ```
   # ceph mon stat
   # ceph osd stat
   # ceph pg stat
   ```

7. List the placement group:

   ```
   # ceph pg dump
   ```

8. List the Ceph pools:

   ```
   # ceph osd lspools
   ```

9. Check the CRUSH map view of OSDs:

   ```
   # ceph osd tree
   ```

10. List the cluster authentication keys:

    ```
    # ceph auth list
    ```

These were some basic commands that we learned in this section. In the upcoming chapters, we will learn advanced commands for Ceph cluster management.

2
Working with Ceph Block Device

In this chapter, we will cover the following recipes:

- ▶ Working with Ceph Block Device
- ▶ Configuring Ceph client
- ▶ Creating Ceph Block Device
- ▶ Mapping Ceph Block Device
- ▶ Ceph RBD resizing
- ▶ Working with RBD snapshots
- ▶ Working with RBD clones
- ▶ A quick look at OpenStack
- ▶ Ceph – the best match for OpenStack
- ▶ Setting up OpenStack
- ▶ Configuring OpenStack as Ceph clients
- ▶ Configuring Glance for Ceph backend
- ▶ Configuring Cinder for Ceph backend
- ▶ Configuring Nova to attach Ceph RBD
- ▶ Configuring Nova to boot instances from Ceph RBD

Introduction

Once you have installed and configured your Ceph storage cluster, the next task is performing storage provisioning. Storage provisioning is the process of assigning storage space or capacity to physical or virtual servers, either in the form of block, file, or object storage. A typical computer system or server comes with a limited local storage capacity that might not be enough for your data storage needs. Storage solutions such as Ceph provide virtually unlimited storage capacity to these servers, making them capable of storing all your data and making sure that you do not run out of space. Using a dedicated storage system instead of local storage gives you the much-needed flexibility in terms of scalability, reliability, and performance.

Ceph can provision storage capacity in a unified way, which includes block, filesystem, and object storage. The following diagram shows storage formats supported by Ceph, and depending on your use case, you can select one or more storage options:

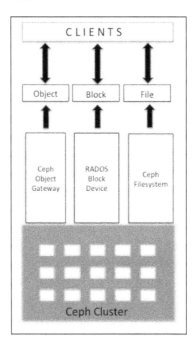

We will discuss each of these options in detail through this book, but in this chapter, we will focus on Ceph block storage.

Working with Ceph Block Device

The **Ceph Block Device**, formerly known as RADOS Block Device, provides reliable, distributed, and high performance block storage disks to clients. A RADOS block device makes use of the `librbd` library and stores a block of data in sequential form striped over multiple OSDs in a Ceph cluster. RBD is backed by the RADOS layer of Ceph, thus every block device is spread over multiple Ceph nodes, delivering high performance and excellent reliability. RBD has native support for Linux kernel, which means that RBD drivers are well integrated with the Linux kernel since past few years. In addition to reliability and performance, RBD also provides enterprise features such as full and incremental snapshots, thin provisioning, copy on write cloning, dynamic resizing, and so on. RBD also supports In-Memory caching, which drastically improves its performance.

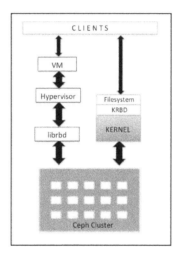

The industry leading open source hypervisors, such as KVM and Zen, provide full support to RBD and leverage its features on their guest virtual machines. Other proprietary hypervisors, such as VMware and Microsoft HyperV will be supported very soon. There has been a lot of work going on in the community to support these hypervisors. The Ceph block device provides full support to cloud platforms such as Open Stack, Cloud Stack, as well as others. It has been proven successful and feature-rich for these cloud platforms. In OpenStack, you can use the Ceph block device with cinder (block) and glance (imaging) components. Doing so, you can spin thousands of **Virtual Machines** (**VMs**) in very little time, taking advantage of the copy on write feature of the Ceph block storage.

All these features make RBD an ideal candidate for cloud platforms such as OpenStack and CloudStack. We will now learn how to create a Ceph block device and make use of it.

Configuring Ceph client

Any regular Linux host (RHEL or Debian-based) can act as a Ceph client. The Client interacts with the Ceph storage cluster over the network to store or retrieve user data. Ceph RBD support has been added to the Linux mainline kernel, starting with 2.6.34 and later versions.

How to do it...

As we have done earlier, we will set up a Ceph client machine using Vagrant and VirtualBox. We will use the same `Vagrantfile` that we cloned in the last chapter. Vagrant will then launch an Ubuntu 14.04 virtual machine that we will configure as a Ceph client:

1. From the directory where we have cloned `ceph-cookbook git repository`, launch the client virtual machine using Vagrant:

   ```
   $ vagrant status client-node1
   ```

   ```
   $ vagrant up client-node1
   ```

   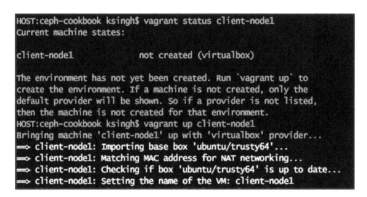

2. Log in to client-node1:

   ```
   $ vagrant ssh client-node1
   ```

    The username and password that Vagrant uses to configure virtual machines is `vagrant`, and Vagrant has sudo rights. The default password for `root` user is `vagrant`.

3. Check OS and kernel release (this is optional):

   ```
   $ lsb_release -a
   ```

   ```
   $ uname -r
   ```

4. Check for RBD support in the kernel:

   ```
   $ sudo modprobe rbd
   ```

   ```
   vagrant@client-node1:~$ lsb_release -a
   No LSB modules are available.
   Distributor ID: Ubuntu
   Description:    Ubuntu 14.04.2 LTS
   Release:        14.04
   Codename:       trusty
   vagrant@client-node1:~$
   vagrant@client-node1:~$ uname -r
   3.13.0-46-generic
   vagrant@client-node1:~$
   vagrant@client-node1:~$ sudo modprobe rbd
   vagrant@client-node1:~$ echo $?
   0
   vagrant@client-node1:~$
   ```

5. Allow `ceph-node1` monitor machine to access `client-node1` over ssh. To do this, copy root ssh keys from `ceph-node1` to `client-node1` Vagrant user. Execute the following commands from `ceph-node1` machine until otherwise specified:

   ```
   ## Login to ceph-node1 machine
   ```

   ```
   $ vagrant ssh ceph-node1
   ```

   ```
   $ sudo su -
   ```

   ```
   # ssh-copy-id vagrant@client-node1
   ```

   Provide a one-time Vagrant user password, that is, `vagrant`, for `client-node1`. Once the ssh keys are copied from `ceph-node1` to `client-node1`, you should able to log in to `client-node1` without a password.

6. Use `ceph-deploy` utility from `ceph-node1` to install Ceph binaries on `client-node1`:

   ```
   # cd /etc/ceph
   ```

   ```
   # ceph-deploy --username vagrant install client-node1
   ```

   ```
   [root@ceph-node1 ceph]# ceph-deploy --username vagrant install client-node1
   [ceph_deploy.conf][DEBUG ] found configuration file at: /root/.cephdeploy.conf
   [ceph_deploy.cli][INFO  ] Invoked (1.5.22): /bin/ceph-deploy --username vagrant install client-node1
   [ceph_deploy.install][DEBUG ] Installing stable version giant on cluster ceph hosts client-node1
   [ceph_deploy.install][DEBUG ] Detecting platform for host client-node1 ...
   [client-node1][DEBUG ] connection detected need for sudo
   [client-node1][DEBUG ] connected to host: vagrant@client-node1
   [client-node1][DEBUG ] detect platform information from remote host
   [client-node1][DEBUG ] detect machine type
   [ceph_deploy.install][INFO  ] Distro info: Ubuntu 14.04 trusty
   [client-node1][INFO  ] installing ceph on client-node1
   ```

7. Copy the Ceph configuration file (`ceph.conf`) to `client-node1`:

   ```
   # ceph-deploy --username vagrant config push client-node1
   ```

8. The client machine will require Ceph keys to access the Ceph cluster. Ceph creates a default user, `client.admin`, which has full access to the Ceph cluster. It's not recommended to share `client.admin` keys with client nodes. The better approach is to create a new Ceph user with separate keys and allow access to specific Ceph pools.

   In our case, we will create a Ceph user, `client.rbd`, with access to the `rbd` pool. By default, Ceph block devices are created on the `rbd` pool:

   ```
   # ceph auth get-or-create client.rbd mon 'allow r' osd 'allow
       class-read object_prefix rbd_children, allow rwx pool=rbd'
   ```

   ```
   [root@ceph-node1 ceph]# ceph auth get-or-create client.rbd mon 'allow r' osd 'allow class-read
    object_prefix rbd_children, allow rwx pool=rbd'
   [client.rbd]
           key = AQCLEg5VeAbGARAAE4ULXC7M5Fwd3BGFDiHRTw==
   [root@ceph-node1 ceph]#
   ```

9. Add the key to `client-node1` machine for `client.rbd` user:

   ```
   # ceph auth get-or-create client.rbd | ssh vagrant@client-node1
   sudo tee /etc/ceph/ceph.client.rbd.keyring
   ```

   ```
   [root@ceph-node1 ceph]# ceph auth get-or-create client.rbd | ssh vagrant@client-node1 sudo tee
    /etc/ceph/ceph.client.rbd.keyring
   [client.rbd]
           key = AQCLEg5VeAbGARAAE4ULXC7M5Fwd3BGFDiHRTw==
   [root@ceph-node1 ceph]#
   ```

10. By this step, `client-node1` should be ready to act as a Ceph client. Check the cluster status from the `client-node1` machine by providing the username and secret key:

    ```
    $ vagrant ssh client-node1
    ```

    ```
    $ sudo su -
    ```

    ```
    # cat /etc/ceph/ceph.client.rbd.keyring >> /etc/ceph/keyring
    ```

    ```
    ### Since we are not using the default user client.admin we need
    to supply username that will connect to Ceph cluster.
    ```

    ```
    # ceph -s --name client.rbd
    ```

    ```
    root@client-node1:~# ceph -s --name client.rbd
        cluster 9609b429-eee2-4e23-af31-28a24fcf5cbc
         health HEALTH_OK
         monmap e3: 3 mons at {ceph-node1=192.168.1.101:6789/0,ceph-node2=192.168.1.102:6789/0,
    ceph-node3=192.168.1.103:6789/0}, election epoch 82, quorum 0,1,2 ceph-node1,ceph-node2,cep
    h-node3
         osdmap e142: 9 osds: 9 up, 9 in
          pgmap v378: 180 pgs, 1 pools, 0 bytes data, 0 objects
                322 MB used, 134 GB / 134 GB avail
                    180 active+clean
    root@client-node1:~#
    ```

Creating Ceph Block Device

Up to now, we have configured Ceph client, and now we will demonstrate creating a Ceph block device from the `client-node1` machine.

How to do it...

1. Create a RADOS Block Device named `rbd1` of size 10240 MB:

   ```
   # rbd create rbd1 --size 10240 --name client.rbd
   ```

2. There are multiple options that you can use to list RBD images:

   ```
   ## The default pool to store block device images is "rbd", you can
   also specify the pool name with the rbd command using -p option:
   # rbd ls --name client.rbd
   # rbd ls -p rbd --name client.rbd
   # rbd list --name client.rbd
   ```

3. Check the details of the rbd image:

   ```
   # rbd --image rbd1 info --name client.rbd
   ```

   ```
   root@client-node1:~# rbd create rbd1 --size 10240 --name client.rbd
   root@client-node1:~# rbd ls --name client.rbd
   rbd1
   root@client-node1:~# rbd --image rbd1 info --name client.rbd
   rbd image 'rbd1':
           size 10240 MB in 2560 objects
           order 22 (4096 kB objects)
           block_name_prefix: rb.0.14f1.238e1f29
           format: 1
   root@client-node1:~#
   ```

Mapping Ceph Block Device

Now that we have created a block device on a Ceph cluster, in order to use this block device, we need to map it to the client machine. To do this, execute the following commands from the `client-node1` machine.

How to do it...

1. Map the block device to the `client-node1`:

   ```
   # rbd map --image rbd1 --name client.rbd
   ```

2. Check the mapped block device:

`rbd showmapped --name client.rbd`

```
root@client-node1:~# rbd map --image rbd1 --name client.rbd
/dev/rbd1
root@client-node1:~# rbd showmapped --name client.rbd
id pool image snap device
1  rbd  rbd1  -    /dev/rbd1
root@client-node1:~#
```

3. To make use of this block device, we should create a filesystem on this and mount it:

`fdisk -l /dev/rbd1`

`mkfs.xfs /dev/rbd1`

`mkdir /mnt/ceph-disk1`

`mount /dev/rbd1 /mnt/ceph-disk1`

`df -h /mnt/ceph-disk1`

```
root@client-node1:~# df -h /mnt/ceph-disk1
Filesystem      Size  Used Avail Use% Mounted on
/dev/rbd1        10G   33M  10G    1% /mnt/ceph-disk1
root@client-node1:~#
```

4. Test the block device by writing data to it:

`dd if=/dev/zero of=/mnt/ceph-disk1/file1 count=100 bs=1M`

```
root@client-node1:~# dd if=/dev/zero of=/mnt/ceph-disk1/file1 count=100 bs=1M
100+0 records in
100+0 records out
104857600 bytes (105 MB) copied, 7.16309 s, 14.6 MB/s
root@client-node1:~# df -h /mnt/ceph-disk1
Filesystem      Size  Used Avail Use% Mounted on
/dev/rbd1        10G  133M  9.9G   2% /mnt/ceph-disk1
root@client-node1:~#
```

5. To map the block device across reboots, you should add `init-rbdmap` script to the system startup, add the Ceph user and keyring details to `/etc/ceph/rbdmap`, and finally, update the `/etc/fstab` file:

`wget https://raw.githubusercontent.com/ksingh7/`
  `ceph-cookbook/master/rbdmap -O /etc/init.d/rbdmap`

`chmod +x /etc/init.d/rbdmap`

`update-rc.d rbdmap defaults`

```
## Make sure you use correct keyring value in /etc/ceph/rbdmap
   file, which is generally unique for an environment.
```

```
# echo "rbd/rbd1 id=rbd,
  keyring=AQCLEg5VeAbGARAAE4ULXC7M5Fwd3BGFDiHRTw==" >>
    /etc/ceph/rbdmap
```

```
# echo "/dev/rbd1 /mnt/ceph-disk1 xfs defaults, _netdev
 0 0 " >> /etc/fstab
```

```
# mkdir /mnt/ceph-disk1
```

```
# /etc/init.d/rbdmap start
```

Ceph RBD resizing

Ceph supports thin provisioned block devices, which means that the physical storage space will not get occupied until you begin storing data on the block device. The Ceph block device is very flexible; you can increase or decrease the size of an RBD on the fly from the Ceph storage end. However, the underlying filesystem should support resizing. Advance filesystems such as XFS, Btrfs, EXT, ZFS, and others support filesystem resizing to a certain extent. Please follow filesystem specific documentation to know more about resizing.

How to do it...

To increase or decrease Ceph RBD image size, use the `--size <New_Size_in_MB>` option with the `rbd resize` command, this will set the new size for the RBD image:

1. The original size of the RBD image that we created earlier was 10 GB. We will now increase its size to 20 GB:

    ```
    # rbd resize --image rbd1 --size 20480 --name client.rbd
    ```

    ```
    # rbd info --image rbd1 --name client.rbd
    ```

    ```
    root@client-node1:~# rbd resize --image rbd1 --size 20480 --name client.rbd
    Resizing image: 100% complete...done.
    root@client-node1:~# rbd info --image rbd1 --name client.rbd
    rbd image 'rbd1':
            size 20480 MB in 5120 objects
            order 22 (4096 kB objects)
            block_name_prefix: rb.0.14f1.238e1f29
            format: 1
    root@client-node1:~#
    ```

2. Grow the filesystem so that we can make use of increased storage space. It's worth knowing that the filesystem resize is a feature of the OS as well as the device filesystem. You should read filesystem documentation before resizing any partition. The XFS filesystem supports online resizing. Check system messages to know the filesystem size change:

```
# dmesg | grep -i capacity
```

```
# xfs_growfs -d /mnt/ceph-disk1
```

```
root@client-node1:~# xfs_growfs -d /mnt/ceph-disk1
meta-data=/dev/rbd1              isize=256    agcount=17, agsize=162816 blks
         =                       sectsz=512   attr=2
data     =                       bsize=4096   blocks=2621440, imaxpct=25
         =                       sunit=1024   swidth=1024 blks
naming   =version 2              bsize=4096   ascii-ci=0
log      =internal               bsize=4096   blocks=2560, version=2
         =                       sectsz=512   sunit=8 blks, lazy-count=1
realtime =none                   extsz=4096   blocks=0, rtextents=0
data blocks changed from 2621440 to 5242880
root@client-node1:~# df -h /mnt/ceph-disk1
Filesystem      Size  Used Avail Use% Mounted on
/dev/rbd1        20G  134M   20G   1% /mnt/ceph-disk1
root@client-node1:~#
```

Working with RBD snapshots

Ceph extends full support to snapshots, which are point-in-time, read-only copies of an RBD image. You can preserve the state of a Ceph RBD image by creating snapshots and restoring the snapshot to get the original data.

How to do it...

Let's see how a snapshot works with Ceph.

1. To test the snapshot functionality of Ceph, let's create a file on the block device that we created earlier:

```
# echo "Hello Ceph This is snapshot test" > /mnt/
  ceph-disk1/snapshot_test_file
```

```
root@client-node1:~# echo "Hello Ceph This is snapshot test" > /mnt/ceph-disk1/snapshot_test_file
root@client-node1:~# ls -l /mnt/ceph-disk1
total 102404
-rw-r--r-- 1 root root 104857600 Mar 22 16:07 file1
-rw-r--r-- 1 root root        33 Mar 22 21:45 snapshot_test_file
root@client-node1:~#
root@client-node1:~# cat /mnt/ceph-disk1/snapshot_test_file
Hello Ceph This is snapshot test
root@client-node1:~#
```

2. Create a snapshot for the Ceph block device:

   Syntax: `rbd snap create <pool-name>/<image-name>@<snap-name>`

   `# rbd snap create rbd/rbd1@snapshot1 --name client.rbd`

3. To list the snapshots of an image, use the following:

   Syntax: `rbd snap ls <pool-name>/<image-name>`

   `# rbd snap ls rbd/rbd1 --name client.rbd`

   ```
   root@client-node1:~# rbd snap create rbd/rbd1@snapshot1 --name client.rbd
   root@client-node1:~# rbd snap ls rbd/rbd1 --name client.rbd
   SNAPID NAME          SIZE
        2 snapshot1 20480 MB
   root@client-node1:~#
   ```

4. To test the snapshot restore functionality of Ceph RBD, let's delete files from the filesystem:

   `# rm -f /mnt/ceph-disk1/*`

5. We will now restore the Ceph RBD snapshot to get back the files that we deleted in the last step. Please note that a rollback operation will overwrite the current version of the RBD image and its data with the snapshot version. You should perform this operation carefully:

   Syntax: `rbd snap rollback <pool-name>/<image-name>@<snap-name>`

   `# rbd snap rollback rbd/rbd1@snapshot1 --name client.rbd`

6. Once the snapshot rollback operation is completed, remount the Ceph RBD filesystem to refresh the filesystem state. You should be able to get your deleted files back:

   `# umount /mnt/ceph-disk1`

   `# mount /dev/rbd1 /mnt/ceph-disk1`

   `# ls -l /mnt/ceph-disk1`

   ```
   root@client-node1:~# rbd snap rollback rbd/rbd1@snapshot1 --name client.rbd
   Rolling back to snapshot: 100% complete...done.
   root@client-node1:~# umount /mnt/ceph-disk1
   root@client-node1:~# mount /dev/rbd1 /mnt/ceph-disk1
   root@client-node1:~# ls -l /mnt/ceph-disk1
   total 102404
   -rw-r--r-- 1 root root 104857600 Mar 22 16:07 file1
   -rw-r--r-- 1 root root        33 Mar 22 21:45 snapshot_test_file
   root@client-node1:~#
   ```

7. When you no longer need snapshots, you can remove a specific snapshot using the following syntax. Deleting the snapshot will not delete your current data on the Ceph RBD image:

    Syntax: `rbd snap rm <pool-name>/<image-name>@<snap-name>`

    `# rbd snap rm rbd/rbd1@snapshot1 --name client.rbd`

8. If you have multiple snapshots of an RBD image and you wish to delete all the snapshots with a single command, then use the `purge` sub command:

    Syntax: `rbd snap purge <pool-name>/<image-name>`

    `# rbd snap purge rbd/rbd1 --name client.rbd`

Working with RBD Clones

Ceph supports a very nice feature for creating **Copy-On-Write** (**COW**) clones from RBD snapshots. This is also known as **Snapshot Layering** in Ceph. Layering allows clients to create multiple instant clones of Ceph RBD. This feature is extremely useful for cloud and virtualization platforms such as OpenStack, CloudStack, Qemu/KVM, and so on. These platforms usually protect Ceph RBD images containing an OS / VM image in the form of a snapshot. Later, this snapshot is cloned multiple times to spawn new virtual machines / instances. Snapshots are read-only, but COW clones are fully writable; this feature of Ceph provides a greater level of flexibility and is extremely useful in cloud platforms. In the later chapters, we will discover more on COW clones for spawning OpenStack instances:

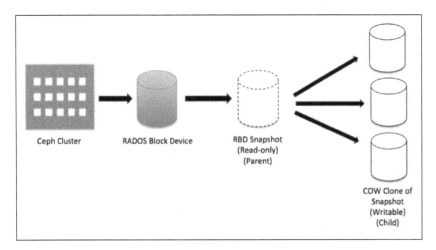

Ceph Cluster   RADOS Block Device   RBD Snapshot
(Read-only)
(Parent)

COW Clone of
Snapshot
(Writable)
(Child)

Every cloned image (child image) stores references of its parent snapshot to read image data. Hence, the parent snapshot should be protected before it can be used for cloning. At the time of data writing on the COW cloned image, it stores new data references to itself. COW cloned images are as good as RBD. They are quite flexible like RBD, which means that they are writable, resizable, and support snapshots and further cloning.

In Ceph RBD, images are of two types: `format-1` and `format-2`. The RBD snapshot feature is available on both types, that is, in `format-1` as well as in `format-2` RBD images. However, the layering feature (the COW cloning feature) is available only for the RBD image with `format-2`. The default RBD image format is `format-1`.

How to do it...

To demonstrate RBD cloning, we will intentionally create a format-2 RBD image, then create and protect its snapshot, and finally, create COW clones out of it:

1. Create a format-2 RBD image and check its detail:

   ```
   # rbd create rbd2 --size 10240 --image-format 2 --name client.rbd
   ```
   ```
   # rbd info --image rbd2 --name client.rbd
   ```

   ```
   root@client-node1:/# rbd create rbd2 --size 10240 --image-format 2 --name client.rbd
   root@client-node1:/#
   root@client-node1:/# rbd info --image rbd2 --name client.rbd
   rbd image 'rbd2':
           size 10240 MB in 2560 objects
           order 22 (4096 kB objects)
           block_name_prefix: rbd_data.20f42ae8944a
           format: 2
           features: layering
   root@client-node1:/#
   ```

2. Create a snapshot of this RBD image:

   ```
   # rbd snap create rbd/rbd2@snapshot_for_cloning --name client.rbd
   ```

3. To create a COW clone, protect the snapshot. This is an important step, we should protect the snapshot because if the snapshot gets deleted, all the attached COW clones will be destroyed:

   ```
   # rbd snap protect rbd/rbd2@snapshot_for_cloning --name client.rbd
   ```

4. Next, we will create a cloned RBD image using this snapshot:

   Syntax: `rbd clone <pool-name>/<parent-image>@<snap-name> <pool-name>/<child-image-name>`

   ```
   # rbd clone rbd/rbd2@snapshot_for_cloning rbd/clone_rbd2 --name client.rbd
   ```

5. Creating a clone is a quick process. Once it's completed, check the new image information. You will notice that its parent pool, image, and snapshot information will be displayed:

```
# rbd info rbd/clone_rbd2 --name client.rbd
```

```
root@client-node1:/# rbd snap create rbd/rbd2@snapshot_for_cloning --name client.rbd
root@client-node1:/# rbd snap protect rbd/rbd2@snapshot_for_cloning --name client.rbd
root@client-node1:/# rbd clone rbd/rbd2@snapshot_for_cloning rbd/clone_rbd2 --name client.rbd
root@client-node1:/# rbd info rbd/clone_rbd2 --name client.rbd
rbd image 'clone_rbd2':
        size 10240 MB in 2560 objects
        order 22 (4096 kB objects)
        block_name_prefix: rbd_data.220b3d1b58ba
        format: 2
        features: layering
        parent: rbd/rbd2@snapshot_for_cloning
        overlap: 10240 MB
root@client-node1:/#
```

At this point, we have a cloned RBD image, which is dependent upon its parent image snapshot. To make the cloned RBD image independent of its parent, we need to *flatten the image*, which involves copying the data from the parent snapshot to the child image. The time it takes to complete the flattening process depends on the size of the data present in the parent snapshot. Once the flattening process is completed, there is no dependency between the cloned RBD image and its parent snapshot.

6. To initiate the flattening process, use the following:

```
# rbd flatten rbd/clone_rbd2 --name client.rbd
```

```
# rbd info --image clone_rbd2 --name client.rbd
```

After the completion of the flattening process, if you check image information, you will notice that the parent image/snapshot name is not present and the clone is independent.

```
root@client-node1:/# rbd flatten rbd/clone_rbd2 --name client.rbd
Image flatten: 100% complete...done.
root@client-node1:/# rbd info --image clone_rbd2 --name client.rbd
rbd image 'clone_rbd2':
        size 10240 MB in 2560 objects
        order 22 (4096 kB objects)
        block_name_prefix: rbd_data.220b3d1b58ba
        format: 2
        features: layering
root@client-node1:/#
```

7. You can also remove the parent image snapshot if you no longer require it. Before removing the snapshot, you first have to unprotect it:

```
# rbd snap unprotect rbd/rbd2@snapshot_for_cloning --name client.
rbd
```

8. Once the snapshot is unprotected, you can remove it:

```
# rbd snap rm rbd/rbd2@snapshot_for_cloning --name client.rbd
```

A quick look at OpenStack

OpenStack is an open source software platform for building and managing public and private cloud infrastructure. It is being governed by an independent, non-profit foundation known as the OpenStack foundation. It has the largest and the most active community, which is backed by technology giants such as HP, Red Hat, Dell, Cisco, IBM, Rackspace, and many more. OpenStack's idea for a cloud is that it should be simple to implement and massively scalable.

OpenStack is considered as the cloud operating system where users are allowed to instantly deploy hundreds of virtual machines in an automated way. It also provides an efficient way of hassle free management of these machines. OpenStack is known for its dynamic scale up, scale out, and distributed architecture capabilities, making your cloud environment robust and future-ready. OpenStack provides an enterprise class **Infrastructure-as-a-Service** (**IaaS**) platform for all your cloud needs.

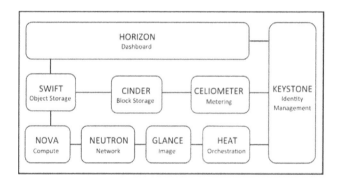

As shown in the preceding diagram, OpenStack is made up of several different software components that work together to provide cloud services. Out of all these components, in this chapter, we will focus on Cinder and Glance, which provide block storage and image services respectively. For more information on OpenStack components, please visit http://www.openstack.org/.

Ceph – the best match for OpenStack

In the last few years, OpenStack has been getting amazingly popular, as it's based on software defined on a wide range, whether it's computing, networking, or even storage. And when you talk about storage for OpenStack, Ceph will get all the attention. An OpenStack user survey, conducted in September 2015, showed Ceph dominating the block storage driver market with a whopping 62% usage.

Ceph provides the robust, reliable storage backend that OpenStack was looking for. Its seamless integration with OpenStack components such as cinder, glance, nova, and keystone provides an all in one cloud storage backend for OpenStack. Here are some key benefits that make Ceph the best match for OpenStack:

- ▶ Ceph provides an enterprise-grade, feature-rich storage backend at a very low cost per gigabyte, which helps to keep the OpenStack cloud deployment price down.

- ▶ Ceph is a unified storage solution for Block, File, or Object storage for OpenStack, allowing applications to use storage as they need.

- ▶ Ceph provides advance block storage capabilities for OpenStack clouds, which includes the easy and quick spawning of instances, as well as the backup and cloning of VMs.

- ▶ It provides default persistent volumes for OpenStack instances that can work like traditional servers, where data will not flush on rebooting the VMs.

- ▶ Ceph supports OpenStack in being host-independent by supporting VM migrations, scaling up storage components without affecting VMs.

- ▶ It provides the snapshot feature to OpenStack volumes, which can also be used as a means of backup.

- ▶ Ceph's copy-on-write cloning feature provides OpenStack to spin up several instances at once, which helps the provisioning mechanism function faster.

- ▶ Ceph supports rich APIs for both Swift and S3 Object storage interfaces.

The Ceph and OpenStack communities have been working closely over the last few years to make the integration more seamless and to make use of new features as they emerge. In the future, we can expect that OpenStack and Ceph will be more closely associated due to Red Hat's acquisition of Inktank, the company behind Ceph; Red Hat is one of the major contributors to the OpenStack project.

OpenStack is a modular system that has a unique component for a specific set of tasks. There are several components that require a reliable storage backend, such as Ceph, and extend full integration to it, as shown in the following diagram. Each of these components uses Ceph in their own way to store block devices and objects. The majority of cloud deployment based on OpenStack and Ceph use the Cinder, glance, and Swift integrations with Ceph. Keystone integration is used when you need an S3-compatible object storage on the Ceph backend. Nova integration allows boot from Ceph volume capabilities for your OpenStack instances.

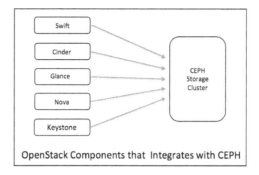

OpenStack Components that Integrates with CEPH

Setting up OpenStack

OpenStack setup and configuration is beyond the scope of this book, however, for ease of demonstration, we will use a virtual machine preinstalled with the OpenStack RDO Juno release. If you like, you can also use your own OpenStack environment and can perform Ceph integration.

How to do it...

In this recipe, we will demonstrate setting up a preconfigured OpenStack environment using Vagrant and accessing it via CLI and GUI:

1. Launch `openstack-node1` using `Vagrantfile` as we did for Ceph nodes in the last chapter. Make sure that you are on the host machine and are under the `ceph-cookbook` repository before bringing up `openstack-node1` using Vagrant:

   # **cd ceph-cookbook**

   # **vagrant up openstack-node1**

```
HOST:ceph-cookbook ksingh$ vagrant up openstack-node1
Bringing machine 'openstack-node1' up with 'virtualbox' provider...
==> openstack-node1: Clearing any previously set forwarded ports...
==> openstack-node1: Clearing any previously set network interfaces...
==> openstack-node1: Preparing network interfaces based on configuration...
    openstack-node1: Adapter 1: nat
    openstack-node1: Adapter 2: hostonly
==> openstack-node1: Forwarding ports...
    openstack-node1: 22 => 2222 (adapter 1)
==> openstack-node1: Running 'pre-boot' VM customizations...
==> openstack-node1: Booting VM...
==> openstack-node1: Waiting for machine to boot. This may take a few minutes...
```

2. Once `openstack-node1` is up, check the Vagrant status, and log in to the node:

   `$ vagrant status openstack-node1`

   `$ vagrant ssh openstack-node1`

```
HOST:ceph-cookbook ksingh$ vagrant status openstack-node1
Current machine states:

openstack-node1            running (virtualbox)

The VM is running. To stop this VM, you can run `vagrant halt` to
shut it down forcefully, or you can run `vagrant suspend` to simply
suspend the virtual machine. In either case, to restart it again,
simply run `vagrant up`.
HOST:ceph-cookbook ksingh$
HOST:ceph-cookbook ksingh$
HOST:ceph-cookbook ksingh$ vagrant ssh openstack-node1
Last login: Sat Mar 28 21:38:07 2015 from 10.0.2.2
[vagrant@os-node1 ~]$
```

3. We assume that you have some knowledge of OpenStack and are aware of its operations. We will source the `keystone_admin` file, which has been placed under `/root`, and to do this, we need to switch to root:

   `$ sudo su -`

   `$ source keystone_admin`

   We will now run some native OpenStack commands to make sure that OpenStack is set up correctly. Please note that some of these commands do not show any information, since this is a fresh OpenStack environment and does not have instances or volumes created:

   `# nova list`

   `# cinder list`

   `# glance image-list`

```
[vagrant@os-node1 ~]$ sudo su -
Last login: Sat Mar 28 22:34:52 EET 2015 on pts/0
[root@os-node1 ~]# source keystonerc_admin
[root@os-node1 ~(keystone_admin)]#
[root@os-node1 ~(keystone_admin)]# nova list
+----+------+--------+------------+-------------+----------+
| ID | Name | Status | Task State | Power State | Networks |
+----+------+--------+------------+-------------+----------+
+----+------+--------+------------+-------------+----------+
[root@os-node1 ~(keystone_admin)]#
[root@os-node1 ~(keystone_admin)]# cinder list
+----+--------+--------------+------+-------------+----------+-------------+
| ID | Status | Display Name | Size | Volume Type | Bootable | Attached to |
+----+--------+--------------+------+-------------+----------+-------------+
+----+--------+--------------+------+-------------+----------+-------------+
[root@os-node1 ~(keystone_admin)]# glance image-list
+--------------------------------------+--------+-------------+------------------+----------+--------+
| ID                                   | Name   | Disk Format | Container Format | Size     | Status |
+--------------------------------------+--------+-------------+------------------+----------+--------+
| 5c261af7-9388-44ad-a8ce-f9ebdad2e5cb | cirros | qcow2       | bare             | 13200896 | active |
+--------------------------------------+--------+-------------+------------------+----------+--------+
[root@os-node1 ~(keystone_admin)]#
```

4. You can also log in to the OpenStack horizon web interface (`https://192.168.1.111/dashboard`) with the username as `admin` and password as `vagrant`.

5. After logging in, the Overview page opens:

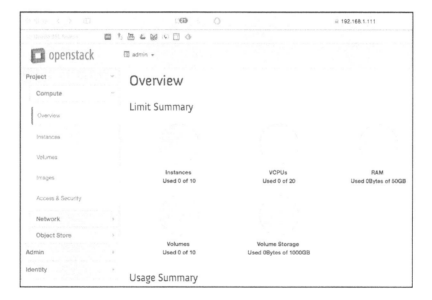

Configuring OpenStack as Ceph clients

OpenStack nodes should be configured as Ceph clients in order to access the Ceph cluster. To do this, install Ceph packages on OpenStack nodes and make sure it can access the Ceph cluster.

How to do it...

In this recipe, we are going to configure OpenStack as a Ceph client, which will be later used to configure cinder, glance, and nova:

1. We will use `ceph-node1` to install Ceph binaries on `os-node1` using `ceph-deploy`, as we have done earlier in *Chapter 1, Ceph – Introduction and Beyond*. To do this, we should set up ssh password-less login to `os-node1`. The root password is again the same (`vagrant`):

```
$ vagrant ssh ceph-node1
$ sudo su -
# ping os-node1 -c 1
# ssh-copy-id root@os-node1
```

```
HOST:ceph-cookbook ksingh$ vagrant ssh ceph-node1
Last login: Sun Mar 29 11:27:53 2015 from 10.0.2.2
[vagrant@ceph-node1 ~]$ sudo su -
Last login: Sun Mar 29 11:27:57 EEST 2015 on pts/1
[root@ceph-node1 ~]# ping os-node1 -c 1
PING os-node1.cephcookbook.com (192.168.1.111) 56(84) bytes of data.
64 bytes from os-node1.cephcookbook.com (192.168.1.111): icmp_seq=1 ttl=64 time=0.568 ms

--- os-node1.cephcookbook.com ping statistics ---
1 packets transmitted, 1 received, 0% packet loss, time 0ms
rtt min/avg/max/mdev = 0.568/0.568/0.568/0.000 ms
[root@ceph-node1 ~]# ssh-copy-id root@os-node1
/bin/ssh-copy-id: INFO: attempting to log in with the new key(s), to filter out any that are already i
nstalled
/bin/ssh-copy-id: INFO: 1 key(s) remain to be installed -- if you are prompted now it is to install th
e new keys
root@os-node1's password:

Number of key(s) added: 1

Now try logging into the machine, with:   "ssh 'root@os-node1'"
and check to make sure that only the key(s) you wanted were added.

[root@ceph-node1 ~]#
```

2. Next, we will install Ceph packages to `os-node1` using `ceph-deploy`:

```
# cd /etc/ceph
# ceph-deploy install os-node1
```

```
[root@ceph-node1 ~]# cd /etc/ceph
[root@ceph-node1 ceph]# ceph-deploy install os-node1
[ceph_deploy.conf][DEBUG ] found configuration file at: /root/.cephdeploy.conf
[ceph_deploy.cli][INFO  ] Invoked (1.5.22): /bin/ceph-deploy install os-node1
[ceph_deploy.install][DEBUG ] Installing stable version giant on cluster ceph hosts os-node1
[ceph_deploy.install][DEBUG ] Detecting platform for host os-node1 ...
[os-node1][DEBUG ] connected to host: os-node1
[os-node1][DEBUG ] detect platform information from remote host
[os-node1][DEBUG ] detect machine type
[ceph_deploy.install][INFO  ] Distro info: CentOS Linux 7.0.1406 Core
[os-node1][INFO  ] installing ceph on os-node1
```

3. Push the Ceph configuration file, `ceph.conf`, from `ceph-node1` to `os-node1`.
    This configuration file helps clients reach the Ceph monitor and OSD machines.
    Please note that you can also manually copy the `ceph.conf` file to `os-node1`
    if you like:

    ```
    # ceph-deploy config push os-node1
    ```

 Make sure that the `ceph.conf` file that we have pushed to `os-node1`
has the permission set to 644.

```
[root@ceph-node1 ceph]# ceph-deploy config push os-node1
[ceph_deploy.conf][DEBUG ] found configuration file at: /root/.cephdeploy.conf
[ceph_deploy.cli][INFO  ] Invoked (1.5.22): /bin/ceph-deploy config push os-node1
[ceph_deploy.config][DEBUG ] Pushing config to os-node1
[os-node1][DEBUG ] connected to host: os-node1
[os-node1][DEBUG ] detect platform information from remote host
[os-node1][DEBUG ] detect machine type
[os-node1][DEBUG ] write cluster configuration to /etc/ceph/{cluster}.conf
[root@ceph-node1 ceph]#
```

4. Create Ceph pools for cinder, glance, and nova. You may use any available pool,
    but it's recommended that you create separate pools for OpenStack components:

    ```
    # ceph osd pool create images 128
    ```

    ```
    # ceph osd pool create volumes 128
    ```

    ```
    # ceph osd pool create vms 128
    ```

    ```
    [root@ceph-node1 ceph]# ceph osd pool create images 128
    pool 'images' created
    [root@ceph-node1 ceph]# ceph osd pool create volumes 128
    pool 'volumes' created
    [root@ceph-node1 ceph]# ceph osd pool create vms 128
    pool 'vms' created
    [root@ceph-node1 ceph]# ceph osd lspools
    0 rbd,1 images,2 volumes,3 vms,
    [root@ceph-node1 ceph]# _
    ```

5. Set up client authentication by creating a new user for cinder and glance:

```
# ceph auth get-or-create client.cinder mon 'allow r' osd 'allow
class-read object_prefix rbd_children, allow rwx pool=volumes,
allow rwx pool=vms, allow rx pool=images'
```

```
# ceph auth get-or-create client.glance mon 'allow r' osd 'allow
class-read object_prefix rbd_children, allow rwx pool=images'
```

```
[root@ceph-node1 ceph]# ceph auth get-or-create client.cinder mon 'allow r' osd 'allow class-read
object_prefix rbd_children, allow rwx pool=volumes, allow rwx pool=vms, allow rx pool=images'
[client.cinder]
        key = AQByVBhVMK2nLxAArOf1ya1hbc23N2kyZv0EXw==
[root@ceph-node1 ceph]# ceph auth get-or-create client.glance mon 'allow r' osd 'allow class-read
object_prefix rbd_children, allow rwx pool=images'
[client.glance]
        key = AQCBVBhVYJEEKBAAhXHTe9Z1202YyhM0jpga2A==
[root@ceph-node1 ceph]#
```

6. Add the keyrings to `os-node1` and change their ownership:

```
# ceph auth get-or-create client.glance | ssh os-node1 sudo tee /
etc/ceph/ceph.client.glance.keyring
```

```
# ssh os-node1 sudo chown glance:glance /etc/ceph/ceph.client.
glance.keyring
```

```
# ceph auth get-or-create client.cinder | ssh os-node1 sudo tee /
etc/ceph/ceph.client.cinder.keyring
```

```
# ssh os-node1 sudo chown cinder:cinder /etc/ceph/ceph.client.
cinder.keyring
```

```
[root@ceph-node1 ceph]# ceph auth get-or-create client.glance | ssh os-node1 sudo tee /etc/ceph/ceph.client.glance.keyring
[client.glance]
        key = AQCBVBhVYJEEKBAAhXHTe9Z1202YyhM0jpga2A==
[root@ceph-node1 ceph]# ssh os-node1 sudo chown glance:glance /etc/ceph/ceph.client.glance.keyring
[root@ceph-node1 ceph]# ceph auth get-or-create client.cinder | ssh os-node1 sudo tee /etc/ceph/ceph.client.cinder.keyring
[client.cinder]
        key = AQByVBhVMK2nLxAArOf1ya1hbc23N2kyZv0EXw==
[root@ceph-node1 ceph]# ssh os-node1 sudo chown cinder:cinder /etc/ceph/ceph.client.cinder.keyring
[root@ceph-node1 ceph]#
```

7. The `libvirt` process requires accessing the Ceph cluster while attaching or detaching a block device from Cinder. We should create a temporary copy of the `client.cinder` key that will be needed for the cinder and nova configuration later in this chapter:

```
# ceph auth get-key client.cinder | ssh os-node1 tee /etc/ceph/
temp.client.cinder.key
```

8. At this point, you can test the previous configuration by accessing the Ceph cluster from `os-node1` using the `client.glance` and `client.cinder` Ceph users. Log in to `os-node1` and run the following commands:

```
$ vagrant ssh openstack-node1

$ sudo su -

# cd /etc/ceph

# ceph -s --name client.glance --keyring ceph.client.glance.
keyring

# ceph -s --name client.cinder --keyring ceph.client.cinder.
keyring
```

```
HOST:ceph-cookbook ksingh$ vagrant ssh openstack-node1
Last login: Sun Mar 29 22:55:20 2015 from 10.0.2.2
[vagrant@os-node1 ~]$ sudo su -
Last login: Sun Mar 29 22:55:35 EEST 2015 on pts/0
[root@os-node1 ~]# cd /etc/ceph
[root@os-node1 ceph]# ceph -s --name client.glance --keyring ceph.client.glance.keyring
    cluster 9609b429-eee2-4e23-af31-28a24fcf5cbc
     health HEALTH_OK
     monmap e3: 3 mons at {ceph-node1=192.168.1.101:6789/0,ceph-node2=192.168.1.102:6789/0,ceph-node3=192.1
68.1.103:6789/0}, election epoch 134, quorum 0,1,2 ceph-node1,ceph-node2,ceph-node3
     osdmap e248: 9 osds: 9 up, 9 in
      pgmap v1189: 564 pgs, 4 pools, 114 MB data, 2629 objects
            745 MB used, 134 GB / 134 GB avail
                 564 active+clean
[root@os-node1 ceph]#
[root@os-node1 ceph]# ceph -s --name client.cinder --keyring ceph.client.cinder.keyring
    cluster 9609b429-eee2-4e23-af31-28a24fcf5cbc
     health HEALTH_OK
     monmap e3: 3 mons at {ceph-node1=192.168.1.101:6789/0,ceph-node2=192.168.1.102:6789/0,ceph-node3=192.1
68.1.103:6789/0}, election epoch 134, quorum 0,1,2 ceph-node1,ceph-node2,ceph-node3
     osdmap e248: 9 osds: 9 up, 9 in
      pgmap v1189: 564 pgs, 4 pools, 114 MB data, 2629 objects
            745 MB used, 134 GB / 134 GB avail
                 564 active+clean
[root@os-node1 ceph]#
```

9. Finally, generate `uuid`, then create, define, and set the secret key to `libvirt` and remove temporary keys:

   1. Generate a uuid by using the following:

      ```
      # cd /etc/ceph

      # uuidgen
      ```

   2. Create a secret file and set this `uuid` number to it:

      ```
      cat > secret.xml <<EOF
      <secret ephemeral='no' private='no'>
        <uuid>bb90381e-a4c5-4db7-b410-3154c4af486e</uuid>
        <usage type='ceph'>
          <name>client.cinder secret</name>
        </usage>
      </secret>
      EOF
      ```

Make sure that you use your own `uuid` generated for
your environment.

3. Define the secret and keep the generated secret value safe. We will require
   this secret value in the next steps:

   ```
   # virsh secret-define --file secret.xml
   ```

   ```
   [root@os-node1 ~]# cd /etc/ceph
   [root@os-node1 ceph]# uuidgen
   bb90381e-a4c5-4db7-b410-3154c4af486e
   [root@os-node1 ceph]# cat > secret.xml <<EOF
   > <secret ephemeral='no' private='no'>
   >    <uuid>bb90381e-a4c5-4db7-b410-3154c4af486e</uuid>
   >    <usage type='ceph'>
   >       <name>client.cinder secret</name>
   >    </usage>
   > </secret>
   > EOF
   [root@os-node1 ceph]# virsh secret-define --file secret.xml
   Secret bb90381e-a4c5-4db7-b410-3154c4af486e created

   [root@os-node1 ceph]#
   ```

4. Set the secret value that was generated in the last step to `virsh` and delete
   temporary files. Deleting the temporary files is optional; it's done just to keep
   the system clean:

   ```
   # virsh secret-set-value --secret bb90381e-a4c5-4db7-b410-
   3154c4af486e --base64 $(cat temp.client.cinder.key) && rm
   temp.client.cinder.key secret.xml
   ```

   ```
   # virsh secret-list
   ```

   ```
   [root@os-node1 ceph]# virsh secret-set-value --secret bb90381e-a4c5-4db7-b410-3154c4af486e
   --base64 $(cat temp.client.cinder.key) && rm temp.client.cinder.key secret.xml
   Secret value set

   rm: remove regular file 'temp.client.cinder.key'? y
   rm: remove regular file 'secret.xml'? y
   [root@os-node1 ceph]#
   [root@os-node1 ceph]# virsh secret-list
    UUID                                     Usage
   ------------------------------------------------------------------------
    bb90381e-a4c5-4db7-b410-3154c4af486e  ceph client.cinder secret

   [root@os-node1 ceph]#
   ```

Configuring Glance for Ceph backend

We have completed the configuration required from the Ceph side. In this recipe, we will configure the OpenStack glance to use Ceph as a storage backend.

How to do it...

This recipe talks about configuring the glance component of OpenStack to store virtual machine images on Ceph RBD:

1. Log in to `os-node1`, which is our glance node, and edit `/etc/glance/glance-api.conf` for the following changes:

    1. Under the `[DEFAULT]` section, make sure that the following lines are present:

        ```
        default_store=rbd
        show_image_direct_url=True
        ```

    2. Execute the following command to verify entries:

        # cat /etc/glance/glance-api.conf | egrep -i "default_store|image_direct"

        ```
        [root@os-node1 ceph]# cat /etc/glance/glance-api.conf | egrep -i "default_store|image_direct"
        default_store=rbd
        show_image_direct_url=True
        [root@os-node1 ceph]#
        ```

    3. Under the `[glance_store]` section, make sure that the following lines are present under **RBD Store Options**:

        ```
        stores = rbd
        rbd_store_ceph_conf=/etc/ceph/ceph.conf
        rbd_store_user=glance
        rbd_store_pool=images
        rbd_store_chunk_size=8
        ```

4. Execute the following command to verify the previous entries:

```
# cat /etc/glance/glance-api.conf | egrep -v "#|default" |
grep -i rbd
```

```
[root@os-node1 ceph]# cat /etc/glance/glance-api.conf | egrep -v "#|default" | grep -i rbd
stores = rbd
rbd_store_ceph_conf=/etc/ceph/ceph.conf
rbd_store_user=glance
rbd_store_pool=images
rbd_store_chunk_size=8
[root@os-node1 ceph]#
```

2. Restart the OpenStack glance services:

```
# service openstack-glance-api restart
```

3. Source the `keystone_admin` file for OpenStack and list the glance images:

```
# source /root/keystonerc_admin
```

```
# glance image-list
```

```
[root@os-node1 ~]# source keystonerc_admin
[root@os-node1 ~(keystone_admin)]#
[root@os-node1 ~(keystone_admin)]# glance image-list
+--------------------------------------+--------+-------------+------------------+----------+--------+
| ID                                   | Name   | Disk Format | Container Format | Size     | Status |
+--------------------------------------+--------+-------------+------------------+----------+--------+
| 5c261af7-9388-44ad-a8ce-f9ebdad2e5cb | cirros | qcow2       | bare             | 13200896 | active |
+--------------------------------------+--------+-------------+------------------+----------+--------+
[root@os-node1 ~(keystone_admin)]#
```

4. Download the `cirros` image from the Internet, which will later be stored in Ceph:

```
# wget http://download.cirros-cloud.net/0.3.1/cirros-0.3.1-x86_64-
disk.img
```

5. Add a new glance image using the following command:

```
# glance image-create --name cirros_image --is-public=true --disk-
format=qcow2 --container-format=bare < cirros-0.3.1-x86_64-disk.
img
```

```
[root@os-node1 ~(keystone_admin)]# glance image-create --name cirros_image --is-public=true --disk-format=qcow2
--container-format=bare < cirros-0.3.1-x86_64-disk.img
+------------------+--------------------------------------+
| Property         | Value                                |
+------------------+--------------------------------------+
| checksum         | d972013792949d0d3ba628fbe8685bce     |
| container_format | bare                                 |
| created_at       | 2015-03-30T10:17:58                  |
| deleted          | False                                |
| deleted_at       | None                                 |
| disk_format      | qcow2                                |
| id               | b2d15e34-7712-4f1d-b48d-48b924e79b0c |
| is_public        | True                                 |
| min_disk         | 0                                    |
| min_ram          | 0                                    |
| name             | cirros_image                         |
| owner            | c9f87abe43ea49239313565ca74ebaa0     |
| protected        | False                                |
| size             | 13147648                             |
| status           | active                               |
| updated_at       | 2015-03-30T10:18:01                  |
| virtual_size     | None                                 |
+------------------+--------------------------------------+
```

6. List the glance images using the following command; you will notice there are now two glance images:

   ```
   # glance image-list
   ```

```
[root@os-node1 ~(keystone_admin)]# glance image-list
+--------------------------------------+--------------+-------------+------------------+----------+--------+
| ID                                   | Name         | Disk Format | Container Format | Size     | Status |
+--------------------------------------+--------------+-------------+------------------+----------+--------+
| 5c261af7-9388-44ad-a8ce-f9ebdad2e5cb | cirros       | qcow2       | bare             | 13200896 | active |
| b2d15e34-7712-4f1d-b48d-48b924e79b0c | cirros_image | qcow2       | bare             | 13147648 | active |
+--------------------------------------+--------------+-------------+------------------+----------+--------+
[root@os-node1 ~(keystone_admin)]#
```

7. You can verify that the new image is stored in Ceph by querying the image ID in the Ceph images pool:

   ```
   # rados -p images ls --name client.glance --keyring /etc/ceph/
   ceph.client.glance.keyring | grep -i id
   ```

```
[root@os-node1 ~]# rados -p images ls --name client.glance --keyring /etc/ceph/ceph.client.glance.keyring | grep -i id
rbd_id.b2d15e34-7712-4f1d-b48d-48b924e79b0c
[root@os-node1 ~]#
```

8. Since we have configured glance to use Ceph for its default storage, all the glance images will now be stored in Ceph. You can also try creating images from the OpenStack horizon dashboard:

9. Finally, we will try to launch an instance using the image that we have created earlier:

   ```
   # nova boot --flavor 1 --image b2d15e34-7712-4f1d-b48d-
   48b924e79b0c vm1
   ```

While you are adding new glance images or creating an instance from the glance image stored on Ceph, you can check the IO on the Ceph cluster by monitoring it using the # `watch ceph -s` command.

Configuring Cinder for Ceph backend

The Cinder program of OpenStack provides block storage to virtual machines. In this recipe, we will configure OpenStack Cinder to use Ceph as a storage backend. OpenStack Cinder requires a driver to interact with the Ceph block device. On the OpenStack node, edit the `/etc/cinder/cinder.conf` configuration file by adding the code snippet given in the following section.

How to do it...

In the last recipe, we learned to configure glance to use Ceph. In this recipe, we will learn to use the Ceph RBD with the Cinder service of OpenStack:

1. Since in this demonstration we are not using multiple backend cinder configurations, comment the `enabled_backends` option from the `/etc/cinder/cinder.conf` file:

2. Navigate to the **Options defined in cinder.volume.drivers.rbd** section of the `/etc/cinder/cinder.conf` file and add the following (replace the secret `uuid` with your environments value):

   ```
   volume_driver = cinder.volume.drivers.rbd.RBDDriver
   rbd_pool = volumes
   rbd_user = cinder
   rbd_secret_uuid = bb90381e-a4c5-4db7-b410-3154c4af486e
   rbd_ceph_conf = /etc/ceph/ceph.conf
   rbd_flatten_volume_from_snapshot = false
   rbd_max_clone_depth = 5
   rbd_store_chunk_size = 4
   rados_connect_timeout = -1
   glance_api_version = 2
   ```

3. Execute the following command to verify the previous entries:

   ```
   # cat /etc/cinder/cinder.conf | egrep "rbd|rados|version" | grep -v "#"
   ```

```
[root@os-node1 ~]# cat /etc/cinder/cinder.conf | egrep "rbd|rados|version" | grep -v "#"
volume_driver = cinder.volume.drivers.rbd.RBDDriver
rbd_pool = volumes
rbd_user = cinder
rbd_secret_uuid = bb90381e-a4c5-4db7-b410-3154c4af486e
rbd_ceph_conf = /etc/ceph/ceph.conf
rbd_flatten_volume_from_snapshot = false
rbd_max_clone_depth = 5
rbd_store_chunk_size = 4
rados_connect_timeout = -1
glance_api_version = 2
[root@os-node1 ~]#
```

4. Restart the OpenStack cinder services:

   ```
   # service openstack-cinder-volume restart
   ```

5. Source the `keystone_admin` files for OpenStack:

   ```
   # source /root/keystonerc_admin
   ```

   ```
   # cinder list
   ```

6. To test this configuration, create your first cinder volume of 2 GB, which should now be created on your Ceph cluster:

   ```
   # cinder create --display-name ceph-volume01 --display-description "Cinder volume on CEPH storage" 2
   ```

7. Check the volume by listing the cinder and Ceph volumes pool:

   ```
   # cinder list
   ```

   ```
   # rados -p volumes --name client.cinder --keyring ceph.client.cinder.keyring ls | grep -i id
   ```

```
[root@os-node1 ceph(keystone_admin)]# cinder list
+--------------------------------------+-----------+---------------+------+-------------+----------+-------------+
|                  ID                  |  Status   | Display Name  | Size | Volume Type | Bootable | Attached to |
+--------------------------------------+-----------+---------------+------+-------------+----------+-------------+
| 1337c866-6ff7-4a56-bfe5-b0b80abcb281 | available | ceph-volume01 |  2   |    None     |  false   |             |
+--------------------------------------+-----------+---------------+------+-------------+----------+-------------+
[root@os-node1 ceph(keystone_admin)]#
[root@os-node1 ceph(keystone_admin)]# rados -p volumes --name client.cinder --keyring ceph.client.cinder.keyring ls | grep -i id
rbd_id.volume-1337c866-6ff7-4a56-bfe5-b0b80abcb281
[root@os-node1 ceph(keystone_admin)]#
```

8. Similarly, try creating another volume using the OpenStack Horizon dashboard.

Configuring Nova to attach Ceph RBD

In order to attach the Ceph RBD to OpenStack instances, we should configure the nova component of OpenStack by adding the `rbd` user and uuid information that it needs to connect to the Ceph cluster. To do this, we need to edit `/etc/nova/nova.conf` on the OpenStack node and perform the steps that are given in the following section.

How to do it...

The cinder service that we configured in the last recipe creates volumes on Ceph, however, to attach these volumes to OpenStack instances, we need to configure Nova:

1. Navigate to the **Options defined in nova.virt.libvirt.volume** section and add the following lines of code (replace the secret uuid with your environments value):

   ```
   rbd_user=cinder
   rbd_secret_uuid= bb90381e-a4c5-4db7-b410-3154c4af486e
   ```

2. Restart the OpenStack nova services:

   ```
   # service openstack-nova-compute restart
   ```

3. To test this configuration, we will attach the cinder volume to an OpenStack instance. List the instance and volumes to get the ID:

   ```
   # nova list
   # cinder list
   ```

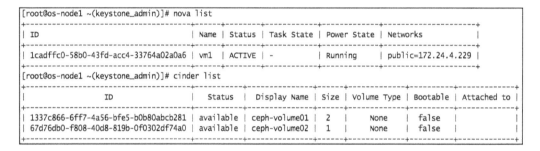

4. Attach the volume to the instance:

   ```
   # nova volume-attach 1cadffc0-58b0-43fd-acc4-33764a02a0a6
   1337c866-6ff7-4a56-bfe5-b0b80abcb281
   # cinder list
   ```

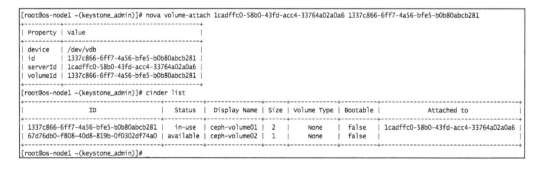

5. You can now use this volume as a regular block disk from your OpenStack instance.

Configuring Nova to boot instances from Ceph RBD

In order to boot all OpenStack instances into Ceph, that is, for the boot-from-volume feature, we should configure an ephemeral backend for nova. To do this, edit `/etc/nova/nova.conf` on the OpenStack node and perform the following changes.

How to do it...

This recipe deals with configuring Nova to store entire virtual machines on the Ceph RBD:

1. Navigate to the `[libvirt]` section and add the following:

   ```
   inject_partition=-2
   images_type=rbd
   images_rbd_pool=vms
   images_rbd_ceph_conf=/etc/ceph/ceph.conf
   ```

2. Verify your changes:

   ```
   # cat /etc/nova/nova.conf|egrep "rbd|partition" | grep -v "#"
   ```

   ```
   [root@os-node1 ~(keystone_admin)]# cat /etc/nova/nova.conf|egrep "rbd|partition" | grep -v "#"
   inject_partition=-2
   images_type=rbd
   images_rbd_pool=vms
   images_rbd_ceph_conf=/etc/ceph/ceph.conf
   rbd_user=cinder
   rbd_secret_uuid=bb90381e-a4c5-4db7-b410-3154c4af486e
   [root@os-node1 ~(keystone_admin)]#
   ```

3. Restart the OpenStack nova services:

   ```
   # service openstack-nova-compute restart
   ```

4. To boot a virtual machine in Ceph, the glance image format must be RAW. We will use the same `cirros` image that we downloaded earlier in this chapter and convert this image from the QCOW to RAW format (this is important). You can also use any other image, as long as it's in the RAW format:

   ```
   # qemu-img convert -f qcow2 -O raw cirros-0.3.1-x86_64-disk.img
   cirros-0.3.1-x86_64-disk.raw
   ```

   ```
   [root@os-node1 ~(keystone_admin)]# qemu-img convert -f qcow2 -O raw cirros-0.3.1-x86_64-disk.img cirros-0.3.1-x86_64-disk.raw
   [root@os-node1 ~(keystone_admin)]#
   [root@os-node1 ~(keystone_admin)]# ls -la cirros-0.3.1-x86_64-disk.raw
   -rw-r--r-- 1 root root 41126400 Apr  3 22:19 cirros-0.3.1-x86_64-disk.raw
   [root@os-node1 ~(keystone_admin)]# file cirros-0.3.1-x86_64-disk.raw
   cirros-0.3.1-x86_64-disk.raw: x86 boot sector; GRand Unified Bootloader, stage1 version 0x3, stage2 address 0x2000, stage2 segment
   0x200; partition 1: ID=0x83, active, starthead 0, startsector 16065, 64260 sectors, code offset 0x48
   [root@os-node1 ~(keystone_admin)]#
   ```

5. Create a glance image using a RAW image:

```
# glance image-create --name cirros_raw_image --is-public=true
--disk-format=raw --container-format=bare < cirros-0.3.1-x86_64-
disk.raw
```

6. To test the boot from the Ceph volume feature, create a bootable volume:

```
# nova image-list
```

```
# cinder create --image-id ff8d9729-5505-4d2a-94ad-7154c6085c97
--display-name cirros-ceph-boot-volume 1
```

```
[root@os-node1 ~(keystone_admin)]# nova image-list
+--------------------------------------+------------------+--------+--------+
| ID                                   | Name             | Status | Server |
+--------------------------------------+------------------+--------+--------+
| 5c261af7-9388-44ad-a8ce-f9ebdad2e5cb | cirros           | ACTIVE |        |
| b2d15e34-7712-4f1d-b48d-48b924e79b0c | cirros_image     | ACTIVE |        |
| ff8d9729-5505-4d2a-94ad-7154c6085c97 | cirros_raw_image | ACTIVE |        |
+--------------------------------------+------------------+--------+--------+
[root@os-node1 ~(keystone_admin)]#
[root@os-node1 ~(keystone_admin)]# cinder create --image-id ff8d9729-5505-4d2a-94ad-7154c6085c97 --display-name cirros-ceph-boot-volume 1
+---------------------+--------------------------------------+
|       Property      |                Value                 |
+---------------------+--------------------------------------+
|     attachments     |                  []                  |
|  availability_zone  |                 nova                 |
|      bootable       |                false                 |
|     created_at      |      2015-04-03T22:47:52.638434      |
| display_description |                 None                 |
|    display_name     |       cirros-ceph-boot-volume        |
|      encrypted      |                False                 |
|         id          | 3a0da68c-d00c-459f-8b52-88c45d6e3bfe |
|      image_id       | ff8d9729-5505-4d2a-94ad-7154c6085c97 |
|      metadata       |                  {}                  |
|        size         |                  1                   |
|     snapshot_id     |                 None                 |
|     source_volid    |                 None                 |
|       status        |               creating              |
|     volume_type     |                 None                 |
+---------------------+--------------------------------------+
[root@os-node1 ~(keystone_admin)]#
```

7. List cinder volumes to check if the bootable field is `true`:

```
# cinder list
```

```
[root@os-node1 ~(keystone_admin)]# cinder list
+--------------------------------------+-----------+--------------------------+------+-------------+----------+--------------------------------------+
|                  ID                  |   Status  |       Display Name       | Size | Volume Type | Bootable |             Attached to              |
+--------------------------------------+-----------+--------------------------+------+-------------+----------+--------------------------------------+
| 1337c866-6ff7-4a56-bfe5-b0b80abcb281 |   in-use  |       ceph-volume01      |  2   |     None    |   false  | 1cadffc0-58b0-43fd-acc4-33764a02a0a6 |
| 3a0da68c-d00c-459f-8b52-88c45d6e3bfe | available | cirros-ceph-boot-volume  |  1   |     None    |   true   |                                      |
| 67d76db0-f808-40d8-819b-0f0302df74a0 | available |       ceph-volume02      |  1   |     None    |   false  |                                      |
+--------------------------------------+-----------+--------------------------+------+-------------+----------+--------------------------------------+
[root@os-node1 ~(keystone_admin)]#
```

8. Now, we have a bootable volume, which is stored on Ceph, so let's launch an instance with this volume:

```
# nova boot --flavor 1 --block_device_mapping vda=fd56314b-
e19b-4129-af77-e6adf229c536::0 --image 964bd077-7b43-46eb-8fe1-
cd979a3370df vm2_on_ceph

--block_device_mapping vda = <cinder bootable volume id >

--image = <Glance image associated with the bootable volume>
```

9. Finally, check the instance status:

```
# nova list
```

```
[root@os-node1 ~(keystone_admin)]# nova list
+--------------------------------------+-------------+---------+------------+-------------+----------------------+
| ID                                   | Name        | Status  | Task State | Power State | Networks             |
+--------------------------------------+-------------+---------+------------+-------------+----------------------+
| 1cadffc0-58b0-43fd-acc4-33764a02a0a6 | vm1         | SHUTOFF | -          | Shutdown    | public=172.24.4.229  |
| 2b35870e-9f7e-4e5f-bd12-9a625797355d | vm2_on_ceph | ACTIVE  | -          | Running     | public=172.24.4.233  |
+--------------------------------------+-------------+---------+------------+-------------+----------------------+
[root@os-node1 ~(keystone_admin)]#
```

10. At this point, we have an instance running from a Ceph volume. Try to log in to the instance from the horizon dashboard:

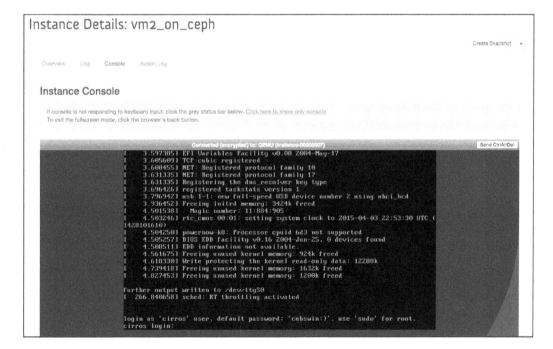

3
Working with Ceph Object Storage

In this chapter, we will cover the following recipes:

- ► Understanding Ceph object storage
- ► RADOS Gateway standard setup, installation, and configuration
- ► Creating the radosgw user
- ► Accessing Ceph object storage using the S3 API
- ► Accessing Ceph object storage using the Swift API
- ► Integrating RADOS Gateway with OpenStack Keystone
- ► Configuring Ceph Federated Gateways
- ► Testing radosgw federated configuration
- ► Building the file sync and share services using the RADOS Gateway

Introduction

Object-based storage has been getting a lot of industry attention as organizations are looking for flexibility for their enormous data. Object storage is an approach to store data in the form of objects rather than traditional files and blocks, and each object stores data, metadata, and a unique identifier. In this chapter, we will understand the object storage part of Ceph and gain practical knowledge by configuring the Ceph RADOS Gateway.

Understanding Ceph object storage

Object storage cannot be directly accessed by an operating system as a disk of filesystem. Rather, it can only be accessed via API at the application level. Ceph is a distributed object storage system that provides an object storage interface via the Ceph object gateway, also known as the **RADOS Gateway** (**RGW**) interface, which has been built on top of the Ceph RADOS layer. The RGW uses **librgw** (**RADOS Gateway Library**) and **librados**, allowing applications to establish a connection with Ceph object storage. The RGW provides applications with a RESTful S3/Swift-compatible API interface to store data in the form of objects in the Ceph cluster. Ceph also supports multitenant object storage, accessible via RESTful API. In addition to this, the RGW also supports Ceph Admin APIs that can be used to manage the Ceph storage cluster using native API calls.

The librados software libraries are very flexible and can allow user applications to directly access the Ceph storage cluster via C, C++, Java, Python, and PHP bindings. Ceph object storage also has multisite capabilities, that is, it provides solutions for disaster recovery.

The following image represents a Ceph object storage:

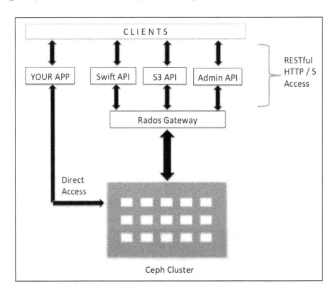

RADOS Gateway standard setup, installation, and configuration

For a production environment, it's recommended that you configure the RGW on a physical, dedicated machine. However, if your object storage workload is not too much, you can consider using any of the monitor machines as an RGW node. The RGW is a separate service that externally connects to a Ceph cluster and provides object storage access to its clients. In a production environment, it's recommended that you run more than one instance of the RGW, masked by a load balancer, as shown in the following diagram:

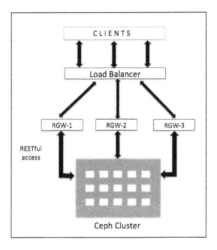

Starting with the Firefly release of Ceph, a new RGW frontend had been introduced: Civetweb, which is a lightweight standalone web server. Civetweb has been embedded directly into the `ceph-radosgw` service, making the Ceph object storage service deployment quicker and easier.

In the following recipes, we will demonstrate the RGW configuration using Civetweb on a virtual machine that will interact with the same Ceph cluster that we have created in *Chapter 1, Ceph – Introduction and Beyond*.

Setting up the RADOS Gateway node

To run the Ceph object storage service, we should have a running Ceph cluster and the RGW node should have access to the Ceph network.

How to do it...

As demonstrated in earlier chapters, we will boot up a virtual machine using Vagrant and configure that as our RGW node.

1. Launch `rgw-node1` using `Vagrantfile`, as we have done for Ceph nodes in *Chapter 1, Ceph – Introduction and Beyond*. Make sure you are on the host machine and under the `ceph-cookbook` repository before bringing up `rgw-node1` using Vagrant:

   # cd ceph-cookbook

   # vagrant up rgw-node1

   ```
   teeri:ceph-cookbook ksingh$ vagrant up rgw-node1
   Bringing machine 'rgw-node1' up with 'virtualbox' provider...
   ==> rgw-node1: Importing base box 'centos7-standard'...
   ==> rgw-node1: Matching MAC address for NAT networking...
   ==> rgw-node1: Setting the name of the VM: rgw-node1
   ==> rgw-node1: Fixed port collision for 22 => 2222. Now on port 2202.
   ==> rgw-node1: Clearing any previously set network interfaces...
   ==> rgw-node1: Preparing network interfaces based on configuration...
       rgw-node1: Adapter 1: nat
       rgw-node1: Adapter 2: hostonly
   ==> rgw-node1: Forwarding ports...
       rgw-node1: 22 => 2202 (adapter 1)
   ==> rgw-node1: Running 'pre-boot' VM customizations...
   ==> rgw-node1: Booting VM...
   ```

2. Once `rgw-node1` is up, check the Vagrant status, and log in to the node:

   $ vagrant status rgw-node1

   $ vagrant ssh rgw-node1

   ```
   teeri:ceph-cookbook ksingh$ vagrant status rgw-node1
   Current machine states:

   rgw-node1                 running (virtualbox)

   The VM is running. To stop this VM, you can run `vagrant halt` to
   shut it down forcefully, or you can run `vagrant suspend` to simply
   suspend the virtual machine. In either case, to restart it again,
   simply run `vagrant up`.
   teeri:ceph-cookbook ksingh$ vagrant ssh rgw-node1
   Last login: Sun Apr  5 19:31:52 2015
   [vagrant@rgw-node1 ~]$
   ```

3. Check if `rgw-node1` can reach the Ceph cluster nodes:

   # ping ceph-node1 -c 3

   # ping ceph-node2 -c 3

   # ping ceph-node3 -c 3

4. Verify the local host file entries, hostname, and FQDN for `rgw-node1`:

   # cat /etc/hosts | grep -i rgw

   # hostname

   # hostname -f

```
[root@rgw-node1 ~]# cat /etc/hosts | grep -i rgw
127.0.0.1    rgw-node1.cephcookbook.com rgw-node1 localhost localhost.localdomain localhost4 localhost4.localdomain4
192.168.1.106 rgw-node1.cephcookbook.com rgw-node1
[root@rgw-node1 ~]#
[root@rgw-node1 ~]# hostname
rgw-node1.cephcookbook.com
[root@rgw-node1 ~]#
[root@rgw-node1 ~]# hostname -f
rgw-node1.cephcookbook.com
[root@rgw-node1 ~]#
```

Installing the RADOS Gateway

The previous recipe was about setting up a virtual machine for RGW. In this recipe, we will learn to set up the `ceph-radosgw` service on this node.

How to do it...

1. First, we should install the Ceph packages on `rgw-node1`. To do this, we will use the `ceph-deploy` tool from `ceph-node1`, which is our Ceph monitor node. Log in to `ceph-node1` and perform the following commands:

   1. Make sure that `ceph-node1` can reach `rgw-node1` over the network using the following command:

      # ping rgw-node1 -c 1

   2. Allow `ceph-node1` a password-less SSH login to `rgw-node1` and test the connection.

The root password for `rgw-node1` is the same as earlier, that is, `vagrant`.

```
# ssh-copy-id rgw-node1
# ssh rgw-node1 hostname
```

```
[root@ceph-node1 ceph]# ping rgw-node1 -c 1
PING rgw-node1.cephcookbook.com (192.168.1.106) 56(84) bytes of data.
64 bytes from rgw-node1.cephcookbook.com (192.168.1.106): icmp_seq=1 ttl=64 time=0.745 ms

--- rgw-node1.cephcookbook.com ping statistics ---
1 packets transmitted, 1 received, 0% packet loss, time 0ms
rtt min/avg/max/mdev = 0.745/0.745/0.745/0.000 ms
[root@ceph-node1 ceph]#
[root@ceph-node1 ceph]# ssh-copy-id rgw-node1
The authenticity of host 'rgw-node1 (192.168.1.106)' can't be established.
ECDSA key fingerprint is af:2a:a5:74:a7:0b:f5:5b:ef:c5:4b:2a:fe:1d:30:8e.
Are you sure you want to continue connecting (yes/no)? yes
/usr/bin/ssh-copy-id: INFO: attempting to log in with the new key(s), to filter out any that are already installed
/usr/bin/ssh-copy-id: INFO: 1 key(s) remain to be installed -- if you are prompted now it is to install the new keys
root@rgw-node1's password:

Number of key(s) added: 1

Now try logging into the machine, with:   "ssh 'rgw-node1'"
and check to make sure that only the key(s) you wanted were added.

[root@ceph-node1 ceph]# ssh rgw-node1 hostname
rgw-node1.cephcookbook.com
[root@ceph-node1 ceph]#
```

3. Using `ceph-node1`, install the Ceph packages and copy the `ceph.conf` file to `rgw-node1`:

```
# cd /etc/ceph
# ceph-deploy install rgw-node1
# ceph-deploy config push rgw-node1
```

2. Finally, log in to `rgw-node1` and install the `ceph-radosgw` package:

```
# yum install ceph-radosgw
```

Configuring RADOS Gateway

Since we are using the Civetweb embedded web server for RGW, most of the things have already been set up with the `ceph-radosgw` service. In this recipe, we will create Ceph authentication keys for the Ceph RGW user and update the `ceph.conf` file.

How to do it...

1. To create the RGW user and keyring, execute the following commands from `ceph-node1`:

    1. Create a keyring using the following command:

       ```
       # cd /etc/ceph
       # ceph-authtool --create-keyring \
       /etc/ceph/ceph.client.radosgw.keyring
       # chmod +r /etc/ceph/ceph.client.radosgw.keyring
       ```

    2. Generate the gateway user and key for the RGW instance; our RGW instance name is `gateway`:

       ```
       # ceph-authtool /etc/ceph/ceph.client.radosgw.keyring \
       -n client.radosgw.gateway --gen-key
       ```

    3. Add capabilities to the key:

       ```
       # ceph-authtool -n client.radosgw.gateway --cap osd 'allow rwx' \
         --cap mon 'allow rwx' /etc/ceph/ceph.client.radosgw.keyring
       ```

    4. Add the key to the Ceph cluster:

       ```
       # ceph auth add client.radosgw.gateway \
       -i /etc/ceph/ceph.client.radosgw.keyring
       ```

    5. Distribute the key to the Ceph RGW node:

       ```
       # scp /etc/ceph/ceph.client.radosgw.keyring \
       rgw-node1:/etc/ceph/ceph.client.radosgw.keyring
       ```

```
[root@ceph-node1 ceph]# ceph-authtool --create-keyring /etc/ceph/ceph.client.radosgw.keyring
creating /etc/ceph/ceph.client.radosgw.keyring
[root@ceph-node1 ceph]#
[root@ceph-node1 ceph]# chmod +r /etc/ceph/ceph.client.radosgw.keyring
[root@ceph-node1 ceph]# ceph-authtool /etc/ceph/ceph.client.radosgw.keyring -n client.radosgw.gateway --gen-key
[root@ceph-node1 ceph]# ceph-authtool -n client.radosgw.gateway --cap osd 'allow rwx' --cap mon 'allow rwx' /etc/ceph ceph.client.radosgw.keyring
[root@ceph-node1 ceph]# ceph auth add client.radosgw.gateway -i /etc/ceph/ceph.client.radosgw.keyring
added key for client.radosgw.gateway
[root@ceph-node1 ceph]#
[root@ceph-node1 ceph]# scp /etc/ceph/ceph.client.radosgw.keyring rgw-node1:/etc/ceph/ceph.client.radosgw.keyring
ceph.client.radosgw.keyring                                              100%  121     0.1KB/s   00:00
[root@ceph-node1 ceph]#
```

2. Add the `client.radosgw.gateway` section to `ceph.conf` on `rgw-node1`.
   Make sure that the hostname is similar to the `# hostname -s` command output:

   ```
   [client.radosgw.gateway]

   host = rgw-node1

   keyring = /etc/ceph/ceph.client.radosgw.keyring

   rgw socket path = /var/run/ceph/ceph.radosgw.gateway.fastcgi.sock

   log file = /var/log/ceph/client.radosgw.gateway.log

   rgw dns name = rgw-node1.cephcookbook.com

   rgw print continue = false
   ```

   ```
   [root@rgw-node1 ceph]# tail -7 ceph.conf
   [client.radosgw.gateway]
   host = rgw-node1
   keyring = /etc/ceph/ceph.client.radosgw.keyring
   rgw socket path = /var/run/ceph/ceph.radosgw.gateway.fastcgi.sock
   log file = /var/log/ceph/client.radosgw.gateway.log
   rgw dns name = rgw-node1.cephcookbook.com
   rgw print continue = false
   [root@rgw-node1 ceph]#
   ```

3. By default, the `ceph-radosgw` startup script executes with the default user,
   `apache`. Change the default user from `apache` to `root`:

   ```
   # sed -i s"/DEFAULT_USER.*=.*'apache'/DEFAULT_USER='root'"/g /etc/
   rc.d/init.d/ceph-radosgw
   ```

   In a production environment, do not run `ceph-radosgw` as the 'root'
   user; instead, use 'apache' or any other non-root user.

4. Start the Ceph `radosgw` service and check its status:

   ```
   # service ceph-radosgw start
   ```

   ```
   # service ceph-radosgw status
   ```

5. The Civetweb webserver that is embedded into the `ceph-radosgw` daemon should
   now be running on the default port, 7480:

   ```
   # netstat -nlp | grep -i 7480
   ```

   ```
   [root@rgw-node1 ceph]# netstat -nlp | grep -i 7480
   tcp        0      0 0.0.0.0:7480            0.0.0.0:*               LISTEN      3635/radosgw
   [root@rgw-node1 ceph]#
   ```

Creating the radosgw user

To use Ceph object storage, we should create an initial Ceph object gateway user for the S3 interface and then create a subuser for the Swift interface

How to do it...

1. Make sure that `rgw-node1` is able to access the Ceph cluster.

    ```
    # ceph -s -k /etc/ceph/ceph.client.radosgw.keyring --name client.
    radosgw.gateway
    ```

2. Create a RADOS Gateway user for S3 access:

    ```
    # radosgw-admin user create --uid=mona --display-name="Monika
    Singh" --email=mona@cephcookbook.com -k /etc/ceph/ceph.client.
    radosgw.keyring --name client.radosgw.gateway
    ```

```
[root@rgw-node1 ceph]# radosgw-admin user create --uid=mona --display-name="Monika Singh" --email=mona@cephcookbook.com -k
/etc/ceph/ceph.client.radosgw.keyring --name client.radosgw.gateway
{ "user_id": "mona",
  "display_name": "Monika Singh",
  "email": "mona@cephcookbook.com",
  "suspended": 0,
  "max_buckets": 1000,
  "auid": 0,
  "subusers": [],
  "keys": [
        { "user": "mona",
          "access_key": "C162E2F8WZ98A0M3KK99",
          "secret_key": "J21mow6EPs6Sz4xtT7h+piDmhQBvlgWqVeicSRMg"}],
  "swift_keys": [],
  "caps": [],
  "op_mask": "read, write, delete",
  "default_placement": "",
  "placement_tags": [],
  "bucket_quota": { "enabled": false,
      "max_size_kb": -1,
      "max_objects": -1},
  "user_quota": { "enabled": false,
      "max_size_kb": -1,
      "max_objects": -1},
  "temp_url_keys": []}
[root@rgw-node1 ceph]#
```

3. The values keys (`access_key`) and the keys (`secret_key`) would be required later in this chapter for access validation.

4. To use Ceph object storage with the Swift API, we need to create a Swift subuser on the Ceph RGW:

```
# radosgw-admin subuser create --uid=mona --subuser=mona:swift
--access=full -k /etc/ceph/ceph.client.radosgw.keyring --name
client.radosgw.gateway
```

```
[root@rgw-node1 ceph]# radosgw-admin subuser create --uid=mona --subuser=mona:swift --access=full -k
/etc/ceph/ceph.client.radosgw.keyring --name client.radosgw.gateway
{ "user_id": "mona",
  "display_name": "Monika Singh",
  "email": "mona@cephcookbook.com",
  "suspended": 0,
  "max_buckets": 1000,
  "auid": 0,
  "subusers": [
        { "id": "mona:swift",
          "permissions": "full-control"}],
  "keys": [
        { "user": "mona:swift",
          "access_key": "58OV73F5AXX3CGNEZ9HV",
          "secret_key": ""},
        { "user": "mona",
          "access_key": "C162E2F8WZ98A0M3KK99",
          "secret_key": "J21mow6EPs6Sz4xtT7h+piDmhQBvlgWqVeicSRMg"}],
  "swift_keys": [],
  "caps": [],
  "op_mask": "read, write, delete",
  "default_placement": "",
  "placement_tags": [],
  "bucket_quota": { "enabled": false,
      "max_size_kb": -1,
      "max_objects": -1},
  "user_quota": { "enabled": false,
      "max_size_kb": -1,
      "max_objects": -1},
  "temp_url_keys": []}
[root@rgw-node1 ceph]#
```

5. Create secret keys for the mona:swift subuser; they will be used later in this chapter:

```
# radosgw-admin key create --subuser=mona:swift --key-type=swift
--gen-secret -k /etc/ceph/ceph.client.radosgw.keyring --name
client.radosgw.gateway
```

```
[root@rgw-node1 ceph]# radosgw-admin key create --subuser=mona:swift --key-type=swift --gen-secret
-k /etc/ceph/ceph.client.radosgw.keyring --name client.radosgw.gateway
{ "user_id": "mona",
  "display_name": "Monika Singh",
  "email": "mona@cephcookbook.com",
  "suspended": 0,
  "max_buckets": 1000,
  "auid": 0,
  "subusers": [
        { "id": "mona:swift",
          "permissions": "full-control"}],
  "keys": [
        { "user": "mona:swift",
          "access_key": "58OV73F5AXX3CGNEZ9HV",
          "secret_key": ""},
        { "user": "mona",
          "access_key": "C162E2F8WZ98A0M3KK99",
          "secret_key": "J21mow6EPs6Sz4xtT7h+piDmhQBvlgWqVeicSRMg"}],
  "swift_keys": [
        { "user": "mona:swift",
          "secret_key": "6vxGDhuEBsPSyX1E7vYvFrTXLVqoJByMHT+jnXPV"}],
  "caps": [],
  "op_mask": "read, write, delete",
  "default_placement": "",
  "placement_tags": [],
  "bucket_quota": { "enabled": false,
     "max_size_kb": -1,
     "max_objects": -1},
  "user_quota": { "enabled": false,
     "max_size_kb": -1,
     "max_objects": -1},
  "temp_url_keys": []}
[root@rgw-node1 ceph]#
```

See also...

> ▸ The *Accessing Ceph object storage using Swift API* recipe.

Accessing Ceph object storage using S3 API

Amazon Web Services offer **Simple Storage Service** (**S3**) that provides storage through web interfaces such as REST. Ceph extends its compatibility with S3 through the RESTful API. S3 client applications can access Ceph object storage based on access and secret keys.

S3 also requires a DNS service in place as it uses the virtual host bucket naming convention, that is, `<object_name>.<RGW_Fqdn>`. For example, if you have a bucket named `jupiter`, then it would be accessible over HTTP via the URL, `http://jupiter.rgw-node1.cephcookbook.com`.

How to do it...

Perform the following steps to configure DNS on the `rgw-node1` node. If you have an existing DNS server, you can skip the DNS configuration and use your DNS server.

Configuring DNS

1. Install bind packages on the `ceph-rgw` node:

   ```
   # yum install bind* -y
   ```

2. Edit `/etc/named.conf` and add information for IP addresses, IP range, and zone, which are mentioned as follows. You can match the changes from the author's version of the `named.conf` file provided with this book:

   ```
   listen-on port 53 { 127.0.0.1;192.168.1.106; };   ### Add DNS IP
   ###

   allow-query    { localhost;192.168.1.0/24; };      ### Add IP Range
   ###
   ```

   ```
   options {
           listen-on port 53 { 127.0.0.1;192.168.1.106; };   ### Add DNS IP ###
           listen-on-v6 port 53 { ::1; };
           directory       "/var/named";
           dump-file       "/var/named/data/cache_dump.db";
           statistics-file "/var/named/data/named_stats.txt";
           memstatistics-file "/var/named/data/named_mem_stats.txt";
           allow-query     { localhost;192.168.1.0/24; };     ### Add IP Range ###
   ```

   ```
   ### Add new zone for domain cephcookbook.com before EOF  ###

   zone "cephcookbook.com" IN {

   type master;

   file "db.cephcookbook.com";

   allow-update { none; };

   };
   ```

   ```
   ### Add new zone for domain cephcookbook.com before EOF   ###
   zone "cephcookbook.com" IN {
   type master;
   file "db.cephcookbook.com";
   allow-update { none; };
   };
   include "/etc/named.rfc1912.zones";
   include "/etc/named.root.key";
   ```

3. Create the zone file, `/var/named/db.cephcookbook.com`, with the following content. You can match the changes from the author's version of the `db.objectstore.com` file provided in the same directory file name `named.conf.rtf` with the code bundle of this chapter:

```
@ 86400 IN SOA cephcookbook.com. root.cephcookbook.com. (
         20091028 ; serial yyyy-mm-dd
         10800 ; refresh every 15 min
         3600 ; retry every hour
         3600000 ; expire after 1 month +
         86400 ); min ttl of 1 day
@ 86400 IN NS cephbookbook.com.
@ 86400 IN A 192.168.1.106
* 86400 IN CNAME @
```

```
[root@rgw-node1 ~]# cat /etc/db.cephcookbook.com
@ 86400 IN SOA cephcookbook.com. root.cephcookbook.com. (
         20091028 ; serial yyyy-mm-dd
         10800 ; refresh every 15 min
         3600 ; retry every hour
         3600000 ; expire after 1 month +
         86400 ); min ttl of 1 day
@ 86400 IN NS cephbookbook.com.
@ 86400 IN A 192.168.1.106
* 86400 IN CNAME @
[root@rgw-node1 ~]#
```

4. Edit `/etc/resolve.conf` and add the following content:

```
search cephcookbook.com
nameserver 192.168.1.106
```

5. Start the `named` service:

```
# service named start
```

6. Test the DNS configuration files for any syntax errors:

```
# named-checkconf /etc/named.conf
# named-checkzone cephcookbook.com /var/named/db.cephcookbook.com
```

```
[root@rgw-node1 ~]# service named start
Redirecting to /bin/systemctl start  named.service
[root@rgw-node1 ~]#
[root@rgw-node1 ~]# named-checkconf /etc/named.conf
[root@rgw-node1 ~]# named-checkzone cephcookbook.com /var/named/db.cephcookbook.com
zone cephcookbook.com/IN: loaded serial 20091028
OK
[root@rgw-node1 ~]#
```

7. Test the DNS server:

```
# dig rgw-node1.cephcookbook.com
# nslookup rgw-node1.cephcookbook.com
```

Configuring the s3cmd client

To access Ceph object storage via the S3 API, we should configure the client machine with `s3cmd` as well as the DNS client settings. Perform the following steps to configure the `s3cmd` client machine:

1. Bring up the `client-node1` virtual machine using Vagrant. This virtual machine will be used as a client machine for S3 object storage:

```
$ vagrant up client-node1
```

2. On the `client-node1` machine, update `/etc/resolve.conf` with DNS server entries:

```
search cephcookbook.com
nameserver 192.168.1.106
```

3. Test DNS settings on `client-node1`:

```
# dig rgw-node1.cephcookbook.com
# nslookup rgw-node1.cephcookbook.com
```

4. `client-node1` should be able to resolve all the subdomains for `rgw-node1.cephcookbook.com`:

```
# ping mj.rgw-node1.cephcookbook.com -c 1
# ping anything.rgw-node1.cephcookbook.com -c 1
```

```
root@client-node1:~# ping mj.rgw-node1.cephcookbook.com -c 1
PING cephcookbook.com (192.168.1.106) 56(84) bytes of data.
64 bytes from 192.168.1.106: icmp_seq=1 ttl=64 time=0.475 ms

--- cephcookbook.com ping statistics ---
1 packets transmitted, 1 received, 0% packet loss, time 0ms
rtt min/avg/max/mdev = 0.475/0.475/0.475/0.000 ms
root@client-node1:~#
root@client-node1:~# ping anything.rgw-node1.cephcookbook.com -c 1
PING cephcookbook.com (192.168.1.106) 56(84) bytes of data.
64 bytes from 192.168.1.106: icmp_seq=1 ttl=64 time=0.413 ms

--- cephcookbook.com ping statistics ---
1 packets transmitted, 1 received, 0% packet loss, time 0ms
rtt min/avg/max/mdev = 0.413/0.413/0.413/0.000 ms
root@client-node1:~#
```

5. Configure the S3 client (`s3cmd`) on client-node1:

   1. Install `s3cmd` using the following command:

      ```
      # apt-get install -y s3cmd
      ```

   2. Configure `s3cmd` by providing the `access_key` and `secret_key` of the user, `mona`, which we created earlier in this chapter. Execute the following command and follow the prompts:

      ```
      # s3cmd --configure
      ```

      ```
      root@client-node1:~# s3cmd --configure

      Enter new values or accept defaults in brackets with Enter.
      Refer to user manual for detailed description of all options.

      Access key and Secret key are your identifiers for Amazon S3
      Access Key: C162E2F8WZ98AOM3KK99
      Secret Key: J21mow6EPs6Sz4xtT7h+piDmhQBvlgWqVeicSRMg

      Encryption password is used to protect your files from reading
      by unauthorized persons while in transfer to S3
      Encryption password:
      Path to GPG program [/usr/bin/gpg]:

      When using secure HTTPS protocol all communication with Amazon S3
      servers is protected from 3rd party eavesdropping. This method is
      slower than plain HTTP and can't be used if you're behind a proxy
      Use HTTPS protocol [No]:

      On some networks all internet access must go through a HTTP proxy.
      Try setting it here if you can't conect to S3 directly
      HTTP Proxy server name:

      New settings:
        Access Key: C162E2F8WZ98AOM3KK99
        Secret Key: J21mow6EPs6Sz4xtT7h+piDmhQBvlgWqVeicSRMg
        Encryption password:
        Path to GPG program: /usr/bin/gpg
        Use HTTPS protocol: False
        HTTP Proxy server name:
        HTTP Proxy server port: 0

      Test access with supplied credentials? [Y/n] n

      Save settings? [y/N] y
      Configuration saved to '/root/.s3cfg'
      root@client-node1:~#
      ```

   3. The `~# s3cmd --configure` command will create `/root/.s3cfg`. Edit this file for the RGW host details. Modify `host_base` and `host_bucket`, as shown as follows. Make sure these lines do not have trailing spaces at the end:

      ```
      host_base = rgw-node1.cephcookbook.com:7480

      host_bucket = %(bucket)s.rgw-node1.cephcookbook.com:7480
      ```

You can refer to the author's version of the `/root/.s3cfg` file provided with the code bundle of this chapter.

```
root@client-node1:~# cat /root/.s3cfg
[default]
access_key = C162E2F8WZ98AOM3KK99
bucket_location = US
cloudfront_host = cloudfront.amazonaws.com
default_mime_type = binary/octet-stream
delete_removed = False
dry_run = False
enable_multipart = True
encoding = UTF-8
encrypt = False
follow_symlinks = False
force = False
get_continue = False
gpg_command = /usr/bin/gpg
gpg_decrypt = %(gpg_command)s -d --verbose --no-use-agent --batch --yes --passphrase-fd %(passphrase_fd)s -o %(output_file)s %(input_file)s
gpg_encrypt = %(gpg_command)s -c --verbose --no-use-agent --batch --yes --passphrase-fd %(passphrase_fd)s -o %(output_file)s %(input_file)s
gpg_passphrase =
guess_mime_type = True
host_base = rgw-node1.cephcookbook.com:7480
host_bucket = %(bucket)s.rgw-node1.cephcookbook.com:7480
human_readable_sizes = False
invalidate_on_cf = False
list_md5 = False
log_target_prefix =
mime_type =
multipart_chunk_size_mb = 15
preserve_attrs = True
progress_meter = True
proxy_host =
proxy_port = 0
recursive = False
recv_chunk = 4096
reduced_redundancy = False
secret_key = J21mow6EPs6Sz4xtT7h+piDmhQBvlgwqVeicSRMg
send_chunk = 4096
simpledb_host = sdb.amazonaws.com
skip_existing = False
socket_timeout = 300
urlencoding_mode = normal
use_https = False
verbosity = WARNING
website_endpoint = http://%(bucket)s.s3-website-%(location)s.amazonaws.com/
website_error =
website_index = index.html
```

6. Finally, we will create buckets and put objects into them:

   # s3cmd mb s3://first-bucket

   # s3cmd ls

   # s3cmd put /etc/hosts s3://first-bucket

   # s3cmd ls s3://first-bucket

```
root@client-node1:~# s3cmd mb s3://first-bucket
Bucket 's3://first-bucket/' created
root@client-node1:~#
root@client-node1:~# s3cmd ls
2015-04-11 23:55  s3://first-bucket
root@client-node1:~#
root@client-node1:~# s3cmd put /etc/hosts s3://first-bucket
WARNING: Module python-magic is not available. Guessing MIME types based on file extensions.
/etc/hosts -> s3://first-bucket/hosts  [1 of 1]
 601 of 601   100% in    1s    436.06 B/s  done
root@client-node1:~#
root@client-node1:~#
root@client-node1:~# s3cmd ls s3://first-bucket
2015-04-11 23:55       601   s3://first-bucket/hosts
root@client-node1:~#
```

Accessing Ceph object storage using the Swift API

Ceph supports RESTful API that is compatible with the basic data access model of the Swift API. In the last section, we covered accessing the Ceph cluster via the S3 API; in this section, we will learn to access it via the Swift API.

How to do it

To use Ceph object storage with the Swift API, we need the Swift subuser and secret keys that we created earlier in this chapter. This user information will then be passed using the Swift CLI tool in order to access Ceph object storage:

1. On `client-node1`, a virtual machine installs the python Swift client:

   ```
   # apt-get install python-setuptools
   # easy_install pip
   # pip install --upgrade setuptools
   # pip install --upgrade python-swiftclient
   ```

2. Get the swift subuser and secret keys:

   ```
   # radosgw-admin user info --uid mona
   ```

3. Access Ceph object storage by listing the default bucket:

   ```
   # swift -A http://192.168.1.106:7480/auth/1.0 -U mona:swift -K 6vx
   GDhuEBsPSyX1E7vYvFrTXLVqoJByMHT+jnXPV list
   ```

4. Add a new bucket, `second-bucket`:

   ```
   # swift -A http://192.168.1.106:7480/auth/1.0 -U mona:swift -K 6vx
   GDhuEBsPSyX1E7vYvFrTXLVqoJByMHT+jnXPV post second-bucket
   ```

5. List the buckets; it should show the new `second-bucket` as well:

   ```
   # swift -A http://192.168.1.106:7480/auth/1.0 -U mona:swift -K 6vx
   GDhuEBsPSyX1E7vYvFrTXLVqoJByMHT+jnXPV list
   ```

   ```
   root@client-node1:~# swift -A http://192.168.1.106:7480/auth/1.0 -U mona:swift -K
   6vxGDhuEBsPSyX1E7vYvFrTXLVqoJByMHT+jnXPV list
   first-bucket
   root@client-node1:~#
   root@client-node1:~# swift -A http://192.168.1.106:7480/auth/1.0 -U mona:swift -K
   6vxGDhuEBsPSyX1E7vYvFrTXLVqoJByMHT+jnXPV post second-bucket
   root@client-node1:~# swift -A http://192.168.1.106:7480/auth/1.0 -U mona:swift -K
   6vxGDhuEBsPSyX1E7vYvFrTXLVqoJByMHT+jnXPV list
   first-bucket
   second-bucket
   root@client-node1:~#
   ```

See also...

▶ The *Creating the RADOS Gateway user* recipe

Integrating RADOS Gateway with OpenStack Keystone

Ceph can be integrated with the OpenStack identity management service, 'Keystone'. With this integration, the Ceph RGW is configured to accept keystone tokens for user authority. So, any user who is validated by Keystone will get rights to access the RGW.

How to do it...

Execute the following command on your `openstack-node1`, unless otherwise specified:

1. Configure OpenStack to point to the Ceph RGW by creating the service and its endpoints:

   ```
   # keystone service-create --name swift --type object-store
   --description "ceph object store"
   ```

   ```
   # keystone endpoint-create --service-
   id 6614554878344bbeaa7fec0d5dccca7f --publicurl
   http://192.168.1.106:7480/swift/v1 --internalurl
   http://192.168.1.106:7480/swift/v1 --adminurl
   http://192.168.1.106:7480/swift/v1 --region RegionOne
   ```

2. Get the keystone admin token, which will be used for the RGW configuration:

   ```
   # cat /etc/keystone/keystone.conf | grep -i admin_token
   ```

3. Create a directory for certificates:

    ```
    # mkdir -p /var/ceph/nss
    ```

4. Generate `openssl` certificates:

    ```
    # openssl x509 -in /etc/keystone/ssl/certs/ca.pem -pubkey|certutil
    -d /var/ceph/nss -A -n ca -t "TCu,Cu,Tuw"
    ```

    ```
    # openssl x509 -in /etc/keystone/ssl/certs/signing_cert.pem
    -pubkey | certutil -A -d /var/ceph/nss -n signing_cert -t "P,P,P"
    ```

    ```
    [root@os-node1 ~(keystone_admin)]# mkdir -p /var/ceph/nss
    [root@os-node1 ~(keystone_admin)]# openssl x509 -in /etc/keystone/ssl/certs/ca.pem -pubkey|certutil -d /var/ceph/nss
     -A -n ca -t "TCu,Cu,Tuw"
    Notice: Trust flag u is set automatically if the private key is present.
    [root@os-node1 ~(keystone_admin)]#
    [root@os-node1 ~(keystone_admin)]# openssl x509 -in /etc/keystone/ssl/certs/signing_cert.pem -pubkey|certutil -A -d
    /var/ceph/nss -n signing_cert -t "P,P,P"
    [root@os-node1 ~(keystone_admin)]# ls -l /var/ceph/nss/
    total 76
    -rw------- 1 root root 65536 Apr 17 00:40 cert8.db
    -rw------- 1 root root 16384 Apr 17 00:40 key3.db
    -rw------- 1 root root 16384 Apr 17 00:38 secmod.db
    [root@os-node1 ~(keystone_admin)]#
    ```

5. Create the `/var/ceph/nss` directory on `rgw-node1`:

    ```
    # mkdir -p /var/ceph/nss
    ```

6. From `openstack-node1`, copy `openssl` certificates to `rgw-node1`. If you are logging in for the first time, you will get an SSH confirmation; type `yes` and then type the root password, which is `vagrant` for all the machines:

    ```
    # scp /var/ceph/nss/* rgw-node1:/var/ceph/nss
    ```

7. On `rgw-node1`, create directories and change the ownership to Apache:

    ```
    # mkdir /var/run/ceph
    ```

    ```
    # chown apache:apache /var/run/ceph
    ```

    ```
    # chown -R apache:apache /var/ceph/nss
    ```

8. Update `/etc/ceph/ceph.conf` on `rgw-node1` with the following entries under the `[client.radosgw.gateway]` section:

    ```
    rgw keystone url = http://192.168.1.111:5000
    ```

    ```
    rgw keystone admin token = f72adb0238d74bb885005744ce526148
    ```

    ```
    rgw keystone accepted roles = admin, Member, swiftoperator
    ```

    ```
            rgw keystone token cache size = 500
    ```

    ```
            rgw keystone revocation interval = 60
    ```

    ```
            rgw s3 auth use keystone = true
    ```

    ```
    nss db path = /var/ceph/nss
    ```

rgw keystone url must be the keystone management URL that can be gotten from the `# keystone endpoint-list` command.

rgw keystone admin token is the token value that we saved in Step 2 of this recipe.

9. Finally, restart the `ceph-radosgw` service:

   ```
   # systemctl restart ceph-radosgw
   ```

10. Now, to test the Keystone and Ceph integration, switch back to `openstack-node1` and run basic Swift commands, and it should not ask for any user keys:

    ```
    # swift list
    ```

    ```
    # swift post swift-test-bucket
    ```

    ```
    # swift list
    ```

    ```
    [root@os-node1 ~(keystone_admin)]# swift list
    [root@os-node1 ~(keystone_admin)]# swift post swift-test-bucket
    [root@os-node1 ~(keystone_admin)]# swift list
    swift-test-bucket
    [root@os-node1 ~(keystone_admin)]#
    ```

11. You should be able to perform all sorts of bucket operations using both `swift cli` as well as from the OpenStack horizon dashboard, the **Object storage** section, without being asked for user credentials for the Ceph RGW; this is because after this configuration changes, Keystone verified tokens are accepted by the Ceph RGW.

Configuring Ceph federated gateways

The Ceph RGW can be deployed in a federated configuration with multiple regions, and with multiple zones for a region. As shown in the following diagram, multiple Ceph radosgw instances can be deployed in a geographically separated fashion. Configuring the Ceph object gateway regions and metadata synchronization agents helps to maintain a single namespace, even though Ceph `radosgw` instances run in a different geographic locale or on a different Ceph storage cluster.

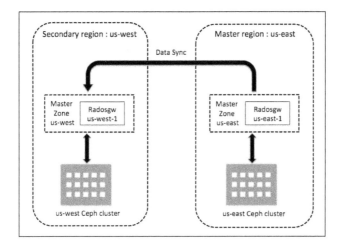

Another approach is to deploy one or more `ceph radosgw` instances that are geographically separated yet are within a region in separated logical containers known as zones. In this case, a data synchronization agent also enables the service to maintain one or more copies of the master zone's data within a region on the same Ceph cluster. These extra copies of data are important for backup or disaster recovery use cases.

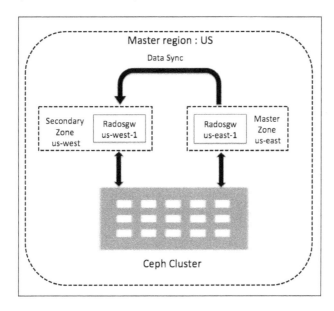

In this recipe, we will learn to deploy the latter method of the Ceph `radosgw` federation. Under this, we will create a master region, US, which will host two zones: `master zone: us-east`, containing the RGW instance `us-east-1`, and `secondary zone: us-west`, containing the RGW instance `us-west-1`. The following are parameters and their values that will be used:

- ▸ Master Region → United States: `us`
- ▸ Master Zone → United States region-East zone: `us-east`
- ▸ Secondary Zone → United States region-West zone: `us-west`
- ▸ Radosgw Instance-1 → United States region-East zone - Instance1: `us-east-1`
- ▸ Radosgw Instance-2 → United States region-West zone - Instance1: `us-west-1`

How to do it...

1. From your host machine, bring up the virtual machines `us-east-1` and `us-west-1` using Vagrant:

```
$ cd ceph-cookbook
$ vagrant status us-east-1 us-west-1
$ vagrant up us-east-1 us-west-1
$ vagrant status us-east-1 us-west-1
```

```
teeri:ceph-cookbook ksingh$ vagrant status us-east-1 us-west-1
Current machine states:

us-east-1                 running (virtualbox)
us-west-1                 running (virtualbox)

This environment represents multiple VMs. The VMs are all listed
above with their current state. For more information about a specific
VM, run `vagrant status NAME`.
teeri:ceph-cookbook ksingh$
```

From now on, we will execute all the commands from any of the Ceph monitor machines until otherwise specified. In our case, we will use `ceph-node1`. Next, we will create Ceph pools that will be used to store a bunch of critical information about object storage data, such as buckets, a bucket index, a global catalog, logs, an S3 user ID, Swift user accounts, e-mails, and so on.

2. Create Ceph pools for the `us-east` zone:

```
# ceph osd pool create .us-east.rgw.root 32 32
# ceph osd pool create .us-east.rgw.control 32 32
# ceph osd pool create .us-east.rgw.gc 32 32
# ceph osd pool create .us-east.rgw.buckets 32 32
# ceph osd pool create .us-east.rgw.buckets.index 32 32
```

```
# ceph osd pool create .us-east.rgw.buckets.extra 32 32

# ceph osd pool create .us-east.log 32 32

# ceph osd pool create .us-east.intent-log 32 32

# ceph osd pool create .us-east.usage 32 32

# ceph osd pool create .us-east.users 32 32

# ceph osd pool create .us-east.users.email 32 32

# ceph osd pool create .us-east.users.swift 32 32

# ceph osd pool create .us-east.users.uid 32 32
```

3. Create Ceph pools for the `us-west` zone:

```
# ceph osd pool create .us-west.rgw.root 32 32

# ceph osd pool create .us-west.rgw.control 32 32

# ceph osd pool create .us-west.rgw.gc 32 32

# ceph osd pool create .us-west.rgw.buckets 32 32

# ceph osd pool create .us-west.rgw.buckets.index 32 32

# ceph osd pool create .us-west.rgw.buckets.extra 32 32

# ceph osd pool create .us-west.log 32 32

# ceph osd pool create .us-west.intent-log 32 32

# ceph osd pool create .us-west.usage 32 32

# ceph osd pool create .us-west.users 32 32

# ceph osd pool create .us-west.users.email 32 32

# ceph osd pool create .us-west.users.swift 32 32

# ceph osd pool create .us-west.users.uid 32 32
```

4. Verify the newly created Ceph pools:

```
# ceph osd lspools
```

```
[root@ceph-node1 ~]# ceph osd lspools
0 rbd,1 images,2 volumes,3 vms,4 .rgw.root,5 .rgw.control,6 .rgw,7 .rgw.gc,8 .users.uid,9 .users.email,10 .users,11
.users.swift,12 .rgw.buckets.index,13 .rgw.buckets,14 .us-east.rgw.root,15 .us-east.rgw.control,16 .us-east.rgw.gc,1
7 .us-east.rgw.buckets,18 .us-east.rgw.buckets.index,19 .us-east.rgw.buckets.extra,20 .us-east.log,21 .us-east.inten
t-log,22 .us-east.usage,23 .us-east.users,24 .us-east.users.email,25 .us-east.users.swift,26 .us-east.users.uid,27 .
us-west.rgw.root,28 .us-west.rgw.control,29 .us-west.rgw.gc,30 .us-west.rgw.buckets,31 .us-west.rgw.buckets.index,32
 .us-west.rgw.buckets.extra,33 .us-west.log,34 .us-west.intent-log,35 .us-west.usage,36 .us-west.users,37 .us-west.u
sers.email,38 .us-west.users.swift,39 .us-west.users.uid,
[root@ceph-node1 ~]#
```

5. The RGW instance requires a user and keys to talk to the Ceph storage cluster:

1. Create a keyring using the following command:

```
# ceph-authtool --create-keyring /etc/ceph/ceph.client.
radosgw.keyring
```

```
# chmod +r /etc/ceph/ceph.client.radosgw.keyring
```

2. Generate a gateway username and key for each instance:

```
# ceph-authtool /etc/ceph/ceph.client.radosgw.keyring -n
client.radosgw.us-east-1 --gen-key
```

```
# ceph-authtool /etc/ceph/ceph.client.radosgw.keyring -n
client.radosgw.us-west-1 --gen-key
```

3. Add capabilities to keys:

```
# ceph-authtool -n client.radosgw.us-east-1 --cap osd
'allow rwx' --cap mon 'allow rwx' /etc/ceph/ceph.client.
radosgw.keyring
```

```
# ceph-authtool -n client.radosgw.us-west-1 --cap osd
'allow rwx' --cap mon 'allow rwx' /etc/ceph/ceph.client.
radosgw.keyring
```

4. Add keys to the Ceph storage cluster:

```
# ceph -k /etc/ceph/ceph.client.admin.keyring auth add
client.radosgw.us-east-1 -i /etc/ceph/ceph.client.radosgw.
keyring
```

```
# ceph -k /etc/ceph/ceph.client.admin.keyring auth add
client.radosgw.us-west-1 -i /etc/ceph/ceph.client.radosgw.
keyring
```

```
[root@ceph-node1 ~]# ceph-authtool --create-keyring /etc/ceph/ceph.client.radosgw.keyring
creating /etc/ceph/ceph.client.radosgw.keyring
[root@ceph-node1 ~]# chmod +r /etc/ceph/ceph.client.radosgw.keyring
[root@ceph-node1 ~]# ceph-authtool /etc/ceph/ceph.client.radosgw.keyring -n client.radosgw.us-east-1 --gen-key
[root@ceph-node1 ~]# ceph-authtool /etc/ceph/ceph.client.radosgw.keyring -n client.radosgw.us-west-1 --gen-key
[root@ceph-node1 ~]# ceph-authtool -n client.radosgw.us-east-1 --cap osd 'allow rwx' --cap mon 'allow rwx' /etc/ceph
/ceph.client.radosgw.keyring
[root@ceph-node1 ~]# ceph-authtool -n client.radosgw.us-west-1 --cap osd 'allow rwx' --cap mon 'allow rwx' /etc/ceph
/ceph.client.radosgw.keyring
[root@ceph-node1 ~]#
[root@ceph-node1 ~]# ceph -k /etc/ceph/ceph.client.admin.keyring auth add client.radosgw.us-east-1 -i /etc/ceph/ceph
.client.radosgw.keyring
added key for client.radosgw.us-east-1
[root@ceph-node1 ~]#
[root@ceph-node1 ~]# ceph -k /etc/ceph/ceph.client.admin.keyring auth add client.radosgw.us-west-1 -i /etc/ceph/ceph
.client.radosgw.keyring
added key for client.radosgw.us-west-1
[root@ceph-node1 ~]#
```

6. Add RGW instances to the Ceph configuration file, that is, `/etc/ceph/ceph.conf`:

```
[client.radosgw.us-east-1]
host = us-east-1
rgw region = us
rgw region root pool = .us.rgw.root
rgw zone = us-east
rgw zone root pool = .us-east.rgw.root
keyring = /etc/ceph/ceph.client.radosgw.keyring
rgw dns name = rgw-node1
rgw socket path = /var/run/ceph/client.radosgw.us-east-1.sock
log file = /var/log/ceph/client.radosgw.us-east-1.log

[client.radosgw.us-west-1]
host = us-west-1
rgw region = us
rgw region root pool = .us.rgw.root
rgw zone = us-west
rgw zone root pool = .us-west.rgw.root
keyring = /etc/ceph/ceph.client.radosgw.keyring
rgw dns name = rgw-ndoe1
rgw socket path = /var/run/ceph/client.radosgw.us-west-1.sock
log file = /var/log/ceph/client.radosgw.us-west-1.log
```

```
[root@ceph-node1 ceph]# tail -22 ceph.conf

[client.radosgw.us-east-1]
host = us-east-1
rgw region = us
rgw region root pool = .us.rgw.root
rgw zone = us-east
rgw zone root pool = .us-east.rgw.root
keyring = /etc/ceph/ceph.client.radosgw.keyring
rgw dns name = rgw-node1
rgw socket path = /var/run/ceph/client.radosgw.us-east-1.sock
log file = /var/log/ceph/client.radosgw.us-east-1.log

[client.radosgw.us-west-1]
host = us-west-1
rgw region = us
rgw region root pool = .us.rgw.root
rgw zone = us-west
rgw zone root pool = .us-west.rgw.root
keyring = /etc/ceph/ceph.client.radosgw.keyring
rgw dns name = rgw-ndoe1
rgw socket path = /var/run/ceph/client.radosgw.us-west-1.sock
log file = /var/log/ceph/client.radosgw.us-west-1.log
[root@ceph-node1 ceph]#
```

7. Next, we will install Ceph packages on the `us-east-1` and `us-west-1` nodes using `ceph-deploy` from the `ceph-node1` machine. Finally, we will add configuration files to these nodes:

    1. Allow `cep-node1` to perform a password-less SSH login to the RGW nodes. The root password is default, that is, `vagrant`:

        ```
        # ssh-copy-id us-east-1
        # ssh-copy-id us-west-1
        ```

    2. Install Ceph packages on the RGW instances:

        ```
        # ceph-deploy install us-east-1 us-west-1
        ```

    3. Once Ceph packages are installed on the RGW instance, push the Ceph configuration files:

        ```
        # ceph-deploy --overwrite-conf config push us-east-1 us-west-1
        ```

    4. Copy the RGW keyrings from `ceph-node` to gateway instance:

        ```
        # scp ceph.client.radosgw.keyring us-east-1:/etc/ceph
        # scp ceph.client.radosgw.keyring us-west-1:/etc/ceph
        ```

    5. Next, install the `ceph-radosgw` and `radosgw-agent` packages on the `us-east-1` and `us-west-1` radosgw instances:

        ```
        # ssh us-east-1 yum install -y ceph-radosgw radosgw-agent
        # ssh us-west-1 yum install -y ceph-radosgw radosgw-agent
        ```

    6. For simplicity, we will disable firewall on the nodes:

        ```
        # ssh us-east-1 systemctl disable firewalld
        # ssh us-east-1 systemctl stop firewalld
        # ssh us-west-1 systemctl disable firewalld
        # ssh us-west-1 systemctl stop firewalld
        ```

8. Create the `us` region. Log in to `us-east-1` and execute the following commands:

    1. Create a region infile called `us.json` under the `/etc/ceph` directory with the following content. You can refer to the author's version of the `us.json` file provided with the code bundle of this chapter:

        ```
        { "name": "us",
          "api_name": "us",
          "is_master": "true",
          "endpoints": [
            "http:\/\/us-east-1.cephcookbook.com:7480\/"],
          "master_zone": "us-east",
          "zones": [
        ```

```
        { "name": "us-east",
          "endpoints": [
            "http:\/\/us-east-1.cephcookbook.com:7480\/"],
            "log_meta": "true",
            "log_data": "true"},
            { "name": "us-west",
              "endpoints": [
                 "http:\/\/us-west-1.cephcookbook.
    com:7480\/"],
              "log_meta": "true",
              "log_data": "true"}],
     "placement_targets": [
      {
        "name": "default-placement",
        "tags": []
      }
      ],
     "default_placement": "default-placement"}
```

```
[root@us-east-1 ceph]# cat us.json
{ "name": "us",
  "api_name": "us",
  "is_master": "true",
  "endpoints": [
        "http:\/\/us-east-1.cephcookbook.com:7480\/"],
  "master_zone": "us-east",
  "zones": [
        { "name": "us-east",
          "endpoints": [
                "http:\/\/us-east-1.cephcookbook.com:7480\/"],
          "log_meta": "true",
          "log_data": "true"},
        { "name": "us-west",
          "endpoints": [
                "http:\/\/us-west-1.cephcookbook.com:7480\/"],
          "log_meta": "true",
          "log_data": "true"}],
  "placement_targets": [
   {
     "name": "default-placement",
     "tags": []
   }
   ],
  "default_placement": "default-placement"}
[root@us-east-1 ceph]#
```

2. Create the `us` region with the `us.json` infile that you just created:

```
# cd /etc/ceph
# radosgw-admin region set --infile us.json --name
client.radosgw.us-east-1
```

3. Delete the default region if it exists:

```
# rados -p .us.rgw.root rm region_info.default --name
client.radosgw.us-east-1
```

4. Set the `us` region as the default region:

```
# radosgw-admin region default --rgw-region=us --name
client.radosgw.us-east-1
```

5. Finally, update the region map:

```
# radosgw-admin regionmap update --name client.radosgw.
us-east-1
```

9. Generate `access_keys` and `secret_keys` for `us-east` and `us-west` zones:

1. Generate an `access_key` for the `us-east` zone:

```
# < /dev/urandom tr -dc A-Z-0-9 | head -c${1:-20};echo;
```

2. Generate a `secret_key` for the `us-east` zone:

```
# < /dev/urandom tr -dc A-Z-0-9-a-z | head -c${1:-
40};echo;
```

```
[root@us-east-1 ceph]# < /dev/urandom tr -dc A-Z-0-9 | head -c${1:-20};echo;
XNKOST8WXTMWZGN29NF9
[root@us-east-1 ceph]#
[root@us-east-1 ceph]# < /dev/urandom tr -dc A-Z-0-9-a-z | head -c${1:-40};echo;
7VJm8uAp71xKQZkjoPZmHu4sACA1SY8jTjay9dP5
[root@us-east-1 ceph]#
```

3. Generate `access_key` for the `us-west` zone:

```
# < /dev/urandom tr -dc A-Z-0-9 | head -c${1:-20};echo;
```

4. Generate `secret_key` for the `us-west` zone:

```
# < /dev/urandom tr -dc A-Z-0-9-a-z | head -c${1:-
40};echo;
```

```
[root@us-east-1 ceph]# < /dev/urandom tr -dc A-Z-0-9 | head -c${1:-20};echo;
AAKOST8WXTMWZGN29NF9
[root@us-east-1 ceph]# < /dev/urandom tr -dc A-Z-0-9-a-z | head -c${1:-40};echo;
AAJm8uAp71xKQZkjoPZmHu4sACA1SY8jTjay9dP5
[root@us-east-1 ceph]#
```

10. Create a zone infile called `us-east.json` for the `us-east` zone. You can refer to the author's version of the `us-east.json` file provided with the code bundle of this chapter:

```
{ "domain_root": ".us-east.domain.rgw",
"control_pool": ".us-east.rgw.control",
"gc_pool": ".us-east.rgw.gc",
"log_pool": ".us-east.log",
"intent_log_pool": ".us-east.intent-log",
"usage_log_pool": ".us-east.usage",
"user_keys_pool": ".us-east.users",
"user_email_pool": ".us-east.users.email",
"user_swift_pool": ".us-east.users.swift",
"user_uid_pool": ".us-east.users.uid",
"system_key": { "access_key": " XNK0ST8WXTMWZGN29NF9", "secret_
key": "7VJm8uAp71xKQZkjoPZmHu4sACA1SY8jTjay9dP5"},
"placement_pools": [
{ "key": "default-placement",
"val": { "index_pool": ".us-east.rgw.buckets.index",
"data_pool": ".us-east.rgw.buckets"}
}
]
}
```

```
[root@us-east-1 ceph]# cat us-east.json
{ "domain_root": ".us-east.domain.rgw",
  "control_pool": ".us-east.rgw.control",
  "gc_pool": ".us-east.rgw.gc",
  "log_pool": ".us-east.log",
  "intent_log_pool": ".us-east.intent-log",
  "usage_log_pool": ".us-east.usage",
  "user_keys_pool": ".us-east.users",
  "user_email_pool": ".us-east.users.email",
  "user_swift_pool": ".us-east.users.swift",
  "user_uid_pool": ".us-east.users.uid",
  "system_key": { "access_key": "XNK0ST8WXTMWZGN29NF9", "secret_key":
"7VJm8uAp71xKQZkjoPZmHu4sACA1SY8jTjay9dP5"},
  "placement_pools": [
    { "key": "default-placement",
      "val": { "index_pool": ".us-east.rgw.buckets.index",
               "data_pool": ".us-east.rgw.buckets"}
    }
  ]
}
[root@us-east-1 ceph]#
```

11. Add the `us-east` zone using an infile in both the east and west pools:

```
# radosgw-admin zone set --rgw-zone=us-east --infile us-east.json
--name client.radosgw.us-east-1
```

```
[root@us-east-1 ceph]# radosgw-admin zone set --rgw-zone=us-east --infile us-east.json
--name client.radosgw.us-east-1
2015-05-03 21:56:38.878117 7fc365bd5880  0 couldn't find old data placement pools conf
ig, setting up new ones for the zone
{ "domain_root": ".us-east.domain.rgw",
  "control_pool": ".us-east.rgw.control",
  "gc_pool": ".us-east.rgw.gc",
  "log_pool": ".us-east.log",
  "intent_log_pool": ".us-east.intent-log",
  "usage_log_pool": ".us-east.usage",
  "user_keys_pool": ".us-east.users",
  "user_email_pool": ".us-east.users.email",
  "user_swift_pool": ".us-east.users.swift",
  "user_uid_pool": ".us-east.users.uid",
  "system_key": { "access_key": "XNKOST8WXTMWZGN29NF9",
      "secret_key": "7VJm8uAp71xKQzkjoPZmHu4sACA1SY8jTjay9dP5"},
  "placement_pools": [
        { "key": "default-placement",
          "val": { "index_pool": ".us-east.rgw.buckets.index",
              "data_pool": ".us-east.rgw.buckets",
              "data_extra_pool": ""}}]}[root@us-east-1 ceph]#
[root@us-east-1 ceph]#
```

Now, run the following command:

```
# radosgw-admin zone set --rgw-zone=us-east --infile us-east.json
--name client.radosgw.us-west-1
```

```
[root@us-east-1 ceph]# radosgw-admin zone set --rgw-zone=us-east --infile us-east.json
--name client.radosgw.us-west-1
2015-05-03 21:58:58.982509 7f4b14f47880  0 couldn't find old data placement pools conf
ig, setting up new ones for the zone
{ "domain_root": ".us-east.domain.rgw",
  "control_pool": ".us-east.rgw.control",
  "gc_pool": ".us-east.rgw.gc",
  "log_pool": ".us-east.log",
  "intent_log_pool": ".us-east.intent-log",
  "usage_log_pool": ".us-east.usage",
  "user_keys_pool": ".us-east.users",
  "user_email_pool": ".us-east.users.email",
  "user_swift_pool": ".us-east.users.swift",
  "user_uid_pool": ".us-east.users.uid",
  "system_key": { "access_key": "XNKOST8WXTMWZGN29NF9",
      "secret_key": "7VJm8uAp71xKQzkjoPZmHu4sACA1SY8jTjay9dP5"},
  "placement_pools": [
        { "key": "default-placement",
          "val": { "index_pool": ".us-east.rgw.buckets.index",
              "data_pool": ".us-east.rgw.buckets",
              "data_extra_pool": ""}}]}[root@us-east-1 ceph]#
[root@us-east-1 ceph]#
```

12. Similarly, for the `us-east` zone, create the `us-west.json` infile with the following contents. You can refer to the author's version of the `us-west.json` file provided with the code bundle of this chapter:

```
{ "domain_root": ".us-west.domain.rgw",
   "control_pool": ".us-west.rgw.control",
   "gc_pool": ".us-west.rgw.gc",
   "log_pool": ".us-west.log",
   "intent_log_pool": ".us-west.intent-log",
   "usage_log_pool": ".us-west.usage",
   "user_keys_pool": ".us-west.users",
   "user_email_pool": ".us-west.users.email",
   "user_swift_pool": ".us-west.users.swift",
   "user_uid_pool": ".us-west.users.uid",
   "system_key": { "access_key": " AAKOST8WXTMWZGN29NF9", "secret_
key": " AAJm8uAp71xKQZkjoPZmHu4sACA1SY8jTjay9dP5"},
   "placement_pools": [
     { "key": "default-placement",
       "val": { "index_pool": ".us-west.rgw.buckets.index",
                 "data_pool": ".us-west.rgw.buckets"}
     }
   ]
}
```

```
[root@us-east-1 ceph]# cat us-west.json
{ "domain_root": ".us-west.domain.rgw",
  "control_pool": ".us-west.rgw.control",
  "gc_pool": ".us-west.rgw.gc",
  "log_pool": ".us-west.log",
  "intent_log_pool": ".us-west.intent-log",
  "usage_log_pool": ".us-west.usage",
  "user_keys_pool": ".us-west.users",
  "user_email_pool": ".us-west.users.email",
  "user_swift_pool": ".us-west.users.swift",
  "user_uid_pool": ".us-west.users.uid",
  "system_key": { "access_key": "AAKOST8WXTMWZGN29NF9", "secret_key": "AAJm8uAp71xKQZk
joPZmHu4sACA1SY8jTjay9dP5"},
  "placement_pools": [
    { "key": "default-placement",
      "val": { "index_pool": ".us-west.rgw.buckets.index",
                "data_pool": ".us-west.rgw.buckets"}
    }
  ]
}
[root@us-east-1 ceph]#
```

13. Add the `us-west` zone using an infile in both the east and west pools:

```
# radosgw-admin zone set --rgw-zone=us-west --infile us-west.json
--name client.radosgw.us-east-1
```

```
[root@us-east-1 ceph]# radosgw-admin zone set --rgw-zone=us-west --infile us-west.json
--name client.radosgw.us-east-1
2015-05-03 22:03:16.279758 7f4ac6bd4880  0 couldn't find old data placement pools conf
ig, setting up new ones for the zone
{ "domain_root": ".us-west.domain.rgw",
  "control_pool": ".us-west.rgw.control",
  "gc_pool": ".us-west.rgw.gc",
  "log_pool": ".us-west.log",
  "intent_log_pool": ".us-west.intent-log",
  "usage_log_pool": ".us-west.usage",
  "user_keys_pool": ".us-west.users",
  "user_email_pool": ".us-west.users.email",
  "user_swift_pool": ".us-west.users.swift",
  "user_uid_pool": ".us-west.users.uid",
  "system_key": { "access_key": "AAK0ST8WXTMWZGN29NF9",
      "secret_key": "AAJm8uAp71xKQZkjoPZmHu4sACA1SY8jTjay9dP5"},
  "placement_pools": [
        { "key": "default-placement",
          "val": { "index_pool": ".us-west.rgw.buckets.index",
              "data_pool": ".us-west.rgw.buckets",
              "data_extra_pool": ""}}]}[root@us-east-1 ceph]#
[root@us-east-1 ceph]#
```

```
# radosgw-admin zone set --rgw-zone=us-west --infile us-west.json
--name     client.radosgw.us-west-1
```

```
[root@us-east-1 ceph]# radosgw-admin zone set --rgw-zone=us-west --infile us-west.json
 --name     client.radosgw.us-west-1
2015-05-03 22:04:48.050644 7f74fd327880  0 couldn't find old data placement pools conf
ig, setting up new ones for the zone
{ "domain_root": ".us-west.domain.rgw",
  "control_pool": ".us-west.rgw.control",
  "gc_pool": ".us-west.rgw.gc",
  "log_pool": ".us-west.log",
  "intent_log_pool": ".us-west.intent-log",
  "usage_log_pool": ".us-west.usage",
  "user_keys_pool": ".us-west.users",
  "user_email_pool": ".us-west.users.email",
  "user_swift_pool": ".us-west.users.swift",
  "user_uid_pool": ".us-west.users.uid",
  "system_key": { "access_key": "AAK0ST8WXTMWZGN29NF9",
      "secret_key": "AAJm8uAp71xKQZkjoPZmHu4sACA1SY8jTjay9dP5"},
  "placement_pools": [
        { "key": "default-placement",
          "val": { "index_pool": ".us-west.rgw.buckets.index",
              "data_pool": ".us-west.rgw.buckets",
              "data_extra_pool": ""}}]}[root@us-east-1 ceph]#
[root@us-east-1 ceph]#
```

14. Delete the default zone if it exists:

    ```
    # rados -p .rgw.root rm zone_info.default --name client.radosgw.
    us-east-1
    ```

15. Update the region map:

    ```
    # radosgw-admin regionmap update --name client.radosgw.us-east-1
    ```

16. After configuring zones, create zone users:

    1. Create the `us-east` zone user for the `us-east-1` gateway instance. Use the same `access_key` and `secret_key` that we generated earlier for the `us-east` zone:

        ```
        # radosgw-admin user create --uid="us-east" --display-
        name="Region-US Zone-East" --name client.radosgw.us-
        east-1 --access_key="XNK0ST8WXTMWZGN29NF9" --secret="7VJm
        8uAp71xKQZkjoPZmHu4sACA1SY8jTjay9dP5" --system
        ```

```
[root@us-east-1 ceph]# radosgw-admin user create --uid="us-east" --display-name="Region-US Zone-East" --name client.radosgw.us-east-1
--access_key="XNK0ST8WXTMWZGN29NF9" --secret="7VJm8uAp71xKQZkjoPZmHu4sACA1SY8jTjay9dP5" --system
{ "user_id": "us-east",
  "display_name": "Region-US Zone-East",
  "email": "",
  "suspended": 0,
  "max_buckets": 1000,
  "auid": 0,
  "subusers": [],
  "keys": [
        { "user": "us-east",
          "access_key": "XNK0ST8WXTMWZGN29NF9",
          "secret_key": "7VJm8uAp71xKQZkjoPZmHu4sACA1SY8jTjay9dP5"}],
  "swift_keys": [],
  "caps": [],
  "op_mask": "read, write, delete",
  "system": "true",
  "default_placement": "",
  "placement_tags": [],
  "bucket_quota": { "enabled": false,
      "max_size_kb": -1,
      "max_objects": -1},
  "user_quota": { "enabled": false,
      "max_size_kb": -1,
      "max_objects": -1},
  "temp_url_keys": []}
[root@us-east-1 ceph]#
```

2. Create the `us-west` zone user for the `us-west-1` gateway instance. Use the same `access_key` and `secret_key` that we generated earlier for the `us-west` zone:

```
# radosgw-admin user create --uid="us-west" --display-name="Region-US Zone-West" --name client.radosgw.us-west-1 --access_key="AAK0ST8WXTMWZGN29NF9" --secret="AAJm8uAp71xKQZkjoPZmHu4sACA1SY8jTjay9dP5" --system
```

```
[root@us-east-1 ceph]# radosgw-admin user create --uid="us-west" --display-name="Region-US Zone-West" --name client.radosgw.us-west-1
--access_key="AAK0ST8WXTMWZGN29NF9" --secret="AAJm8uAp71xKQZkjoPZmHu4sACA1SY8jTjay9dP5" --system
{ "user_id": "us-west",
  "display_name": "Region-US Zone-West",
  "email": "",
  "suspended": 0,
  "max_buckets": 1000,
  "auid": 0,
  "subusers": [],
  "keys": [
      { "user": "us-west",
        "access_key": "AAK0ST8WXTMWZGN29NF9",
        "secret_key": "AAJm8uAp71xKQZkjoPZmHu4sACA1SY8jTjay9dP5"}],
  "swift_keys": [],
  "caps": [],
  "op_mask": "read, write, delete",
  "system": "true",
  "default_placement": "",
  "placement_tags": [],
  "bucket_quota": { "enabled": false,
      "max_size_kb": -1,
      "max_objects": -1},
  "user_quota": { "enabled": false,
      "max_size_kb": -1,
      "max_objects": -1},
  "temp_url_keys": []}
[root@us-east-1 ceph]#
```

3. Create the `us-east` zone user for the `us-west-1` gateway instance. Use the same `access_key` and `secret_key` that we generated earlier for the `us-east` zone:

```
# radosgw-admin user create --uid="us-east" --display-name="Region-US Zone-East" --name client.radosgw.us-west-1 --access_key="XNK0ST8WXTMWZGN29NF9" --secret="7VJm8uAp71xKQZkjoPZmHu4sACA1SY8jTjay9dP5" --system
```

```
[root@us-east-1 ceph]# radosgw-admin user create --uid="us-east" --display-name="Region-US Zone-East" --name client.radosgw.us-west-1
--access_key="XNK0ST8WXTMWZGN29NF9" --secret="7VJm8uAp71xKQZkjoPZmHu4sACA1SY8jTjay9dP5" --system
{ "user_id": "us-east",
  "display_name": "Region-US Zone-East",
  "email": "",
  "suspended": 0,
  "max_buckets": 1000,
  "auid": 0,
  "subusers": [],
  "keys": [
      { "user": "us-east",
        "access_key": "XNK0ST8WXTMWZGN29NF9",
        "secret_key": "7VJm8uAp71xKQZkjoPZmHu4sACA1SY8jTjay9dP5"}],
  "swift_keys": [],
  "caps": [],
  "op_mask": "read, write, delete",
  "system": "true",
  "default_placement": "",
  "placement_tags": [],
  "bucket_quota": { "enabled": false,
      "max_size_kb": -1,
      "max_objects": -1},
  "user_quota": { "enabled": false,
      "max_size_kb": -1,
      "max_objects": -1},
  "temp_url_keys": []}
[root@us-east-1 ceph]#
```

4. Create the `us-west` zone user for the `us-east-1` gateway instance. Use the same `access_key` and `secret_key` that we generated earlier for the `us-west` zone:

```
# radosgw-admin user create --uid="us-west" --display-
name="Region-US Zone-West" --name client.radosgw.us-
east-1 --access_key="AAK0ST8WXTMWZGN29NF9" --secret="AAJm
8uAp71xKQZkjoPZmHu4sACA1SY8jTjay9dP5" --system
```

```
[root@us-east-1 ceph]# radosgw-admin user create --uid="us-west" --display-name="Region-US Zone-West" --name client.radosgw.us-east-1
--access_key="AAK0ST8WXTMWZGN29NF9" --secret="AAJm8uAp71xKQZkjoPZmHu4sACA1SY8jTjay9dP5" --system
{ "user_id": "us-west",
  "display_name": "Region-US Zone-West",
  "email": "",
  "suspended": 0,
  "max_buckets": 1000,
  "auid": 0,
  "subusers": [],
  "keys": [
       { "user": "us-west",
         "access_key": "AAK0ST8WXTMWZGN29NF9",
         "secret_key": "AAJm8uAp71xKQZkjoPZmHu4sACA1SY8jTjay9dP5"}],
  "swift_keys": [],
  "caps": [],
  "op_mask": "read, write, delete",
  "system": "true",
  "default_placement": "",
  "placement_tags": [],
  "bucket_quota": { "enabled": false,
      "max_size_kb": -1,
      "max_objects": -1},
  "user_quota": { "enabled": false,
      "max_size_kb": -1,
      "max_objects": -1},
  "temp_url_keys": []}
[root@us-east-1 ceph]#
```

17. Update the `ceph-radosgw` init script and set the default user as `root`. By default, `ceph-radosgw` runs using the Apache user, and you might encounter errors if the Apache user is not present:

```
# sed -i s"/DEFAULT_USER.*=.*'apache'/DEFAULT_USER='root'"/g /etc/
rc.d/init.d/ceph-radosgw
```

```
[root@us-east-1 ceph]# cat /etc/rc.d/init.d/ceph-radosgw | grep -i root
DEFAULT_USER='root'
[root@us-east-1 ceph]#
```

18. Log in to the `us-east-1` and `us-west-1` nodes and restart the `ceph-radosgw` service:

```
# systemctl restart ceph-radosgw
```

19. To verify if the region, zone, and `radosgw` configurations are correct, execute the following commands from the `us-east-1` node:

```
# radosgw-admin regions list --name client.radosgw.us-east-1
```

```
# radosgw-admin regions list --name client.radosgw.us-west-1
```

```
# radosgw-admin zone list --name client.radosgw.us-east-1
```

```
# radosgw-admin zone list --name client.radosgw.us-west-1
# curl http://us-east-1.cephcookbook.com:7480
# curl http://us-west-1.cephcookbook.com:7480
```

```
[root@us-east-1 ceph]# radosgw-admin regions list --name client.radosgw.us-east-1
{ "default_info": { "default_region": "us"},
  "regions": [
        "us"]}
[root@us-east-1 ceph]# radosgw-admin regions list --name client.radosgw.us-west-1
{ "default_info": { "default_region": "us"},
  "regions": [
        "us"]}
[root@us-east-1 ceph]# radosgw-admin zone list --name client.radosgw.us-east-1
{ "zones": [
        "us-west",
        "us-east"]}
[root@us-east-1 ceph]# radosgw-admin zone list --name client.radosgw.us-west-1
{ "zones": [
        "us-west",
        "us-east"]}
[root@us-east-1 ceph]# curl http://us-east-1.cephcookbook.com:7480
<?xml version="1.0" encoding="UTF-8"?><ListAllMyBucketsResult xmlns="http://s3.amazona
ws.com/doc/2006-03-01/"><Owner><ID>anonymous</ID><DisplayName></DisplayName></Owner><B
uckets></Buckets></ListAllMyBucketsResult>[root@us-east-1 ceph]#
[root@us-east-1 ceph]# curl http://us-west-1.cephcookbook.com:7480
<?xml version="1.0" encoding="UTF-8"?><ListAllMyBucketsResult xmlns="http://s3.amazona
ws.com/doc/2006-03-01/"><Owner><ID>anonymous</ID><DisplayName></DisplayName></Owner><B
uckets></Buckets></ListAllMyBucketsResult>[root@us-east-1 ceph]#
[root@us-east-1 ceph]# _
```

20. Set up multisite data replication by creating the `cluster-data-sync.conf` file with the following contents:

```
src_zone: us-east
source: http://us-east-1.cephcookbook.com:7480
src_access_key: XNK0ST8WXTMWZGN29NF9
src_secret_key: 7VJm8uAp71xKQZkjoPZmHu4sACA1SY8jTjay9dP5
dest_zone: us-west
destination: http://us-west-1.cephcookbook.com:7480
dest_access_key: AAK0ST8WXTMWZGN29NF9
dest_secret_key: AAJm8uAp71xKQZkjoPZmHu4sACA1SY8jTjay9dP5
log_file: /var/log/radosgw/radosgw-sync-us-east-west.log
```

```
[root@us-east-1 ceph]# cat cluster-data-sync.conf
src_zone: us-east
source: http://us-east-1.cephcookbook.com:7480
src_access_key: XNKOST8WXTMWZGN29NF9
src_secret_key: 7VJm8uAp71xKQZkjoPZmHu4sACA1SY8jTjay9dP5
dest_zone: us-west
destination: http://us-west-1.cephcookbook.com:7480
dest_access_key: AAKOST8WXTMWZGN29NF9
dest_secret_key: AAJm8uAp71xKQZkjoPZmHu4sACA1SY8jTjay9dP5
log_file: /var/log/radosgw/radosgw-sync-us-east-west.log
[root@us-east-1 ceph]#
```

21. Activate the data synchronization agent. Once the data sync has started, you should see an output similar to the one shown as follows:

```
# radosgw-agent -c cluster-data-sync.conf
```

```
2015-05-02 21:05:44,144 5420 [radosgw_agent.sync][INFO ] Starting sync
2015-05-02 21:05:44,161 5423 [radosgw_agent.worker][INFO ] 5423 is processing shard number 0
2015-05-02 21:05:44,210 5423 [radosgw_agent.worker][INFO ] finished processing shard 0
2015-05-02 21:05:44,211 5423 [radosgw_agent.worker][INFO ] 5423 is processing shard number 1
2015-05-02 21:05:44,222 5420 [radosgw_agent.sync][INFO ] 1/64 items processed
2015-05-02 21:05:44,326 5423 [radosgw_agent.worker][INFO ] finished processing shard 1
2015-05-02 21:05:44,326 5423 [radosgw_agent.worker][INFO ] 5423 is processing shard number 2
2015-05-02 21:05:44,386 5420 [radosgw_agent.sync][INFO ] 2/64 items processed
2015-05-02 21:06:09,277 5423 [radosgw_agent.worker][INFO ] finished processing shard 2
2015-05-02 21:06:09,278 5423 [radosgw_agent.worker][INFO ] 5423 is processing shard number 3
2015-05-02 21:06:09,285 5420 [radosgw_agent.sync][INFO ] 3/64 items processed
```

Testing the radosgw federated configuration

To test the federated configuration, we will first add some objects to the us-east zone via the radosgw instance, us-east-1, using Swift. Then, after the data synchronization between the us-east and us-west zones, we will access the same objects from the us-west zone via the us-west-1 gateway interface.

How to do it...

1. For the `us-east` zone user, create a Swift subuser:

    ```
    # radosgw-admin subuser create --uid="us-east"  --subuser="us-
    east:swift" --access=full --name client.radosgw.us-east-1 --key-
    type swift --secret="7VJm8uAp71xKQZkjoPZmHu4sACA1SY8jTjay9dP5"
    ```

    ```
    # radosgw-admin subuser create --uid="us-east"  --subuser="us-
    east:swift" --access=full --name client.radosgw.us-west-1 --key-
    type swift --secret="7VJm8uAp71xKQZkjoPZmHu4sACA1SY8jTjay9dP5"
    ```

    ```
    [root@us-east-1 ceph]# radosgw-admin subuser create --uid="us-east"  --subuser="us-east:swift" --access=full
    --name client.radosgw.us-east-1 --key-type swift --secret="7VJm8uAp71xKQZkjoPZmHu4sACA1SY8jTjay9dP5"
    { "user_id": "us-east",
      "display_name": "Region-US Zone-East",
      "email": "",
      "suspended": 0,
      "max_buckets": 1000,
      "auid": 0,
      "subusers": [
            { "id": "us-east:swift",
              "permissions": "full-control"}],
      "keys": [
            { "user": "us-east",
              "access_key": "XNK0ST8WXTMWZGN29NF9",
              "secret_key": "7VJm8uAp71xKQZkjoPZmHu4sACA1SY8jTjay9dP5"}],
      "swift_keys": [
            { "user": "us-east:swift",
              "secret_key": "7VJm8uAp71xKQZkjoPZmHu4sACA1SY8jTjay9dP5"}],
      "caps": [],
      "op_mask": "read, write, delete",
      "system": "true",
      "default_placement": "",
      "placement_tags": [],
      "bucket_quota": { "enabled": false,
          "max_size_kb": -1,
          "max_objects": -1},
      "user_quota": { "enabled": false,
          "max_size_kb": -1,
          "max_objects": -1},
      "temp_url_keys": []}
    [root@us-east-1 ceph]#
    ```

2. Similarly, for the `us-west` zone user, create the Swift subuser:

    ```
    # radosgw-admin subuser create --uid="us-west"  --subuser=
    "us-west:swift" --access=full --name client.radosgw.us-east-1
    --key-type swift --secret=
    "AAJm8uAp71xKQZkjoPZmHu4sACA1SY8jTjay9dP5"
    ```

    ```
    # radosgw-admin subuser create --uid="us-west"  --subuser=
    "us-west:swift" --access=full --name client.radosgw.us-west-1
    --key-type swift --secret=
    "AAJm8uAp71xKQZkjoPZmHu4sACA1SY8jTjay9dP5"
    ```

3. Install the `python-swift` client on the `us-east-1` and `us-west-1` nodes:

   ```
   # yum install python-swift
   # yum install python-setuptools
   # easy_install pip
   # pip install --upgrade setuptools
   # pip install python-swiftclient
   ```

4. Set up `python-swiftclient` on the `us-east-1` node:

   ```
   # export ST_AUTH="http://us-east-1.cephcookbook.com:7480/auth/1.0"
   # export ST_KEY=7VJm8uAp71xKQZkjoPZmHu4sACA1SY8jTjay9dP5
   # export ST_USER=us-east:swift
   ```

5. List and create some objects from the `us-east-1` node:

   ```
   # swift list
   # swift  upload container-1 us.json
   # swift list
   # swift list container-1
   ```

   ```
   [root@us-east-1 ceph]# export ST_AUTH="http://us-east-1.cephcookbook.com:7480/auth/1.0"
   [root@us-east-1 ceph]# export ST_KEY=7VJm8uAp71xKQZkjoPZmHu4sACA1SY8jTjay9dP5
   [root@us-east-1 ceph]# export ST_USER=us-east:swift
   [root@us-east-1 ceph]# swift list
   [root@us-east-1 ceph]# swift  upload container-1 us.json
   us.json
   [root@us-east-1 ceph]# swift list
   container-1
   [root@us-east-1 ceph]#
   [root@us-east-1 ceph]# swift list container-1
   us.json
   [root@us-east-1 ceph]#
   ```

6. Activate the data synchronization agent:

   ```
   # radosgw-agent -c cluster-data-sync.conf
   ```

7. Once the data synchronization completes, try to access the objects from the us-west zone using the us-west-1 gateway instance. At this stage, the data should be accessible to you from the us-west-1 gateway instance:

```
# export ST_AUTH="http://us-west-1.cephcookbook.com:
7480/auth/1.0"

# export ST_KEY=7VJm8uAp71xKQZkjoPZmHu4sACA1SY8jTjay9dP5

# export ST_USER=us-east:swift

# swift list
```

```
[root@us-west-1 ceph]# export ST_AUTH="http://us-west-1.cephcookbook.com:7480/auth/1.0"
[root@us-west-1 ceph]# export ST_KEY=7VJm8uAp71xKQZkjoPZmHu4sACA1SY8jTjay9dP5
[root@us-west-1 ceph]# export ST_USER=us-east:swift
[root@us-west-1 ceph]# swift list
container-1
[root@us-west-1 ceph]# swift list container-1
us.json
[root@us-west-1 ceph]#
```

Building file sync and share service using RGW

File sync and share services, such as Dropbox, Box, Google Drive, and many more, have become extremely popular in the last few years. With Ceph, you can deploy on-premise file sync and share services using any S3- or Swift-based frontend applications. In this recipe, we will demonstrate how to build up a file sync and share services based on Ceph and ownCloud.

To build this service, we would require a running Ceph cluster, a RGW instance that can access Ceph storage via S3, and an ownCloud frontend environment, as shown next:

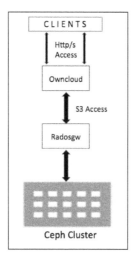

Getting ready...

In the last recipe, we configured the `radosgw` instance, `us-east-1`; we will use the same gateway instance in this section to build the file sync and share service. We will also use our DNS service, which is configured on `rgw-node1` to support S3 subdomain calls for the `us-east-1` RGW instance; however, you can also use any DNS server until it resolves subdomains for `us-east-1`.

How to do it...

1. Log in to `rgw-node1`, which is also our DNS server, and create a file, `/var/named/us-east-1.cephcookbook.com`, with the following contents:

```
@ 86400 IN SOA cephcookbook.com. root.cephcookbook.com. (
        20091028 ; serial yyyy-mm-dd
        10800 ; refresh every 15 min
        3600 ; retry every hour
        3600000 ; expire after 1 month +
        86400 ); min ttl of 1 day
@ 86400 IN NS cephbookbook.com.
@ 86400 IN A 192.168.1.107
* 86400 IN CNAME @
```

```
[root@rgw-node1 ~]# cat /var/named/us-east-1.cephcookbook.com
@ 86400 IN SOA cephcookbook.com. root.cephcookbook.com. (
        20091028 ; serial yyyy-mm-dd
        10800 ; refresh every 15 min
        3600 ; retry every hour
        3600000 ; expire after 1 month +
        86400 ); min ttl of 1 day
@ 86400 IN NS cephbookbook.com.
@ 86400 IN A 192.168.1.107
* 86400 IN CNAME @
[root@rgw-node1 ~]#
```

2. Configure the `us-east-1` node to use the DNS server. Update `/etc/resolve.conf` with the `rgw-node1` address and ping any subdomain; it should resolve to the `us-east-1` address.

```
[root@us-east-1 ~]# cat /etc/resolv.conf
# Generated by NetworkManager
search cephcookbook.com
nameserver 192.168.1.106
[root@us-east-1 ~]#
[root@us-east-1 ~]# ping anything.us-east-1.cephcookbook.com -c 1
PING us-east-1.cephcookbook.com (192.168.1.107) 56(84) bytes of data.
64 bytes from us-east-1.cephcookbook.com (192.168.1.107): icmp_seq=1 ttl=64 time=0.038 ms

--- us-east-1.cephcookbook.com ping statistics ---
1 packets transmitted, 1 received, 0% packet loss, time 0ms
rtt min/avg/max/mdev = 0.038/0.038/0.038/0.000 ms
[root@us-east-1 ~]#
```

3. Make sure that the `us-east-1` node can connect to the Ceph storage cluster over S3. We created a user in the last recipe with the name `us-east`, and we will use its access and secret keys with `s3cmd`:

   1. Install `s3cmd`:

      ```
      # yum install -y s3cmd
      ```

   2. Configure `s3cmd` and provide `access_key` as XNK0ST8WXTMWZGN29NF9 and `secret_key` as 7VJm8uAp71xKQZkjoPZmHu4sACA1SY8jTjay9dP5:

      ```
      # s3cmd --configure
      ```

   3. Edit `/root/.s3cmd` for host details:

      ```
      host_base = us-east-1.cephcookbook.com:7480
      ```

      ```
      host_bucket = %(bucket)s.us-east-1.cephcookbook.com:7480
      ```

   4. Test the `s3cmd` connection:

      ```
      # s3cmd ls
      ```

   5. Create an S3 bucket for ownCloud, which will be used to store ownCloud objects:

      ```
      # s3cmd mb s3://owncloud
      ```

4. Next, we will install ownCloud, which will provide us with the frontend/user interface to the file sync and share service:

   1. Bring up the ownCloud virtual machine using Vagrant and log in to the VM:

      ```
      # vagrant up owncloud
      ```

      ```
      # vagrant ssh owncloud
      ```

2. Install the ownCloud repositories as follows:

```
# cd /etc/yum.repos.d/
```

```
# wget http://download.opensuse.org/repositories/
isv:ownCloud:community/CentOS_CentOS-7/
isv:ownCloud:community.repo
```

3. Install ownCloud as follows:

```
# yum install owncloud -y
```

4. Since this is a test setup, disable the firewall:

```
# systemctl disable firewalld
```

```
# systemctl stop firewalld
```

5. Try accessing the ownCloud web interface by accessing
   `http://192.168.1.120/owncloud/` in your host web browser.
   Create an admin account called `owncloud` with the password as `owncloud`:

6. The first login screen will look like the following one; you can use ownCloud as a desktop or mobile app any time:

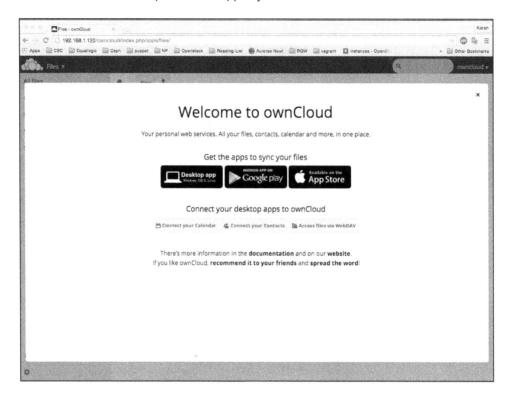

5. Configure ownCloud to use Ceph as an S3 external storage:

   1. Enable external storage from the ownCloud admin account by navigating to **Files** | **Apps** | **Not enabled** | **External Storage** and clicking on **Enable it**.

   2. Next, set up the external storage to use Ceph. To do this, navigate to the top-right-hand side of the window and select the ownCloud user, then select **admin**, and then navigate to the left-hand side panel and select **External Storage**.

   3. Configure Amazon S3 and the compliant storage with ownCloud by checking **Enable User External Storage** and then navigating to **Amazon S3 and compliant** | **Add Storage** | **Amazon S3 and Compliant**.

6. Provide the Ceph `radosgw` user detail with the access key, secret key, and hostname:

    ❑ **Folder name**: Enter the folder name that you want to show on your ownCloud files page.

    ❑ **Access key**: Enter your S3 Access Key, `XNK0ST8WXTMWZGN29NF9`

    ❑ **Secret key**: Enter your S3 Secret key, `7VJm8uAp71xKQZkjoPZmHu4sACA1SY8jTjay9dP5"`

    ❑ **Bucket**: Enter the name of your S3 bucket that we created in step 3

    ❑ **Hostname**: Enter `us-east-1.cephcookbook.com`

    ❑ **Port**: Enter `7480`

    ❑ **Region** (optional): Enter `US` (optional)

    ❑ **Available for**: Enter `owncloud` (optional)

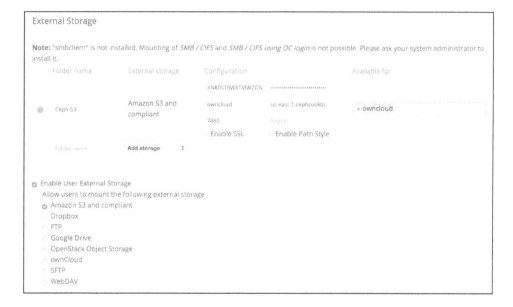

7. As soon as you enter the preceding details, ownCloud should connect to the Ceph cluster over S3, and you should see a green circle just before the folder name, as shown in the preceding image.

8. Next, upload your files via the ownCloud web user interface. To do this, navigate to **Files | External Storage** and click on the `ceph-s3` upload files or directory.

9. Verify that the files have been added to the Ceph storage cluster by switching to us-east-1 node and performing the s3cmd ls s3://owncloud command; you should get the file you uploaded from the ownCloud web user interface.

```
[root@us-east-1 ~]# s3cmd ls s3://owncloud
                        DIR    s3://owncloud/mona/
2015-05-05 21:32    148481    s3://owncloud/eknumber.jpg
[root@us-east-1 ~]#
```

10. Congratulations! You have learned how to build your own private file sync and share service using Ceph S3 object storage and ownCloud.

See also...

For more information on ownCloud, visit https://owncloud.org/.

4
Working with the Ceph Filesystem

In this chapter, we will cover the following recipes:

- ▶ Understanding the Ceph Filesystem and MDS
- ▶ Deploying Ceph MDS
- ▶ Accessing CephFS via kernel driver
- ▶ Accessing CephFS via FUSE client
- ▶ Exporting Ceph Filesystem as an NFS
- ▶ ceph-dokan – CephFS for Windows clients
- ▶ CephFS – a drop-in replacement for HDFS

Introduction

The Ceph Filesystem, also known as CephFS, is a POSIX-compliant filesystem that uses the Ceph storage cluster to store user data. CephFS supports the native Linux kernel driver, which makes CephFS highly adaptive across any flavor of the Linux OS. In this chapter, we will cover the Ceph Filesystem in detail, including its deployment, understanding the kernel driver and FUSE, as well as CephFS for Windows clients.

Understanding Ceph Filesystem and MDS

The Ceph Filesystem offers the POSIX-compliant distributed filesystem of any size that uses Ceph RADOS to store its data. To implement Ceph filesystem, you need a running Ceph storage cluster and at least one Ceph **Metadata Serer** (**MDS**) to manage its metadata and keep it separated from data, which helps in reducing complexity and improves reliability. The following diagram depicts the architectural view of CephFS and its interfaces:

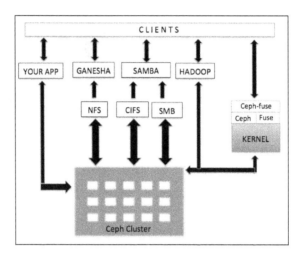

`libcephfs` libraries play an important role in supporting its multiple client implementations. It has the native Linux kernel driver support and thus clients can use native filesystem mounting, for example, using the `mount` command. It has tight integration with SAMBA and support for CIFS and SMB. CephFS extends its support to **Filesystem in USErspace** (**FUSE**) using cephfuse modules. It also allows direct application interaction with the RADOS cluster using libcephfs libraries. CephFS is gaining popularity as a replacement for Hadoop HDFS. Previous versions of HDFS only supported the single name node, which impacts its scalability and creates a single point of failure; however, this has been changed in current versions of HDFS. Unlike HDFS, CephFS can be implemented over multiple MDS in an active-active state, thus making it highly scalable, high performing, and with no single point of failure.

Ceph MDS stands for Metadata Server and is required only for the Ceph Filesystem (CephFS); other storage methods' block- and object-based storage do not require MDS services. Ceph MDS operates as a daemon, which allows the client to mount a POSIX filesystem of any size. MDS does not serve any data directly to the client; data serving is done only by OSD. MDS provides a shared coherent filesystem with a smart caching layer, hence drastically reducing reads and writes. It extends its benefits towards dynamic subtree partitioning and a single MDS for a piece of metadata. It is dynamic in nature; daemons can join and leave, and the takeover to failed nodes is quick.

MDS does not store local data, which is quite useful in some scenarios. If an MDS daemon dies, we can start it up again on any system that has cluster access. The Metadata server's daemons are configured as active or passive. The primary MDS node becomes active and the rest will go into "standby". In the event of primary MDS failure, the second node takes charge and is promoted to active. For even faster recovery, you can specify that a standby node should follow one of your active nodes, which will keep the same data in memory to pre-populate the cache.

CephFS is not production ready at the moment, as it lacks robust **fsck** check/repair functions, multiple active MDS, and snapshots. Its development is going at a very fast pace, and we can expect it to be production ready starting Ceph Jewel. For your no critical workloads you can consider using CephFS with single MDS and no snapshots.

Deploying Ceph MDS

To configure the Meta Data Server for the Ceph Filesystem, you should have a running Ceph cluster. In earlier chapters, we learned to deploy the Ceph storage cluster; we will use the same cluster for MDS deployment.

How to do it...

1. Use `ceph-deploy` from `ceph-node1` to deploy and configure MDS on `ceph-node2`:

   ```
   # ceph-deploy --overwrite-conf mds create ceph-node2
   ```

```
[root@ceph-node1 ceph]# ceph-deploy --overwrite-conf mds create ceph-node2
[ceph_deploy.conf][DEBUG ] found configuration file at: /root/.cephdeploy.conf
[ceph_deploy.cli][INFO  ] Invoked (1.5.22): /usr/bin/ceph-deploy --overwrite-conf mds create ceph-node2
[ceph_deploy.mds][DEBUG ] Deploying mds, cluster ceph hosts ceph-node2:ceph-node2
[ceph-node2][DEBUG ] connected to host: ceph-node2
[ceph-node2][DEBUG ] detect platform information from remote host
[ceph-node2][DEBUG ] detect machine type
[ceph_deploy.mds][INFO  ] Distro info: CentOS Linux 7.0.1406 Core
[ceph_deploy.mds][DEBUG ] remote host will use sysvinit
[ceph_deploy.mds][DEBUG ] deploying mds bootstrap to ceph-node2
[ceph-node2][DEBUG ] write cluster configuration to /etc/ceph/{cluster}.conf
[ceph-node2][DEBUG ] create path if it doesn't exist
[ceph-node2][INFO  ] Running command: ceph --cluster ceph --name client.bootstrap-mds --keyring /var/lib/c
eph/bootstrap-mds/ceph.keyring auth get-or-create mds.ceph-node2 osd allow rwx mds allow mon allow profile
 mds -o /var/lib/ceph/mds/ceph-ceph-node2/keyring
[ceph-node2][INFO  ] Running command: service ceph start mds.ceph-node2
[ceph-node2][DEBUG ] === mds.ceph-node2 ===
[ceph-node2][DEBUG ] Starting Ceph mds.ceph-node2 on ceph-node2...
[ceph-node2][WARNIN] Running as unit run-4697.service.
[ceph-node2][INFO  ] Running command: systemctl enable ceph
[ceph-node2][WARNIN] ceph.service is not a native service, redirecting to /sbin/chkconfig.
[ceph-node2][WARNIN] Executing /sbin/chkconfig ceph on
[ceph-node2][WARNIN] The unit files have no [Install] section. They are not meant to be enabled
[root@ceph-node1 ceph]#
```

2. The command should deploy the MDS and start its daemon on `ceph-node2`; however, we need to carry out a few more steps to get CephFS accessible:

   # **ssh ceph-node2 service ceph status mds**

   ```
   [root@ceph-node1 ceph]# ssh ceph-node2 service ceph status mds
   === mds.ceph-node2 ===
   mds.ceph-node2: running {"version":"0.87.1"}
   [root@ceph-node1 ceph]#
   ```

3. Create data and metadata pools for the Ceph Filesystem:

   # **ceph osd pool create cephfs_data 64 64**

   # **ceph osd pool create cephfs_metadata 64 64**

4. Finally, create the Ceph Filesystem; once this command is executed the MDS should attain an active state and CephFS should be ready for use:

   # **ceph fs new cephfs cephfs_metadata cephfs_data**

   ```
   [root@ceph-node1 ceph]# ceph osd pool create cephfs_data 64 64
   pool 'cephfs_data' created
   [root@ceph-node1 ceph]# ceph osd pool create cephfs_metadata 64 64
   pool 'cephfs_metadata' created
   [root@ceph-node1 ceph]#
   [root@ceph-node1 ceph]# ceph fs new cephfs cephfs_metadata cephfs_data
   new fs with metadata pool 44 and data pool 43
   [root@ceph-node1 ceph]#
   ```

5. To verify the status of CephFS and MDS, use the following commands:

   # **ceph mds stat**

   # **ceph fs ls**

   ```
   [root@ceph-node1 ceph]# ceph mds stat
   e10: 1/1/1 up {0=ceph-node2=up:active}
   [root@ceph-node1 ceph]# ceph fs ls
   name: cephfs, metadata pool: cephfs_metadata, data pools: [cephfs_data ]
   [root@ceph-node1 ceph]#
   ```

6. It's recommended that you don't share `client.admin` user keyrings with Ceph clients, so we will create a user `client.cephfs` on the Ceph cluster and will allow this user access to CephFS pools:

   # **ceph auth get-or-create client.cephfs mon 'allow r' osd 'allow rwx pool=cephfs_metadata,allow rwx pool=cephfs_data' -o /etc/ceph/ client.cephfs.keyring**

```
# ceph-authtool -p -n client.cephfs /etc/ceph/client.cephfs.
keyring > /etc/ceph/client.cephfs

# cat /etc/ceph/client.cephfs
```

```
[root@ceph-node1 ~]# ceph auth get-or-create client.cephfs mon 'allow r' osd 'allow rwx pool=cephfs_metadata,allow
rwx pool=cephfs_data' -o /etc/ceph/client.cephfs.keyring
[root@ceph-node1 ~]#
[root@ceph-node1 ~]# ceph-authtool -p -n client.cephfs /etc/ceph/client.cephfs.keyring > /etc/ceph/client.cephfs
[root@ceph-node1 ~]#
[root@ceph-node1 ~]# cat /etc/ceph/client.cephfs
AQAGSF5VMIDWHhAAox9s/oHg/6FPzf4xRQV73Q==
[root@ceph-node1 ~]#
```

Accessing CephFS via kernel driver

Native support for Ceph has been added in Linux kernel 2.6.34 and the later versions.
In this recipe, we will demonstrate how to access CephFS via the Linux kernel driver on
`ceph-client1`.

How to do it...

1. Check your client's Linux kernel version:

    `# uname -r`

2. Create a mount point directory:

    `# mkdir /mnt/cephfs`

3. Get the keys for the `clieht.cephfs` user, which we created in the last section.
    Execute the following command from the Ceph monitor node to get the user keys:

    `# ceph auth get-key client.cephfs`

4. Mount CephFS using the native Linux mount call with the following syntax:

    Syntax: `mount -t ceph <Monitor_IP>:<Monitor_port>:/ <mount_point_name> -o name=admin,secret=<admin_user_key>`

    `# mount -t ceph ceph-node1:6789:/ /mnt/cephfs -o name=cephfs,secret=AQAGSF5VMIDWHhAAox9s/oHg/6FPzf4xRQV73Q==`

```
root@client-node1:/etc/ceph# mount -t ceph ceph-node1:6789:/ /mnt/cephfs -o name=cephfs,secret=
AQAGSF5VMIDWHhAAox9s/oHg/6FPzf4xRQV73Q==
root@client-node1:/etc/ceph# df -h /mnt/cephfs
Filesystem           Size  Used Avail Use% Mounted on
192.168.1.101:6789:/ 135G  7.3G  128G   6% /mnt/cephfs
root@client-node1:/etc/ceph#
```

5. To mount CephFS more securely, avoiding the admin key being visible in the command history, store the admin keyring as plain text in a separate file and use this file as a mount option for `secretkey`:

```
# echo AQAGSF5VMIDWHhAAox9s/oHg/6FPzf4xRQV73Q== > /etc/ceph/
cephfskey
```

```
# mount -t ceph ceph-node1:6789:/ /mnt/cephfs -o
name=cephfs,secretfile=/etc/ceph/cephfskey
```

```
root@client-node1:/etc/ceph# echo AQAGSF5VMIDWHhAAox9s/oHg/6FPzf4xRQV73Q== > /etc/ceph/cephfskey
root@client-node1:/etc/ceph# umount /mnt/cephfs
root@client-node1:/etc/ceph# mount -t ceph ceph-node1:6789:/ /mnt/cephfs -o name=cephfs,secretfile=
/etc/ceph/cephfskey
root@client-node1:/etc/ceph# df -h /mnt/cephfs
Filesystem            Size  Used Avail Use% Mounted on
192.168.1.101:6789:/  135G  7.3G  128G   6% /mnt/cephfs
root@client-node1:/etc/ceph#
```

6. To allow the CephFS mount during the OS startup, add the following lines in the `/etc/fstab` file on `client-node1`:

   Syntax: `<Mon_ipaddress>:<monitor_port>:/ <mount_point> <filesystem-name> [name=username,secret=secretkey|secretfile=/path/to/secretfile],[{mount.options}]`

```
# echo "ceph-node1:6789:/ /mnt/cephfs ceph
name=cephfs,secretfile=/etc/ceph/cephfskey,noatime 02" >> /etc/
fstab
```

7. Umount and mount CephFS again:

```
# umount /mnt/cephfs
```

```
# mount /mnt/cephfs
```

```
root@client-node1:/etc/ceph# echo "ceph-node1:6789:/ /mnt/cephfs ceph name=cephfs,secretfile
=/etc/ceph/cephfskey,noatime 02" >> /etc/fstab
root@client-node1:/etc/ceph# cat /etc/fstab | grep -i cephfs
ceph-node1:6789:/ /mnt/cephfs ceph name=cephfs,secretfile=/etc/ceph/cephfskey,noatime 02
root@client-node1:/etc/ceph# umount /mnt/cephfs
root@client-node1:/etc/ceph# mount /mnt/cephfs
root@client-node1:/etc/ceph# df -h /mnt/cephfs
Filesystem            Size  Used Avail Use% Mounted on
192.168.1.101:6789:/  135G  7.3G  128G   6% /mnt/cephfs
root@client-node1:/etc/ceph#
```

8. Perform some IO on the Ceph Filesystem and then umount it:

```
# dd if=/dev/zero of=/mnt/cephfs/file1 bs=1M count=1024
```

```
# umount /mnt/cephfs
```

```
root@client-node1:~# dd if=/dev/zero of=/mnt/cephfs/file1 bs=1M count=1024
1024+0 records in
1024+0 records out
1073741824 bytes (1.1 GB) copied, 58.9853 s, 18.2 MB/s
root@client-node1:~#
root@client-node1:~# ls -l /mnt/cephfs/file1
-rw-r--r-- 1 root root 1073741824 May 20 21:15 /mnt/cephfs/file1
root@client-node1:~#
```

Accessing CephFS via FUSE client

The Ceph Filesystem is natively supported by the LINUX kernel; however, if your host is running on a lower kernel version, or if you have any application dependency, then you can always use the FUSE (Filesystem in User Space) client for Ceph to mount CephFS.

How to do it...

1. Install the Ceph FUSE package on the `client-node1` machine:

    # apt-get install -y ceph-fuse

2. Create the CephFS keyring file, `/etc/ceph/client.cephfs.keyring`, with the following contents:

    ```
    [client.cephfs]
    key = AQAGSF5VMIDWHhAAox9s/oHg/6FPzf4xRQV73Q==
    ```

3. Mount CephFS using the Ceph FUSE client:

    # ceph-fuse --keyring /etc/ceph/client.cephfs.keyring --name client.cephfs -m ceph-node1:6789 /mnt/cephfs

```
root@client-node1:/etc/ceph# ceph-fuse --keyring /etc/ceph/client.cephfs.keyring --name client.cephfs
-m ceph-node1:6789  /mnt/cephfs
ceph-fuse[3356]: starting ceph client
2015-05-21 21:46:05.599027 7fc80ea017c0 -1 init, newargv = 0x45663a0 newargc=11
ceph-fuse[3356]: starting fuse
root@client-node1:/etc/ceph#
root@client-node1:/etc/ceph# df -h /mnt/cephfs
Filesystem      Size  Used Avail Use% Mounted on
ceph-fuse       135G  7.3G  128G   6% /mnt/cephfs
root@client-node1:/etc/ceph#
```

4. To mount CephFS at the OS boot, add the following lines in the `/etc/fstab` file on `client-node1`:

    ```
    id=cephfs,keyring=client.cephfs.keyring          /mnt/cephfs fuse.
    ceph defaults 00
    ```

5. Umount and mount CephFS again:

```
# umount /mnt/cephfs
# mount /mnt/cephfs
```

Exporting Ceph Filesystem as NFS

The **Network Filesystem** (**NFS**) is one of the most popular sharable filesystem protocols that can be used with every Unix-based system. Unix-based clients that do not understand the CephFS type can still access the Ceph Filesystem using NFS. To do this, we would require an NFS server in place that can re-export CephFS as an NFS share. NFS-Ganesha is an NFS server that runs in user space and supports the CephFS **FSAL** (**File System Abstraction Layer**) using `libcephfs`.

In this recipe, we will demonstrate creating `ceph-node1` as an NFS-Ganesha server and exporting CephFS as an NFS and mounting it on `client-node1`.

How to do it...

1. On `ceph-node1`, install packages required for `nfs-ganesha`:

   ```
   # yum install -y  nfs-utils nfs-ganesha nfs-ganesha-fsal-ceph
   ```

2. Since this is a test setup, disable firewall. For the production setup, you might consider enabling the required ports over a firewall, which is generally `2049`:

   ```
   # systemctl stop firewalld; systemctl disable firewalld
   ```

3. Enable the `rpc` services required by NFS:

   ```
   # systemctl start rpcbind; systemctl enable rpcbind
   # systemctl start rpc-statd.service
   ```

4. Create the NFS-Ganesha configuration file, `/etc/ganesha.conf`, with the following contents:

   ```
   EXPORT
   {
       Export_ID = 1;
       Path = "/";
       Pseudo = "/";
       Access_Type = RW;
       NFS_Protocols = "3";
       Squash = No_Root_Squash;
       Transport_Protocols = TCP;
       SecType = "none";
   ```

```
        FSAL {
            Name = CEPH;
        }
    }
```

5. Finally, start the `ganesha nfs` daemon by providing the `ganesha.conf` file that we created in the last step. You can verify the exported NFS share using the `showmount` command:

```
# ganesha.nfsd -f /etc/ganesha.conf -L /var/log/ganesha.log -N
NIV_DEBUG -d
```

```
# showmount -e
```

```
[root@ceph-node1 ~]# ganesha.nfsd -f /etc/ganesha.conf -L /var/log/ganesha.log -N NIV_DEBUG -d
[root@ceph-node1 ~]#
[root@ceph-node1 ~]# ps -ef | grep -i nfs
root      7975     1  0 00:55 ?        00:00:00 ganesha.nfsd -f /etc/ganesha.conf -L /var/log/ganesha.log -N NIV_DEBUG -d
root      8023  5901  0 00:56 pts/0    00:00:00 grep --color=auto -i nfs
[root@ceph-node1 ~]#
```

Let's recall the steps that we have taken: `ceph-node2` has been configured as Ceph MDS, and `ceph-node1` has been configured as the NFS-Ganesha server.

Next, in order to mount the NFS share on client machines, we just need to install the NFS client packages and mount the share exported by `ceph-node1`, as shown next:

Install the `nfs` client packages on `client-node1` and `mount`:

```
# apt-get install nfs-common
```

```
# mkdir /mnt/cephfs
```

```
# mount -o rw,noatime 192.168.1.101:/ /mnt/cephfs
```

```
root@client-node1:~# mount -o rw,noatime 192.168.1.101:/ /mnt/cephfs
root@client-node1:~# df -h
Filesystem       Size  Used Avail Use% Mounted on
/dev/sda1         40G  1.1G   37G   3% /
none             4.0K     0  4.0K   0% /sys/fs/cgroup
udev             241M   12K  241M   1% /dev
tmpfs             49M  356K   49M   1% /run
none             5.0M     0  5.0M   0% /run/lock
none             245M     0  245M   0% /run/shm
none             100M     0  100M   0% /run/user
192.168.1.101:/  135G  7.3G  128G   6% /mnt/cephfs
root@client-node1:~#
```

ceph-dokan – CephFS for Windows clients

Up to now, we have learned different methods of accessing CephFS, such as the Ceph FUSE, the Ceph kernel driver, and NFS Ganesha; however, these methods could be used only on Linux-based systems and are not supposed to work on Windows-based client machines.

An open source project such as Ceph has its own advantages; Ceph has developed a thriving community around it. `ceph-dokan` is a native Windows Ceph client developed by Meng Shengzhi, working as the principal storage engineer at UnitedStack. In addition to OpenStack and Ceph development, Meng manages the `ceph-dokan` project.

`ceph-dokan` allows CephFS access on a Windows platform. To do this, `ceph-dokan` makes use of two key components: `libcephfs.dll`, which is an application to access CephFS, and `ceph-dokan.exe,` which is based on the Dokan project to provide a FUSE-like filesystem service on a Windows platform, which helps in mounting CephFS as a local drive on Windows systems. In the background, `ceph-dokan.exe` uses `dokan.dll` and `libcephfs.dll` for the win32 filesystem user space implementation. Like Ceph, `ceph-dokan` is also an open source project and is available on GitHub at `https://github.com/ceph/ceph-dokan`. Pull requests for contribution to this project can be sent anytime. You can build `ceph-dokan` from the source available at GitHub; however, for the sake of simplicity, you can use `ceph-dokan.exe`, which can be found under the `ceph-dokan` directory on the `ceph-cookbook` GitHub repository that you have already cloned in an earlier chapter.

How to do it...

1. Configure a Windows 7 or 8 machine and attach it to the network, the same as your Ceph cluster (`192.168.1.0/24`).

2. Make sure you can reach the Ceph monitor nodes by verifying access using the `telnet` command from the command prompt:

    telnet 192.168.1.101 6789

3. Once the access to Ceph cluster is through, download `ceph-dokan.exe` and `DokanInstall_0.6.0.exe` from `https://github.com/ksingh7/ceph-cookbook/tree/master/ceph-dokan` on the Windows client.

4. Install `DokanInstall_0.6.0.ex`; if you are using the Windows 8 OS, you might need to install it in compatibility mode.

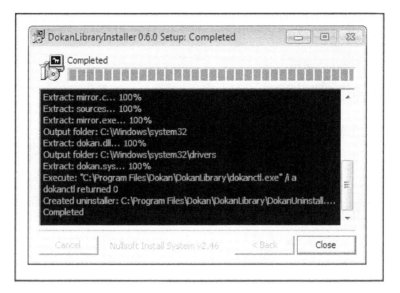

5. Open the Windows command prompt and change the directory to the absolute path where you downloaded `ceph-dokan.exe`.

6. Create a `ceph.conf` file with the following contents on the Windows client, which will tell `ceph-dokan` about the Ceph cluster monitors:

```
[global]
auth client required = none
log_file = dokan.log
mon_initial_members = ceph-node1
mon_host = 192.168.1.101
[mon]
[mon.ceph-node1]
mon addr = 192.168.1.101:6789
```

 Since `ceph-dokan` can only read `ceph.conf` if it's in the Unix format, you should convert `ceph.conf` to the Unix format using the **dos2unix** utility. For more information, refer http://sourceforge.net/projects/dos2unix/.

7. `ceph-dokan` currently does not support **cephx** authentication. So, to use `ceph-dokan`, you need to disable cephx from all of your Ceph cluster monitor machines.

8. To disable cephx from the Ceph cluster, modify the `/etc/ceph/ceph.conf` file with the auth related entries as none:

```
auth_cluster_required = none
auth_service_required = none
auth_client_required = none
```

9. After changing `ceph.conf`, restart the ceph services on all the monitor nodes:

   ```
   # service ceph restart
   ```

10. Make sure cephx is disabled:

    ```
    # ceph --admin-daemon /var/run/ceph/ceph-osd.0.asok config show |
    grep -i auth | grep -i none
    ```

    ```
    [root@ceph-node1 ceph]# ceph --admin-daemon /var/run/ceph/ceph-osd.0.asok
    config show | grep -i auth | grep -i none
      "auth_cluster_required": "none",
      "auth_service_required": "none",
      "auth_client_required": "none",
    [root@ceph-node1 ceph]#
    ```

11. Finally, on the Windows client, run `ceph-dokan.exe` to mount CephFS as a drive. Using the command prompt, execute the following:

    ```
    ceph-dokan.exe -c ceph.conf -l m
    ```

    ```
    [root@ceph-node1 ~]# ganesha.nfsd -f /etc/ganesha.conf -L /var/log/ganesha.log -N NIV_DEBUG -d
    [root@ceph-node1 ~]#
    [root@ceph-node1 ~]# ps -ef | grep -i nfs
    root      7975     1  0 00:55 ?        00:00:00 ganesha.nfsd -f /etc/ganesha.conf -L /var/log/ganesha.log -N NIV_DEBUG -d
    root      8023  5901  0 00:56 pts/0    00:00:00 grep --color=auto -i nfs
    [root@ceph-node1 ~]#
    ```

    This command should mount CephFS as a local drive on your Windows client.

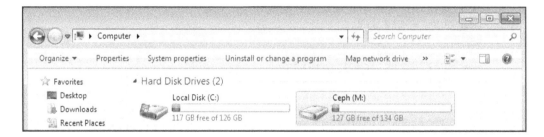

Both CephFS and `ceph-dokan` require more contribution and development to gain enough maturity to support production workloads. However, they are good candidates for testing and POC.

CephFS a drop-in replacement for HDFS

Hadoop is a programming framework that supports the processing and storage of large data sets in a distributed computing environment. The Hadoop core includes the analytics Map-Reduce engine and the distributed file system known as HDFS (Hadoop Distributed File System), which has several weaknesses that are listed as follows:

- It had a single point of failure until the recent versions of HDFS
- It isn't POSIX compliant
- It stores at least 3 copies of data
- It has a centralized name server resulting in scalability challenges

The Apache Hadoop project and other software vendors are working independently to fix these gaps in HDFS.

The Ceph community has done some development in this space, and it has a file system plugin for Hadoop that possibly overcomes the limitations of HDFS and can be used as a drop-in replacement for it. There are three requirements for using CephFS with HDFS; they are as follows:

- Running the Ceph cluster
- Running the Hadoop cluster
- Installing the CephFS Hadoop plugin

The Hadoop and HDFS implementation is beyond the scope of this book, however, in this section, we will superficially discuss how CephFS can be used in conjunction with HDFS. Hadoop clients can access CephFS through a java-based plugin named `hadoop-cephfs.jar`. The two-java classes that follow are required to support Hadoop connectivity to CephFS.

- `libcephfs.jar`: This file should be placed in `/usr/share/java/`, and the path should be added to `HADOOP_CLASSPATH` in the `Hadoop_env.sh` file.
- `libcephfs_jni.so`: This file should be added to the `LD_LIBRARY_PATH` environment parameter and placed in `/usr/lib/hadoop/lib`. You should also soft link it to `/usr/lib/hadoop/lib/native/Linux-amd64-64/libcephfs_jni.so`.

In addition to this, the native CephFS client must be installed on each node of the Hadoop cluster. For more of the latest information on using CephFS for Hadoop, please visit the official Ceph documentation at `http://ceph.com/docs/master/cephfs/hadoop`, and Ceph GitHub at `https://github.com/ceph/cephfs-hadoop`.

5
Monitoring Ceph Clusters using Calamari

In this chapter, we will cover the following recipes:

- ▶ Ceph cluster monitoring – the classic way
- ▶ Monitoring Ceph Cluster
- ▶ Introducing Ceph Calamari
- ▶ Building Calamari server packages
- ▶ Building Calamari client packages
- ▶ Setting up the Calamari master server
- ▶ Adding Ceph nodes to Calamari
- ▶ Monitoring Ceph clusters from the Calamari dashboard
- ▶ Troubleshooting Calamari

Introduction

Whether you have a small, medium, or exascale cluster, monitoring is the most critical part of your infrastructure. As soon as you have done the designing, deployment, and production service implementation of your Ceph cluster, monitoring becomes the key responsibility of the storage administrator. In this chapter, we will learn multiple ways to monitor your Ceph cluster and its components. We will cover both the CLI and GUI monitoring of Ceph using its native CLI tools; we will also implement Calamari, which is an open source Ceph cluster management dashboard.

Ceph cluster monitoring – the classic way

As a storage administrator, you would need to keep an eye on your Ceph storage cluster and find out what's going on at a given time. Regular and disciplined monitoring keeps you updated with your cluster health. Based on monitoring notifications, you would get a bit more time to take necessary action before service outages.

Monitoring a Ceph cluster is an everyday task that includes the monitoring of MON, OSD, MDS, PG, as well as storage provisioning services such as RBD, Radosgw, CephFS, and Ceph clients. Ceph, by default, comes with a rich set of native command line tools and API to perform monitoring on these components. In addition to this, there are also open source projects that are intentionally developed for monitoring Ceph clusters on a GUI one-view dashboard. In the following recipes, we will focus on Ceph CLI tools for cluster monitoring.

Monitoring Ceph clusters

In this recipe, we will learn commands that are used to monitor the overall Ceph cluster.

How to do it...

Here is how we go about monitoring the Ceph cluster. The steps are explained topic-wise as follows.

Checking the cluster's health

To check the health of your cluster, use the `ceph` command followed by `health` as the command option:

```
# ceph health
```

The output of this command would be divided into several sections separated by a semicolon:

```
[root@ceph-node1 ~]# ceph health
HEALTH_WARN 64 pgs degraded; 1408 pgs stuck unclean; recovery 1/5744 objects degraded (0.017%)
[root@ceph-node1 ~]#
```

The first section of the output shows that your cluster is in the warning state, HEALTH_WARN, as 64 **placement groups** (**PGs**) are degraded. The second section represents that 1408 PGs are not clean, and the third section of the output represents that cluster recovery is going on for 1 out of 5744 objects and the cluster is 0.017% degraded. If your cluster is healthy, you will receive the output as HEALTH_OK.

To find out more details of your cluster health, use the `ceph health detail` command. This command will tell you all the PGs that are not active and clean, that is, all the PGs that are unclean, inconsistent, and degraded will be listed here with their details. If your cluster is healthy, you will receive the output as `HEALTH_OK`.

```
[root@ceph-node2 ceph]# ceph health detail
HEALTH_ERR 61 pgs degraded; 6 pgs inconsistent; 1312 pgs stuck unclean; recovery 3/5746 objects degraded (0.052%); 8 scrub errors
pg 9.76 is stuck unclean since forever, current state active+remapped, last acting [7,3,2]
pg 8.77 is stuck unclean since forever, current state active+remapped, last acting [4,6,8]
pg 7.78 is stuck unclean for 788849.714074, current state active+remapped, last acting [6,5,1]
pg 6.79 is stuck unclean since forever, current state active+remapped, last acting [4,7,8]
pg 5.7a is stuck unclean since forever, current state active+remapped, last acting [7,4,2]
pg 4.7b is stuck unclean since forever, current state active+remapped, last acting [7,3,1]
pg 11.74 is stuck unclean for 788413.925336, current state active+remapped, last acting [4,7,8]
pg 10.75 is stuck unclean for 788412.797947, current state active+remapped, last acting [7,3,0]
```

Monitoring cluster events

You can monitor cluster events using the `ceph` command with the `-w` option. This command will display all the cluster events' messages including information (INF), warning (WRN), and error (ERR) in real time. The output of this command will be continuous, live cluster changes; you can use *Ctrl + C* to get on to the shell:

`ceph -w`

```
[root@ceph-node1 ~]# ceph -w
    cluster 9609b429-eee2-4e23-af31-28a24fcf5cbc
     health HEALTH_OK
     monmap e3: 3 mons at {ceph-node1=192.168.1.101:6789/0,ceph-node2=192.168.1.102:6789/0
,ceph-node3=192.168.1.103:6789/0}, election epoch 640, quorum 0,1,2 ceph-node1,ceph-node2,
ceph-node3
     mdsmap e68: 1/1/1 up {0=ceph-node2=up:active}
     osdmap e1821: 9 osds: 9 up, 9 in
      pgmap v20731: 1628 pgs, 45 pools, 2422 MB data, 3742 objects
            7605 MB used, 127 GB / 134 GB avail
               1628 active+clean

2015-06-06 20:13:27.047075 mon.0 [INF] pgmap v20731: 1628 pgs: 1628 active+clean; 2422 MB
data, 7605 MB used, 127 GB / 134 GB avail; 7931 kB/s, 1 objects/s recovering
2015-06-06 20:14:25.958762 mon.0 [INF] from='client.? 192.168.1.103:0/1008239' entity='cli
ent.admin' cmd=[{"prefix": "pg repair", "pgid": "43.29"}]: dispatch
2015-06-06 20:14:32.031029 mon.0 [INF] pgmap v20732: 1628 pgs: 1628 active+clean; 2422 MB
data, 7605 MB used, 127 GB / 134 GB avail
2015-06-06 20:14:57.541278 mon.0 [INF] pgmap v20733: 1628 pgs: 1628 active+clean; 2422 MB
data, 7621 MB used, 127 GB / 134 GB avail
2015-06-06 20:15:02.371735 mon.0 [INF] pgmap v20734: 1628 pgs: 1628 active+clean; 2422 MB
data, 7633 MB used, 127 GB / 134 GB avail
```

There are other options that can be used with the `ceph` command to gather different types of event details. They are as follows:

- ► **--watch-debug**: to watch debug events
- ► **--watch-info**: to watch info events
- ► **--watch-sec**: to watch security events
- ► **--watch-warn**: to watch warning events
- ► **--watch-error**: to watch error events

The cluster utilization statistics

To know your cluster's space utilization statistics, use the `ceph` command with the `df` option. This command will show the total cluster size, the available size, the used size, and the percentage. This will also display pool information, such as the pool name, ID, utilization, and number of objects in each pool:

```
# ceph df
```

The output is as follows:

```
[root@ceph-node1 ~]# ceph df
GLOBAL:
    SIZE      AVAIL     RAW USED     %RAW USED
    134G      127G       7440M          5.39
POOLS:
    NAME                     ID     USED      %USED     MAX AVAIL     OBJECTS
    rbd                      0      114M      0.08        42924M         2629
    images                   1      53002k    0.04        42924M           12
    volumes                  2      47        0           42924M            8
    vms                      3      208M      0.15        42924M           31
    .rgw.root                4      162       0           42924M            2
    .rgw.control             5      0         0           42924M            8
    .rgw                     6      2731      0           42924M           15
    .rgw.gc                  7      0         0           42924M           32
    .users.uid               8      736       0           42924M            4
    .users.email             9      8         0           42924M            1
    .users                   10     16        0           42924M            2
    .users.swift             11     8         0           42924M            1
    .rgw.buckets.index       12     0         0           42924M            9
    .rgw.buckets             13     1744      0           42924M            4
```

Checking the cluster's status

Checking the cluster's status is the most common and the most frequent operation when managing a Ceph cluster. You can check the status of your cluster using the `ceph` command and `status` as the option:

```
# ceph status
```

Instead of the `status` subcommand, you can also use a shorter version, `-s`, as an option:

```
# ceph -s
```

The following screenshot shows the status of our cluster:

```
[root@ceph-node1 ~]# ceph -s
    cluster 9609b429-eee2-4e23-af31-28a24fcf5cbc
     health HEALTH_OK
     monmap e3: 3 mons at {ceph-node1=192.168.1.101:6789/0,ceph-node2=192.168.1.102:6789/0,
ceph-node3=192.168.1.103:6789/0}, election epoch 640, quorum 0,1,2 ceph-node1,ceph-node2,ce
ph-node3
     mdsmap e73: 1/1/1 up {0=ceph-node2=up:active}
     osdmap e1823: 9 osds: 9 up, 9 in
      pgmap v20762: 1628 pgs, 45 pools, 2422 MB data, 3742 objects
            7440 MB used, 127 GB / 134 GB avail
                 1628 active+clean
[root@ceph-node1 ~]#
```

This command will dump a lot of useful information for your Ceph cluster:

- **cluster**: This command represents the Ceph unique cluster ID.
- **health**: This command shows cluster health.
- **monmap**: This command represents the monitor map epoch version, monitor information, monitor election epoch version, and monitor quorum status.
- **mdsmap**: This command represent the `mdsmap` epoch version and the `mdsmap` status.
- **osdmap**: This command represents the `osdmap` epoch, OSD total, up and in count.
- **pgmap**: This command shows the `pgmap` version, total number of PGs, pool count, capacity in use for a single copy, and total objects. It also displays information about cluster utilization including used size, free size, and total size. Finally, it will display the PG status.

 In order to view the real time cluster status, you can use **ceph status** with the LINUX `watch` command to get continuous output:

```
# watch ceph -s
```

The cluster authentication entries

Ceph works on an authentication system based on keys. All cluster components interact with each other once they undergo a key-based authentication system. You can use the `ceph` command with the `auth list` subcommand to get a list of all the keys:

```
# ceph auth list
```

 To know more about command operation, you can use `help` with the sub option. For instance, run # `ceph auth --help` and use the command as directed in the help.

Monitoring Ceph MON

Usually a Ceph cluster is deployed with more than one MON instance for high availability. Since there is a large number of monitors, they should attain a quorum to make the cluster function properly.

How to do it...

We will now focus on Ceph commands for OSD monitoring. The steps will be explained topic-wise as follows:

Checking the MON status

To display the cluster's MON status and MON map, use the `ceph` command with either `mon stat` or the `mon dump` suboption:

```
# ceph mon stat
# ceph mon dump
```

The following screenshot displays the output of this command:

```
[root@ceph-node1 ~]# ceph mon stat
e3: 3 mons at {ceph-node1=192.168.1.101:6789/0,ceph-node2=192.168.1.102:6789/0,ceph-node3
=192.168.1.103:6789/0}, election epoch 640, quorum 0,1,2 ceph-node1,ceph-node2,ceph-node3
[root@ceph-node1 ~]#
[root@ceph-node1 ~]# ceph mon dump
dumped monmap epoch 3
epoch 3
fsid 9609b429-eee2-4e23-af31-28a24fcf5cbc
last_changed 2015-03-18 00:20:07.092486
created 0.000000
0: 192.168.1.101:6789/0 mon.ceph-node1
1: 192.168.1.102:6789/0 mon.ceph-node2
2: 192.168.1.103:6789/0 mon.ceph-node3
[root@ceph-node1 ~]#
```

Checking the MON quorum status

To maintain a quorum between Ceph MONs, the cluster should always have more than half of the available monitors in a Ceph cluster. Checking the quorum status of a cluster is very useful at the time of MON troubleshooting. You can check the quorum status by using the `ceph` command and the `quorum_status` subcommand:

```
# ceph quorum_status -f json-pretty
```

The following screenshot displays the output of this command:

```
[root@ceph-node1 ~]# ceph quorum_status -f json-pretty

{ "election_epoch": 640,
  "quorum": [
        0,
        1,
        2],
  "quorum_names": [
        "ceph-node1",
        "ceph-node2",
        "ceph-node3"],
  "quorum_leader_name": "ceph-node1",
  "monmap": { "epoch": 3,
        "fsid": "9609b429-eee2-4e23-af31-28a24fcf5cbc",
        "modified": "2015-03-18 00:20:07.092486",
        "created": "0.000000",
        "mons": [
            { "rank": 0,
              "name": "ceph-node1",
              "addr": "192.168.1.101:6789\/0"},
            { "rank": 1,
              "name": "ceph-node2",
              "addr": "192.168.1.102:6789\/0"},
            { "rank": 2,
              "name": "ceph-node3",
              "addr": "192.168.1.103:6789\/0"}]}}
[root@ceph-node1 ~]#
```

The quorum status displays election_epoch, which is the election version number, and quorum_leader_name, which denotes the hostname of the quorum leader. It also displays the MON map epoch and cluster ID. Each cluster monitor is allocated with a rank. For I/O operations, clients first connect to the quorum lead monitor; if the leader MON is unavailable, the client then connects to the next rank monitor:

> To generate the formatted output for Ceph commands, use the -f json-pretty option.

Monitoring Ceph OSDs

Monitoring OSDs is a crucial task and requires a lot of attention, as there are a lot of OSDs to monitor and take care of. The bigger your cluster, the more OSDs it would have, and the more rigorous the monitoring it would require. Generally, Ceph clusters host a lot of disks, so the chances of facing an OSD failure are quite high.

How to do it...

We will now focus on Ceph commands for OSD monitoring. The steps will be explained topic-wise as follows:

OSD tree view

The tree view in OSD is quite useful for knowing OSD statuses such as IN or OUT and UP or DOWN. The tree view in OSD displays each node with all its OSDs and its location in the CRUSH map. You can check the tree view of OSD using the following command:

```
# ceph osd tree
```

```
[root@ceph-node1 ~]# ceph osd tree
# id    weight  type name          up/down reweight
-1      0.08995 root default
-2      0.02998         host ceph-node1
0       0.009995                        osd.0   up      1
1       0.009995                        osd.1   up      1
2       0.009995                        osd.2   up      1
-3      0.02998         host ceph-node2
3       0.009995                        osd.3   up      1
4       0.009995                        osd.4   up      1
5       0.009995                        osd.5   up      1
-4      0.02998         host ceph-node3
6       0.009995                        osd.6   up      1
7       0.009995                        osd.7   up      1
8       0.009995                        osd.8   up      1
[root@ceph-node1 ~]#
```

This command displays various useful information for Ceph OSDs, such as weight, UP/DOWN status, and IN/OUT status. The output will be beautifully formatted as per your Ceph crush map. If you were maintaining a big cluster, this format would be beneficial to locating your OSDs and their hosting server from a long list.

OSD statistics

To check OSD statistics, use # `ceph osd stat`; this command will help you get the OSD map epoch, total OSD count, and their IN and UP statuses.

To get detailed information about the Ceph cluster and OSD, execute the following command:

```
# ceph osd dump
```

This is a very useful command that will output the OSD map epoch, pool details including pool ID, pool name, pool type, that is, replicated or erasure, crush ruleset, and PGs. This command will also display information for each OSD, such as the OSD ID, status, weight, last clean interval epoch, and so on. All this information is extremely helpful for cluster monitoring and troubleshooting.

You can also make an OSD blacklist to prevent it from connecting to other OSDs so that no heartbeat process can take place. It's mostly used to prevent a lagging metadata server from making bad changes to data on the OSD. Usually, blacklists are maintained by Ceph itself and shouldn't need manual intervention, but it's good to know.

To display blacklisted clients, execute the following command:

```
# ceph osd blacklist ls
```

Checking the crush map

We can query the crush map directly from the `ceph osd` commands. The crush map command line utility can save a lot of the system administrator's time as compared to the conventional way of viewing and editing it after the decompilation of the crush map:

- ▶ To view the crush map, execute the following command:

  ```
  # ceph osd crush dump
  ```

- ▶ To view the crush map rules, execute the following command:

  ```
  # ceph osd crush rule list
  ```

- ▶ To view the detailed crush rule, execute the following command:

  ```
  # ceph osd crush rule dump <crush_rule_name>
  ```

The following figure displays the output of our query crush map:

```
[root@ceph-node1 ~]# ceph osd crush rule list
[
    "replicated_ruleset"]
[root@ceph-node1 ~]#
[root@ceph-node1 ~]# ceph osd crush rule dump replicated_ruleset
{ "rule_id": 0,
  "rule_name": "replicated_ruleset",
  "ruleset": 0,
  "type": 1,
  "min_size": 1,
  "max_size": 10,
  "steps": [
        { "op": "take",
          "item": -1,
          "item_name": "default"},
        { "op": "chooseleaf_firstn",
          "num": 0,
          "type": "host"},
        { "op": "emit"}]}
[root@ceph-node1 ~]#
```

If you are managing a large Ceph cluster with several hundreds of OSDs, it's sometimes difficult to find the location of a specific OSD in the crush map. It's also difficult if your crush map contains multiple bucket hierarchy. You can use `ceph osd find` to search for an OSD and its location in a crush map:

```
# ceph osd find <Numeric_OSD_ID>
```

```
[root@ceph-node1 ~]# ceph osd find 4
{ "osd": 4,
  "ip": "192.168.1.102:6811\/3897",
  "crush_location": { "host": "ceph-node2",
      "root": "default"}}[root@ceph-node1 ~]#
[root@ceph-node1 ~]#
[root@ceph-node1 ~]#
```

Monitoring PGs

OSDs store PGs, and each PG contains objects. The overall health of a cluster depends majorly on PGs. The cluster will remain in a `HEALTH_OK` status only if all the PGs are on the status, `active + clean`. If your Ceph cluster is not healthy, then there are chances that the PGs are not `active + clean`. Placement groups can exhibit multiple states, and even combination of states. The following are some states that a PG can be:

- `Creating`: The PG is being created.

- `Peering`: The process of bringing all of the OSDs that store PGs into agreement about the state of all objects including their metadata in that PG.

- `Active`: Once the peering operation is completed, Ceph lists the PG as active. Under the active state, the data in the PG data is available on the primary PG and its replica for the I/O operation.

- `Clean`: A clean state means that the primary and secondary OSDs have successfully peered and no PG moves away from their correct location. It also shows that PGs are replicated the correct number of times.

- `Down`: This means that the replica with the necessary data is down, so the PG is offline.

- `Degraded`: Once an OSD is DOWN, Ceph changes the state of all the PGs that are assigned to that OSD to DEGRADED. After the OSD comes UP, it has to peer again to make the degraded PGs clean. If the OSD remains DOWN and out for more than 300 seconds, Ceph recovers all the PGs that are degraded from their replica PGs to maintain the replication count. Clients can perform I/O even after PGs are in the degraded stage.

- `Recovering`: When an OSD goes DOWN, the content of the PGs of that OSD fall behind the contents of the replica PGs on other OSDs. Once the OSD comes UP, Ceph initiates a recovery operation on the PGs to keep them up to date with the replica PGs in other OSDs.

- ► `Backfilling`: As soon as a new OSD is added to the cluster, Ceph tries to rebalance the data by moving some PGs from other OSDs to this new OSD; this process is known as backfilling. Once the backfilling is completed for the PGs, the OSD can participate in the client I/O.

- ► `Remapped`: Whenever there is a change in the PG acting set, data migration happens from the old acting set OSD to the new acting set OSD. This operation might take some time depending on the data size that is being migrated to the new OSD. During this time, the old primary OSD of the old acting group serves to client request. As soon as the data migration operation completes, Ceph uses new primary OSDs from the acting group.

 An acting set refers to a group of OSDs responsible for PGs. The primary OSD is known as the first OSD from the acting set and is responsible for the peering operation for each PG with its secondary/tertiary OSD. It also entertains write operations from clients. The OSD, which is up, remains in the acting set. Once the primary OSD is `DOWN`, it's first removed from the up set; the secondary OSD is then promoted to be the primary OSD.

- ► `Stale`: Ceph OSD reports their statistics to the Ceph monitor every 0.5 seconds; by any chance, if the primary OSDs of the PG acting set fail to report their statistics to the monitors, or if other OSDs have reported the primary OSD `DOWN`, the monitor will consider those PGs as stale.

You can monitor PGs using the following commands:

- ► To get the PG status, run `# ceph pg stat`:

```
[root@ceph-node1 ~]# ceph pg stat
v20780: 1628 pgs: 1628 active+clean; 2422 MB data, 7440 MB used, 127 GB / 134 GB avail
[root@ceph-node1 ~]#
```

The output of the `pg stat` command will display a lot of information in a specific format: `vNNNN: X pgs: Y active+clean; R MB data, U MB used, F GB / T GB avail`.

Where the variables are defined as follows:

- ❑ **vNNNN**: This is the PG map version number
- ❑ **X**: The total number of PGs
- ❑ **Y**: The number of PGs that have an `active+clean` state
- ❑ **R**: The raw data stored
- ❑ **U**: The real data stored after replication

- ❏ **F**: The free capacity remaining
- ❏ **T**: The total capacity

▸ To get the PG list, execute the following:

```
# ceph pg dump -f json-pretty
```

This command will generate a lot of essential information with respect to PGs, such as the PG map version, PG ID, PG state, acting set, acting set primary, and so on. The output of this command can be huge depending on the number of PGs in your cluster.

▸ To query a particular PG for detailed information, execute the following command, which has the syntax as `ceph pg <PG_ID> query`:

```
# ceph pg 2.7d query
```

▸ To list stuck PGs, execute the following command that has the syntax as `ceph pg dump_stuck < unclean | Inactive | stale >`:

```
# ceph pg dump_stuck unclean
```

Monitoring Ceph MDS

Metadata servers are used only for CephFS, which is not production ready as of now. The Metadata server has several states, such as UP, DOWN, ACTIVE, and INACTIVE. While performing the monitoring of MDS, you should make sure the state of MDS is UP and ACTIVE. The following commands will help you get information related to the Ceph MDS.

How to do it...

1. Check the CephFS filesystem list:

   ```
   # ceph fs ls
   ```

2. Check the MDS status:

   ```
   # ceph mds stat
   ```

3. Display the details of the metadata server:

   ```
   # ceph mds dump
   ```

The output is shown in the following screenshot:

```
[root@ceph-node1 ~]# ceph fs ls
name: cephfs, metadata pool: cephfs_metadata, data pools: [cephfs_data ]
[root@ceph-node1 ~]#
[root@ceph-node1 ~]# ceph mds stat
e73: 1/1/1 up {0=ceph-node2=up:active}
[root@ceph-node1 ~]#
[root@ceph-node1 ~]# ceph mds dump
dumped mdsmap epoch 73
epoch   73
flags   0
created 2015-05-19 00:18:45.398790
modified        2015-06-06 20:15:21.386153
tableserver     0
root    0
session_timeout 60
session_autoclose       300
max_file_size   1099511627776
last_failure    0
last_failure_osd_epoch  1822
compat  compat={},rocompat={},incompat={1=base v0.20,2=client writeable ranges,3=default
file layouts on dirs,4=dir inode in separate object,5=mds uses versioned encoding,6=dirfr
ag is stored in omap,8=no anchor table}
max_mds 1
in      0
up      {0=47181}
failed
stopped
data_pools      43
metadata_pool   44
inline_data     disabled
47181:  192.168.1.102:6800/7314 'ceph-node2' mds.0.15 up:active seq 6
[root@ceph-node1 ~]# █
```

Introducing Ceph Calamari

Calamari is the management platform for Ceph; an attractive dashboard for monitoring and managing your Ceph cluster. It was initially developed by Inktank as a proprietary software, and it was a product of the Inktank Ceph Enterprise that was offered to their customers. Just after the acquisition of Inktank by Red Hat, it was open sourced on 30 May, 2014, by Red Hat. Calamari has several great feature sets, and its future roadmap is quite impressive. Calamari has two parts, and each part has its own repositories:

▸ **Frontend**: This is the browser-based Graphical User Interface, which is majorly implemented in JavaScript. The frontend part makes use of Calamari's REST API and is constructed in a modular approach so that each component of the fronted can be updated or undergo maintenance independently. The Calamari frontend has been open sourced with an MIT license; you can find the repository at `https://github.com/ceph/calamari-clients`.

▶ **Backend**: This Calamari backend is the core part of the platform, which is written in Python. It also makes use of other components, such as SaltStack, ZeroRPC, graphite, the Django-rest-framework, Django, gevent, and so on, and provides a new REST API for integration with Ceph and other systems. Calamari has been reinvented in its new version where it uses new Calamari REST API to interact with the Ceph cluster. The previous release of Calamari uses the Ceph REST API, which is a bit restrictive for this purpose. The Calamari backend has been open sourced with an LGPL2+ license; you can find the repository at `https://github.com/ceph/calamari`.

Calamari has good documentation available at `http://calamari.readthedocs.org`; whether you are a Calamari operator or a developer working on Calamari or a developer using the Calamari REST API, this documentation is a good source of information to get you started with Calamari. Like Ceph, Calamari has also been developed as an upstream product; you can get involved with Calamari on IRC at `irc://irc.oftc.net/ceph`, register to mailing lists at `ceph-calamari@ceph.com`, or by send pull requests on the Calamari GitHub account at `https://github.com/ceph/calamari` and `https://github.com/ceph/calamari-clients`.

Calamari currently does not provide ready-to-install packages, so you need to build them for your environment. In this recipe, we will learn about building the Ceph Calamari server packages from source. Building these packages is sometimes a challenging task, as you might not get it done in one shot. So, in order to reduce this complexity, I have built the packages for you, which you can download from `https://github.com/ksingh7/ceph-calamari-packages`, so can skip the following two recipes, directly jumping to the installing prerequisite. For those who are interested in building the packages from source, let's get started.

Building Calamari server packages

Calamari provides ready-to-use Vagrant configurations for some OS types. Identify your Calamari host operating type for which you wish to build packages against; in our case, it's CentOS7.

How to do it...

1. Clone the Calamari server repository using the following command:

   ```
   $ git clone https://github.com/ceph/calamari.git
   ```

2. Diamond is a Python daemon that collects system metrics and publishes them to Graphite. It is capable of collecting CPU, memory, network, I/O, load, and disk metrics. For more information on diamond, visit `http://diamond.readthedocs.org/`. Calamari currently provides its own fork of diamond. To get diamond, clone the following repository:

   ```
   $ git clone https://github.com/ceph/Diamond.git --branch=calamari
   ```

3. Under the `calamari` repository, you will find the `vagrant` directory, which provides development environments for various operating system types. Navigate to the following path for CentOS:

   `$ cd calamari/vagrant/centos-build`

```
teeri:git ksingh$ git clone https://github.com/ceph/calamari.git
Cloning into 'calamari'...
remote: Counting objects: 11265, done.
remote: Total 11265 (delta 0), reused 0 (delta 0), pack-reused 11265
Receiving objects: 100% (11265/11265), 20.83 MiB | 1.62 MiB/s, done.
Resolving deltas: 100% (6064/6064), done.
Checking connectivity... done.
teeri:git ksingh$
teeri:git ksingh$ git clone https://github.com/ceph/Diamond.git --branch=calamari
Cloning into 'Diamond'...
remote: Counting objects: 18182, done.
remote: Total 18182 (delta 0), reused 0 (delta 0), pack-reused 18182
Receiving objects: 100% (18182/18182), 4.15 MiB | 2.28 MiB/s, done.
Resolving deltas: 100% (7151/7151), done.
Checking connectivity... done.
teeri:git ksingh$
teeri:git ksingh$ cd calamari/vagrant/centos-build
teeri:centos-build ksingh$
teeri:centos-build ksingh$ ls -l
total 8
-rw-r--r--  1 ksingh  staff  1114 Jun  7 21:05 Vagrantfile
drwxr-xr-x  4 ksingh  staff   136 Jun  7 21:05 salt
teeri:centos-build ksingh$
```

4. At the time of writing this chapter, Vagrant did not provide build configuration to CentOS7. Rather, it was provided to CentOS6. So, we will modify the CentOS6 Vagrant environment by setting `config.vm.box` as `config.vm.box = "boxcutter/centos71"`.

5. Bring up the Vagrant box using the following command:

   `$ vagrant up`

```
==> default: Running provisioner: salt...
Copying salt minion config to vm.
Checking if salt-minion is installed
salt-minion was not found.
Checking if salt-call is installed
salt-call was not found.
Bootstrapping Salt... (this may take a while)


Salt successfully configured and installed!
run_overstate set to false. Not running state.overstate.
run_highstate set to false. Not running state.highstate.
```

6. At this point, our CentOS7 development environment is ready; we should now log in to this machine and run `salt-call` to start building the package:

```
$ vagrant ssh
```

```
$ sudo salt-call state.highstate
```

```
[vagrant@localhost ~]$
[vagrant@localhost ~]$ sudo salt-call state.highstate
[INFO    ] Loading fresh modules for state activity
[INFO    ] Fetching file from saltenv 'base', ** done ** 'top.sls'
```

7. The package build process will take some time; finally, you should get output something like the following:

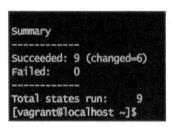

```
Summary
-------------
Succeeded: 9 (changed=6)
Failed:    0
-------------
Total states run:    9
[vagrant@localhost ~]$
```

8. At this point, you have successfully completed package building for the Calamari server and diamond. You can find the installable RPM files one directory up from your cloned `calamari` repository.

Building Calamari client packages

In this recipe, we will learn about building Calamari client packages. Most of the steps are similar to what we did in the last section, that is, with the Calamari server package build.

How to do it...

1. Clone the Calamari client repository:

```
$ git clone https://github.com/ceph/calamari-clients.git
```

2. Change the working directory to the one provided for the Centos Vagrant environment:

```
$ cd calamari-clients/vagrant/centos-package
```

3. Modify `Vagrantfile` and set `config.vm.box` to CentOS7 as follows:

```
config.vm.box = "boxcutter/centos71"
```

4. Next, bring up the machine:

```
$ vagrant up
```

5. At this stage, the development environment for the Calamari client is ready; we should now log in to this machine and run `salt-call` to starting building the package:

    ```
    $ vagrant ssh
    ```

    ```
    $ sudo salt-call state.highstate
    ```

6. The package build process will take some time; finally, you should get an output something like the following:

    ```
    ----------
              ID: copyout_build_product
        Function: cmd.run
            Name: cp calamari-clients*tar.gz /git/
          Result: True
         Comment: Command "cp calamari-clients*tar.gz /git/" run
         Changes:
                  ----------
                  pid:
                      25090
                  retcode:
                      0
                  stderr:
                  stdout:
    Summary
    -------------
    Succeeded: 13
    Failed:     0
    -------------
    Total:     13
    ```

7. At this point, you have successfully completed the package building for the Calamari client, and the RPM files can be found one directory up from your cloned `calamari` repository directory.

Setting up Calamari master server

In the last recipe, we compiled the packages required for Calamari, which includes the `calamari-server`, `calamari-client`, and `diamond`. If you have not compiled these packages by yourself, you can download them from my GitHub repository at `https://github.com/ksingh7/ceph-calamari-packages/tree/master/CentOS-el7`.

How to do it...

In this demonstration, we will be configuring `ceph-node1` as the Calamari master server, as well as the `salt-minion` node, `ceph-node2`, and `ceph-node3` as salt-minion nodes only. At the time of writing this recipe, Calamari did not support salt version 2015, so I have intentionally used salt version 2014.

Let's now begin the installation of the Calamari server:

1. On `ceph-node1`, install the dependency packages required by salt and the Calamari server:

    ```
    # yum install -y python-crypto PyYAML systemd-python yum-utils
    m2crypto pciutils python-msgpack systemd-python python-zmq
    ```

2. By default, CentOS7 will install salt's latest version, so in order to install salt version 2014, set up the salt repo:

    ```
    # wget https://copr.fedoraproject.org/coprs/saltstack/salt/repo/
    epel-7/saltstack-salt-epel-7.repo -O /etc/yum.repos.d/saltstack-
    salt-epel-7.repo
    ```

3. Install the salt master and salt minion version 2014.7.5:

    ```
    # yum --disablerepo="*" --enablerepo="salt*" install -y salt-
    master-2014.7.5-1.el7.centos
    ```

4. Since this is a test setup, we will stop and disable the firewall:

    ```
    # systemctl stop firewalld
    ```

    ```
    # systemctl disable firewalld
    ```

5. Next, install the Calamari server packages. Make sure this does not update the salt version to 2015:

    ```
    # yum install https://github.com/ksingh7/ceph-calamari-packages/
    raw/master/CentOS-el7/calamari-server-1.3.0.1-49_g828960a.el7.
    centos.x86_64.rpm
    ```

6. Next, we will install the Calamari server package that installs the dashboard component of Calamari:

    ```
    # yum install -y https://github.com/ksingh7/ceph-calamari-
    packages/raw/master/CentOS-el7/calamari-clients-1.2.2-32_g931ee58.
    el7.centos.x86_64.rpm
    ```

7. Enable and start the `salt-master` service:

    ```
    # systemctl enable salt-master
    ```

    ```
    # systemctl restart salt-master
    ```

8. At this point, our Calamari server is installed, and we should now configure it by running the following command:

    ```
    # calamari-ctl initialize
    ```

    ```
    [root@ceph-node1 ~]# calamari-ctl initialize
    [INFO] Loading configuration..
    [INFO] Starting/enabling salt...
    [INFO] Starting/enabling postgres...
    [INFO] Initializing database...
    [INFO] You will now be prompted for login details for the administrative user account.
    This is the account you will use to log into the web interface once setup is complete.
    Username (leave blank to use 'root'): root
    Email address: karan_singh1@live.com
    Password:
    Password (again):
    Superuser created successfully.
    [INFO] Initializing web interface...
    [INFO] Starting/enabling services...
    [INFO] Restarting services...
    [INFO] Complete.
    [root@ceph-node1 ~]#
    ```

9. At the time of writing this section, Calamari had a known bug (updating the connected minion), which will end up with an error during the Calamari initialize step. You can skip this step if your `calamari-ctl` initialize command went fine. To fix this bug, edit the `/opt/calamari/venv/lib/python2.7/site-packages/calamari_cthulhu-0.1-py2.7.egg/cthulhu/calamari_ctl.py` file and comment out line 255 that says `update_connected_minions()`:

```
[root@ceph-node1 cthulhu]# cat calamari_ctl.py | grep "update_connected_minions()" | grep -v def
    # update_connected_minions()
[root@ceph-node1 cthulhu]#
```

10. Next, visit the Calamari dashboard by pointing your browser at `http://192.168.1.101/dashboard/`, and provide the username as `root` and the password as what you set in the last step.

11. Once you are logged into the Calamari dashboard, you will see a screen similar to the following; as this is a fresh installation of Calamari, we need to add Ceph nodes to it, and it has been described in the following recipe:

Adding Ceph nodes to Calamari

At this stage, we have a running Calamari master server. In order to monitor your Ceph cluster with Calamari, we need to add Ceph nodes to Calamari. Let's begin that.

Since `ceph-node1` plays the dual role of being a Calamari master server and Calamari Ceph node, we have already performed the first two steps on `ceph-node1`. Execute the steps on `ceph-node2` and `ceph-node3` until otherwise specified.

How to do it...

1. On `ceph-node2` and `ceph-node3`, enable the salt 2014 `yum` repositories:

   ```
   # wget https://copr.fedoraproject.org/coprs/saltstack/salt/
   repo/epel-7/saltstack-salt-epel-7.repo -O /etc/yum.repos.d/
   saltstack-salt-epel-7.repo
   ```

2. Install the dependent packages manually:

   ```
   # yum install -y python-crypto PyYAML systemd-python yum-utils
   m2crypto pciutils python-msgpack systemd-python python-zmq
   ```

From now on, perform these steps on `ceph-node1`, `ceph-node2`, as well as `ceph-node3`:

1. Install the `salt-minion-2014` package:

   ```
   # yum --disablerepo="*" --enablerepo="salt*" install -y salt-
   minion-2014.7.5-1.el7.centos
   ```

2. Install the diamond package:

   ```
   # yum install -y https://github.com/ksingh7/ceph-calamari-
   packages/raw/master/CentOS-el7/diamond-3.4.582-0.noarch.rpm
   ```

3. Enable and start the diamond service:

   ```
   # systemctl enable diamond
   # systemctl restart diamond
   ```

4. Next, configure salt-minions to use `ceph-node1` as the Calamari master node:

   ```
   # echo "master: ceph-node1" > /etc/salt/minion.d/calamari.conf
   ```

5. Enable and start the `salt-minion` service:

   ```
   # systemctl enable salt-minion
   # systemctl restart salt-minion
   ```

   Now, salt-minions, that is, Calamari Ceph nodes, have been configured to use the Calamari master server. Next, we should log in to the Calamari master server, that is, `ceph-node1`, to list and accept the new salt keys of minions.

6. On `ceph-node1`, list salt-keys as follows:

   ```
   # salt-key -L
   ```

7. Next, accept the minion salt-keys:

   ```
   # salt-key -A
   ```

8. Check for accepted minion keys:

   ```
   # salt-key -L
   ```

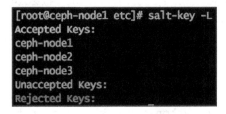

9. Finally, open your browser and visit the Calamari dashboard to check for your Ceph cluster.

 It sometimes happens that Calamari could not find the Ceph cluster just after accepting the salt-minion keys. In such a case, give some time to Calamari and salt to discover the Ceph cluster.

Monitoring Ceph clusters from the Calamari dashboard

Monitoring the Ceph cluster from the Calamari dashboard is fairly straightforward. Let's see how:

1. The dashboard screen shows a lot of useful information.

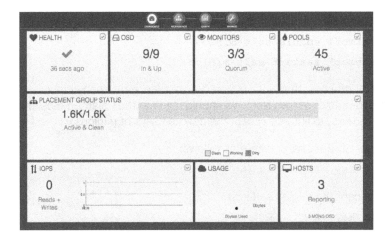

2. OSDs can be monitored using the OSD workbench option.

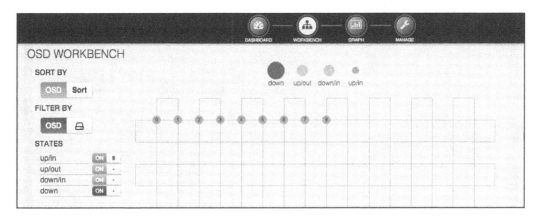

3. Calamari gives some nice options to monitor the host resource usage in the form of graphs. The following graph represents the CPU summary for `ceph-node1`:

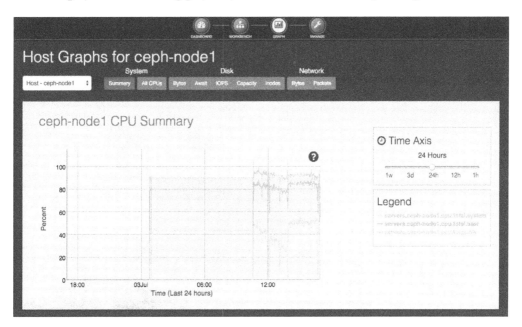

4. This graph represents the load average for `ceph-node1`; do follow the legend for better understanding:

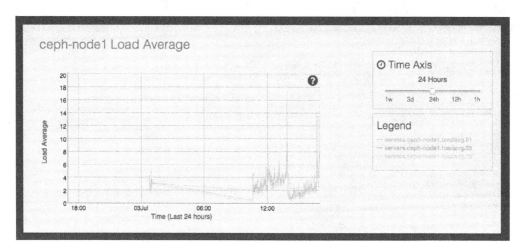

5. Finally, the following is the memory usage graph from `ceph-node1`. You can also view the memory usage in a timeline manner by adjusting the **Time Axis** option on the right-hand side:

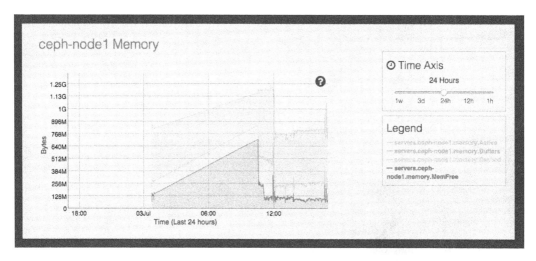

Troubleshooting Calamari

Troubleshooting Calamari is sometimes very tricky. In this recipe, I have collected some recipes that will help you troubleshoot your Calamari environment.

How to do it...

1. Check if the Calamari server, that is, the salt-master, could reach salt-minions:

    ```
    # salt '*' test.ping
    ```

2. Check if salt-master can query the Ceph cluster and get cluster information:

    ```
    # salt '*' ceph.get_heartbeats output
    ```

3. Check if the salt-minion node (Ceph cluster node) could reach the salt-master:

    ```
    # salt-minion -l debug
    ```

4. Salt-minion throws an error, **The Salt Master server's public key did not authenticate!**, under the `salt-minion` log file, that is, `/var/log/salt`.

    ```
    2015-06-26 09:57:27,531 [salt.crypt][CRITICAL] The Salt Master server's public key did
    not authenticate!
    The master may need to be updated if it is a version of Salt lower than 2014.7.5, or
    If you are confident that you are connecting to a valid Salt Master, then remove the
    master public key and restart the Salt Minion.
    The master public key can be found at:
    /etc/salt/pki/minion/minion_master.pub
    ```

5. To solve this problem, we need to delete the `minion` salt-key as well as the master public key and recreate both of them using the following commands:

    ```
    # rm -rf /etc/salt/pki/minion/minion_master.pub
    # systemctl stop salt-minion
    ```

    Now, perform the following set of steps:

    1. On salt-master, delete the minion key:

        ```
        # salt-key -L
        # slat-key -D <minion name>
        ```

    2. Start the `salt-minion` service:

        ```
        # systemctl start salt-minion
        ```

3. On salt-master, accept the new key for minion:

   `# salt-key -L`

   `# salt-key -A`

4. Finally, on salt-minion, use `# salt-minion -l` and make sure you do not get this error again.

6. Execute the `calamari-ctl initialize` command that will throw the **could not connect to server: Connection refused** error as follows:

```
[root@ceph-node1]# calamari-ctl initialize
[INFO] Loading configuration..
[INFO] Starting/enabling salt...
[INFO] Starting/enabling postgres...
[ERROR] (OperationalError) could not connect to server: Connection refused
  Is the server running on host "localhost" (::1) and accepting
  TCP/IP connections on port 5432?
could not connect to server: Connection refused
  Is the server running on host "localhost" (127.0.0.1) and accepting
  TCP/IP connections on port 5432?
 None None
[ERROR] We are sorry, an unexpected error occurred.  Debugging information has
been written to a file at '/tmp/2015-06-24_1919.txt', please include this when seeking technical
support.
[root@ceph-node1]#
```

Then, perform the set of steps mentioned as follows:

1. First, check if the postgres services are running:

   `# systemctl status postgres`

2. Log in to postgres and check whether the Calamari database exists or not:

   `# sudo -u postgres psql`

   `List postgres databases # \l`

```
[root@ceph-node1]# sudo -u postgres psql
psql (9.2.10)
Type "help" for help.
postgres=#
postgres=# \l
                                List of databases
    Name    |  Owner   | Encoding |   Collate   |    Ctype    |   Access privileges
------------+----------+----------+-------------+-------------+-----------------------
 postgres   | postgres | UTF8     | en_US.UTF-8 | en_US.UTF-8 |
 template0  | postgres | UTF8     | en_US.UTF-8 | en_US.UTF-8 | =c/postgres          +
            |          |          |             |             | postgres=CTc/postgres
 template1  | postgres | UTF8     | en_US.UTF-8 | en_US.UTF-8 | =c/postgres          +
            |          |          |             |             | postgres=CTc/postgres
(3 rows)

postgres=#
```

3. You might see that there is no database called `calamari`; now you should invoke `salt` to create a `calamari` user and database in postgres:

   ```
   # salt-call --local state.template /opt/calamari/salt-local/
   postgres.sls
   ```

4. Finally, re-run # `calamari-ctl initialize`; it should work this time.

7. The `calamari-ctl initialize` command line fails to throw the **Updating already connected nodes. failed with rc=2** error, as seen in the following screenshot:

```
[root@ceph-node1 ~]# calamari-ctl initialize
[INFO] Loading configuration..
[INFO] Starting/enabling salt...
[INFO] Starting/enabling postgres...
[INFO] Initializing database...
[INFO] You will now be prompted for login details for the administrative user account.
This is the account you will use to log into the web interface once setup is complete.
Username (leave blank to use 'root'):
Email address: karan_singh1@live.com
Password:
Password (again):
Superuser created successfully.
[INFO] Initializing web interface...
[INFO] Starting/enabling services...
[INFO] Updating already connected nodes.
[ERROR] Updating already connected nodes. failed with rc=2
[ERROR] We are sorry, an unexpected error occurred.  Debugging information has
been written to a file at '/tmp/2015-06-22_1855.txt', please include this when seeking
technical
support.
```

8. To fix this error, edit the `/opt/calamari/venv/lib/python2.7/site-packages/calamari_cthulhu-0.1-py2.7.egg/cthulhu/calamari_ctl.py` file, and comment out line 255, which says `update_connected_minions()`.

```
[root@ceph-node1 cthulhu]# cat calamari_ctl.py | grep "update_connected_minions()" | grep -v def
   # update_connected_minions()
[root@ceph-node1 cthulhu]#
```

6
Operating and Managing a Ceph Cluster

In this chapter, we will cover the following recipes:

- Understanding Ceph service management
- Managing the cluster configuration file
- Running Ceph with SYSVINIT
- Running Ceph as a service
- Scale-up versus scale-out
- Scaling out your Ceph cluster
- Scaling down your Ceph cluster
- Replacing a failed disk in the Ceph cluster
- Upgrading your Ceph cluster
- Maintaining a Ceph cluster

Introduction

At this point, I'm sure you are pretty confident in Ceph cluster deployment, provisioning, as well as monitoring. In this chapter, we will cover standard topics such as Ceph service management. We will also cover advanced topics such as scaling up your cluster by adding OSD and MON nodes, and finally, upgrading the Ceph cluster followed by some maintenance operations.

Understanding Ceph service management

Every component of Ceph, whether it's MON, OSD, MDS, or RGW, runs as a service on top of an underlying operating system. As a Ceph storage administrator, you should know about the Ceph services and how to operate them. On Red-Hat-based distributions, Ceph daemons can be managed in different ways: as a traditional **SYSVINIT** or **as a service**. Each time you **start**, **restart**, and **stop** Ceph daemons (or your entire cluster), you must specify at least one option and one command. You may also specify a daemon type or a daemon instance. The general syntax for this is as follows:

```
{ceph service command} [options] [command] [daemons]
```

The Ceph options include:

- `--verbose` or `-v`: This is for verbose logging.
- `--valgrind`: (It's used for Dev and QA only.) This is for valgrind debugging.
- `--allhosts` or `-a`: This executes on all nodes that are mentioned in `ceph.conf`, otherwise on localhost.
- `--conf` or `-c`: This is to use and alternate the configuration file.
- `--restart`: Automatically restarts the daemon if it core dumps.
- `--norestart`: This command says to not restart the daemon if it core dumps.

The Ceph commands include the following:

- `status`: Shows status of the daemon
- `start`: Starts the daemon
- `stop`: Stops the daemon
- `restart`: Stops and then starts the daemon
- `forcestop`: Forces the daemon to stop; similar to `kill-9`
- `killall`: Kills all daemons of a particular type
- `cleanlogs`: Cleans out the log directory
- `cleanalllogs`: Cleans out *everything* in the log directory

The Ceph daemons include the following:

- `mon`
- `osd`
- `msd`

Managing the cluster configuration file

If you are managing a large cluster, it's good practice to keep your cluster configuration file (`/etc/ceph/ceph.conf`) updated with information about cluster monitors, OSDs, MDSs, and RGW nodes. With these entries in place, you can manage all your cluster services from a single node.

How to do it...

To better understand this, we will update the Ceph configuration file on `ceph-node1` and add details of all monitor, OSD, and MDS nodes.

Adding monitor nodes to the Ceph configuration file

Since we have three monitor nodes, add their details to the `/etc/ceph/ceph.conf` file from `ceph-node1`.

```
[mon]
        mon data = /var/lib/ceph/mon/$cluster-$id
[mon.ceph-node1]
        host = ceph-node1
        mon addr = ceph-node1:6789
[mon.ceph-node2]
        host = ceph-node2
        mon addr = ceph-node2:6789
[mon.ceph-node3]
        host = ceph-node3
        mon addr = ceph-node3:6789
```

Adding an MDS node to the Ceph configuration file

Like in monitor, let's add MDS node details to the `/etc/ceph/ceph.conf` file from `ceph-node1`.

```
[mds]

[mds.ceph-node2]
        host = ceph-node2
```

Adding OSD nodes to the Ceph configuration file

Now, let's add the OSD nodes' details to the `/etc/ceph/ceph.conf` file from `ceph-node1`.

```
[osd]
        osd data = /var/lib/ceph/osd/$cluster-$id
        osd journal = /var/lib/ceph/osd/$cluster-$id/journal
[osd.0]
        host = ceph-node1
[osd.1]
        host = ceph-node1
[osd.2]
        host = ceph-node1
[osd.3]
        host = ceph-node2
[osd.4]
        host = ceph-node2
[osd.5]
        host = ceph-node2
[osd.6]
        host = ceph-node3
[osd.7]
        host = ceph-node3
[osd.8]
        host = ceph-node3
```

Running Ceph with SYSVINIT

SYSVINIT is a traditional yet recommended method of managing Ceph daemons on Red-Hat-based systems as well as for some older Debian/Ubuntu-based distributions. The general syntax for managing Ceph daemons using `sysvinit` is `/etc/init.d/ceph [options] [command] [daemons]`.

Starting and stopping all daemons

To start or stop all Ceph daemons, perform the following set of commands.

How to do it...

Let's see how to start and stop all Ceph daemons:

1. To start your Ceph cluster, execute Ceph with the `start` command. This command will start all Ceph services that you have deployed for all the hosts mentioned in the `ceph.conf` file:

   ```
   # /etc/init.d/ceph -a start
   ```

2. To stop your Ceph cluster, execute Ceph using the `stop` command. This command will stop all Ceph services that you have deployed for all the hosts mentioned in the `ceph.conf` file. The `-a` option is to execute on all nodes:

   ```
   # /etc/init.d/ceph -a stop
   ```

If you are using the -a option for service management, make sure that your ceph.conf file has all your Ceph hosts defined there and that the current node can ssh to all those other nodes. If the -a option is not used, then the command will only be executed on localhost.

Starting and stopping all daemons by type

To start or stop all Ceph daemons by their types, perform the following set of commands.

How to do it...

Let's see how to start and stop daemons by type:

Starting daemons by type

1. To start the Ceph monitor daemons on localhost, execute Ceph with the start command followed by the daemon type:

   ```
   # /etc/init.d/ceph start mon
   ```

2. To start the Ceph monitor daemons on all the hosts, execute the same command with the -a option:

   ```
   # /etc/init.d/ceph -a start mon
   ```

3. Similarly, you can start daemons of other types, that is, osd, mds, and ceph-radosgw:

   ```
   # /etc/init.d/ceph start osd
   # /etc/init.d/ceph start mds
   # /etc/init.d/ceph start ceph-radosgw
   ```

Stopping daemons by type

1. To stop the Ceph monitor daemons on localhost, execute Ceph with the stop command followed by the daemon type:

   ```
   # /etc/init.d/ceph stop mon
   ```

2. To stop the Ceph monitor daemons on all the hosts, execute the same command with the -a option:

   ```
   # /etc/init.d/ceph -a stop mon
   ```

3. Similarly, you can stop daemons of other types, that is, `osd`, `mds`, and `ceph-radosgw`:

```
# /etc/init.d/ceph stop osd
# /etc/init.d/ceph stop mds
# /etc/init.d/ceph stop ceph-radosgw
```

Starting and stopping a specific daemon

To start or stop a specific Ceph daemon, perform the following set of commands.

How to do it...

Let's see how to start and stop specific daemons.

Starting a specific daemon

To start a specific daemon on localhost, execute Ceph with the `start` command followed by `{daemon_type}.{instance}`, for example:

1. Start the `mon.0` daemon:

```
# /etc/init.d/ceph start mon.ceph-node1
```

2. Similarly, you can start other daemons and their instances:

```
# /etc/init.d/ceph start osd.1
# /etc/init.d/ceph -a start mon.ceph-node2
# /etc/init.d/ceph start ceph-radosgw.gateway1
```

Stopping a specific daemon

To stop a specific Ceph daemon on localhost, execute Ceph with the `stop` command followed by `{daemon_type}.{instance}`, for example:

1. Stop the `mon.0` daemon:

```
# /etc/init.d/ceph start mon.ceph-node1
```

2. Similarly, you can stop other daemons and their instances:

```
# /etc/init.d/ceph stop osd.1
# /etc/init.d/ceph stop -a mds.ceph-node2
# /etc/init.d/ceph stop ceph-radosgw.gateway1
```

Running Ceph as a service

In the last recipe, we learned about Ceph service management using `sysvinit`; in this recipe, we will understand managing Ceph as a service, that is, using the Linux `service` command. Starting from the Ceph Argonaut release, we can manage Ceph daemons using the Linux `service` command with the following syntax:

```
service ceph [options] [command] [daemons]
```

Starting and stopping all daemons

To start or stop all Ceph daemons, perform the following set of commands.

How to do it...

Let's see how to start and stop all Ceph daemons:

1. To start your Ceph cluster, execute Ceph with the `start` command. This command will start all Ceph services that you have deployed for all the hosts mentioned in the `ceph.conf` file. Once you start Ceph with the `-a` option, Ceph should begin operating:

   ```
   # service ceph -a start
   ```

2. To stop your Ceph cluster, execute Ceph with the `stop` command. This command will stop all Ceph services that you have deployed for all the hosts mentioned in the `ceph.conf` file. Once you stop Ceph using the `-a` option, Ceph should shut down:

   ```
   # service ceph -a stop
   ```

Starting and stopping all daemons by type

To start or stop all Ceph daemons by their types, perform the following set of commands.

How to do it...

Let's see how to start and stop daemons by type.

Starting daemons by type

1. To start the Ceph monitor daemons on localhost, execute the Ceph service with the `start` command followed by the daemon type:

    ```
    # service ceph start mon
    ```

2. To start the Ceph monitor daemons on all the hosts, execute the same command with the `-a` option:

    ```
    # service ceph -a start mon
    ```

3. Similarly, you can start daemons of other types, that is, `osd`, `mds`, and `ceph-radosgw`:

    ```
    # service ceph start osd
    # service ceph start mds
    # service ceph start ceph-radosgw
    ```

Stopping daemons by type

1. To stop the Ceph monitor daemons on localhost, execute `service ceph` with the `stop` command followed by the daemon type:

    ```
    # service ceph stop mon
    ```

2. To stop the Ceph monitor daemons on all the hosts, execute the same command with the `-a` option:

    ```
    # service ceph -a stop mon
    ```

3. Similarly, you can stop daemons of other types, that is, `osd`, `mds`, and `ceph-radosgw`:

    ```
    # service ceph stop osd
    # service ceph stop mds
    # service ceph stop ceph-radosgw
    ```

Starting and stopping a specific daemon

To start or stop a specific Ceph daemon, perform the following set of commands.

How to do it...

Let's see how to start and stop specific daemons.

Starting a specific daemon

To start a specific daemon on localhost, execute Ceph with the `start` command followed by `{daemon_type}.{instance}`, for example:

1. Start the `mon.0` daemon:

    ```
    # service ceph start mon.ceph-node1
    ```

2. Similarly, you can start other daemons and their instances:

    ```
    # service ceph start osd.1
    # service ceph -a start mds.ceph-node2
    # service ceph start ceph-radosgw.gateway1
    ```

Stopping a specific daemon

To stop a specific Ceph daemon on localhost, execute Ceph with the `stop` command followed by `{daemon_type}.{instance}`, for example:

1. Stop the `mon.0` daemon:

    ```
    # service ceph start mon.ceph-node1
    ```

2. Similarly, you can stop other daemons and their instances:

    ```
    # service ceph stop osd.1
    # service ceph -a stop mds.ceph-node2
    # service ceph stop ceph-radosgw.gateway1
    ```

Scale-up versus scale-out

When you are building up a storage infrastructure, scalability is one of the most important design aspects. The storage solution that you have chosen for your infrastructure should be scalable enough to accommodate your future data needs. Usually, a storage system starts with small to medium capacity and grows gradually into a large storage solution.

Traditional storage systems were based on scale-up design and were limited by a certain storage capacity. If you try to expand these storage systems over a certain limit, you might need to compromise the performance, reliability, and availability. The scale-up design methodology for storage involves adding disk resources to the existing controller systems, which becomes a bottleneck for performance, capacity, and manageability when it reaches a certain level.

On the other hand, scale-out design focuses on adding entire new devices containing disks, CPU, memory, and other resources to the existing storage cluster. With this type of design, you would not face the challenges that have been seen in scale-up design; it is rather benefited by linear performance improvement. The following diagram explains the scale-up and scale-out design of a storage system:

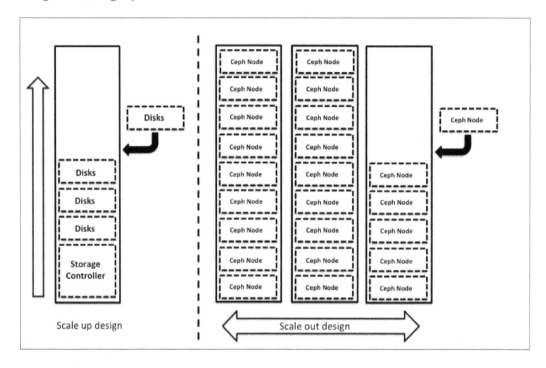

Ceph is a seamless scalable storage system based on scale out design, where you can add a compute node with a bunch of disks to an existing Ceph cluster and extend your storage system to a larger storage capacity.

Scaling out your Ceph cluster

From the roots, Ceph has been designed to grow from a few nodes to several hundreds, and it's supposed to scale on the fly without any downtime. In this recipe, we will dive deep into the Ceph scale-out feature by adding MON, OSD, MDS, and RGW nodes.

Adding the Ceph OSD

Adding an OSD node to the Ceph cluster is an online process. To demonstrate this, we would require a new virtual machine named `ceph-node4` with three disks that will act as OSDs. This new node will then be added to our existing Ceph cluster.

How to do it...

Run the following commands from `ceph-node1` until otherwise specified:

1. Create a new node, `ceph-node4`, with three disks (OSD). You can follow the process of creating a new virtual machine with disks and the OS configuration, as mentioned in the *Setting up virtual infrastructure* recipe in *Chapter 1, Ceph – Introduction and Beyond*, and make sure `ceph-node1` can SSH into `ceph-node4`.

   Before adding the new node to the Ceph cluster, let's check the current OSD tree. As shown in the following screenshot, the cluster has three nodes and a total of nine OSDs:

   # ceph osd tree

   ```
   [root@ceph-node1 ~]# ceph osd tree
   # id    weight  type name        up/down reweight
   -1      0.08998 root default
   -3      0.03            host ceph-node2
   3       0.009995                        osd.3   up      1
   4       0.009995                        osd.4   up      1
   5       0.009995                        osd.5   up      1
   -4      0.03            host ceph-node3
   6       0.009995                        osd.6   up      1
   7       0.009995                        osd.7   up      1
   8       0.009995                        osd.8   up      1
   -2      0.02998         host ceph-node1
   0       0.009995                        osd.0   up      1
   1       0.009995                        osd.1   up      1
   2       0.009995                        osd.2   up      1
   [root@ceph-node1 ~]#
   ```

2. Make sure that the new nodes have the Ceph packages installed. It's a recommended practice to keep all cluster nodes on the same Ceph version. From `ceph-node1`, install the Ceph packages on `ceph-node4`:

   # ceph-deploy install ceph-node4 --release giant

    We are intentionally installing the Ceph Giant release here so that one can learn how to upgrade the Ceph cluster from Giant to Hammer later in this chapter.

3. List the disks of `ceph-node4`:

   # ceph-deploy disk list ceph-node4

4. Let's add disks from `ceph-node4` to our existing Ceph cluster:

   # ceph-deploy disk zap ceph-node4:sdb ceph-node4:sdc ceph-node4:sdd

   # ceph-deploy osd create ceph-node4:sdb ceph-node4:sdc ceph-node4:sdd

5. As soon as you add new OSDs to the Ceph cluster, you will notice that the Ceph cluster starts rebalancing existing data to the new OSDs. You can monitor rebalancing using the following command; after a while, you will notice that your Ceph cluster becomes stable:

```
# watch ceph -s
```

6. Finally, once the `ceph-node4` disks' addition is complete, you will notice the cluster's new storage capacity:

```
# rados df
```

7. Check the OSD tree; it will give you a better understanding of your cluster. You should notice the new OSDs under `ceph-node4`, which have been recently added:

```
# ceph osd tree
```

```
[root@ceph-node1 ceph]# ceph osd tree
# id    weight  type name          up/down reweight
-1      0.12    root default
-3      0.03            host ceph-node2
3       0.009995                    osd.3   up      1
4       0.009995                    osd.4   up      1
5       0.009995                    osd.5   up      1
-4      0.03            host ceph-node3
6       0.009995                    osd.6   up      1
7       0.009995                    osd.7   up      1
8       0.009995                    osd.8   up      1
-2      0.02998         host ceph-node1
0       0.009995                    osd.0   up      1
1       0.009995                    osd.1   up      1
2       0.009995                    osd.2   up      1
-5      0.02998         host ceph-node4
9       0.009995                    osd.9   up      1
10      0.009995                    osd.10  up      1
11      0.009995                    osd.11  up      1
[root@ceph-node1 ceph]#
```

This command outputs some valuable information such as OSD weight, which Ceph node hosts which OSD, the UP/DOWN status of an OSD, and the OSD IN/OUT status represented by 1 or 0.

Just now, we have learned how to add a new node to the existing Ceph cluster. It's a good time to understand that as the number of OSDs increases, choosing the right value for the PG becomes more important because it has a significant influence on the behavior of the cluster. Increasing the PG count on a large cluster can be an expensive operation. I encourage you to take a look at http://docs.ceph.com/docs/master/rados/operations/placement-groups/#choosing-the-number-of-placement-groups for any updated information on **Placement Groups** (**PGs**).

Adding the Ceph MON

In an environment where you have deployed a large Ceph cluster, you might want to increase your monitor count. Like in an OSD, adding new monitors to the Ceph cluster is an online process. In this recipe, we will configure `ceph-node4` as a monitor node.

Since this is a test Ceph cluster, we will add `ceph-node4` as the fourth monitor node, however, in production setup, you should always have an odd number of monitor nodes in your Ceph cluster; this improves resiliency.

How to do it...

1. To configure `ceph-node4` as a monitor node, execute the following command from `ceph-node1`:

    ```
    # ceph-deploy mon create ceph-node4
    ```

2. Once `ceph-node4` is configured as a monitor node, check the Ceph status to see the cluster status. Please notice that `ceph-node4` is your new monitor node.

    ```
    [root@ceph-node1 ceph]# ceph -s
        cluster 9609b429-eee2-4e23-af31-28a24fcf5cbc
         health HEALTH_OK
         monmap e6: 4 mons at {ceph-node1=192.168.1.101:6789/0,ceph-node2=192.168.1.102:6789/0,
    ceph-node3=192.168.1.103:6789/0,ceph-node4=192.168.1.104:6789/0}, election epoch 958, quoru
    m 0,1,2,3 ceph-node1,ceph-node2,ceph-node3,ceph-node4
         mdsmap e217: 1/1/1 up {0=ceph-node2=up:active}
         osdmap e3951: 12 osds: 12 up, 12 in
          pgmap v32414: 1628 pgs, 45 pools, 2422 MB data, 3742 objects
                7920 MB used, 172 GB / 179 GB avail
                    1628 active+clean
    [root@ceph-node1 ceph]#
    ```

3. Check the Ceph monitor status and notice `ceph-node4` as the new Ceph monitor.

```
[root@ceph-node1 ceph]# ceph mon stat
e6: 4 mons at {ceph-node1=192.168.1.101:6789/0,ceph-node2=192.168.1.102:6789/0,ceph-node3=192.168.1.103:6789/0,ceph-node4
=192.168.1.104:6789/0}, election epoch 958, quorum 0,1,2,3 ceph-node1,ceph-node2,ceph-node3,ceph-node4
[root@ceph-node1 ceph]#
```

Adding the Ceph RGW

For an object storage use case, you have to deploy the Ceph RGW component, and to make your object storage service highly available and performing, you should deploy more than one instance of the Ceph RGW. A Ceph object storage service can easily scale from one to several nodes of RGW. The following diagram shows how multiple RGW instances can be deployed and scaled to provide the HA object storage service:

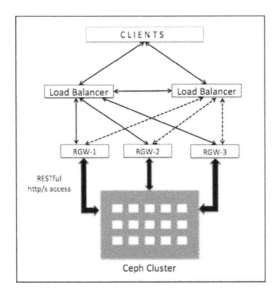

Scaling RGW is the same as adding additional RGW nodes; please refer to the *Installing Rados Gateway* recipe from *Chapter 3, Working with Ceph Object Storage*, to add more RGW nodes to your Ceph environment.

Scaling down your Ceph cluster

One of the most important features of a storage system is its flexibility. A good storage solution should be flexible enough to support its expansion and reduction without causing any downtime to the services. Traditional storage systems had limited flexibility; the expansion and reduction of such systems is a tough job. Sometimes, you feel locked with storage capacity and cannot perform changes as per your needs.

Ceph is an absolutely flexible storage system that supports on-the-fly changes to storage capacity, whether expansion or reduction. In the last recipe, we learned how easy it is to scale out a Ceph cluster. In this recipe, we will scale down a Ceph cluster, without any impact on its accessibility, by removing `ceph-node4` from the Ceph cluster.

Removing the Ceph OSD

Before proceeding with the cluster size reduction, scaling it down, or removing the OSD node, make sure that the cluster has enough free space to accommodate all the data present on the node you are planning to move out. The cluster should not be at its full ratio, which is the percentage of used disk space in an OSD. So, as a best practice, do not remove the OSD or OSD node without considering the impact on the full ratio.

How to do it...

1. As we need to scale down the cluster, we will remove `ceph-node4` and all of its associated OSDs out of the cluster. Ceph OSDs should be set out so that Ceph can perform data recovery. From any of the Ceph nodes, take the OSDs out of the cluster:

   `# ceph osd out osd.9`

   `# ceph osd out osd.10`

   `# ceph osd out osd.11`

```
[root@ceph-node1 ~]# ceph osd out osd.9
marked out osd.9.
[root@ceph-node1 ~]# ceph osd out osd.10
marked out osd.10.
[root@ceph-node1 ~]# ceph osd out osd.11
marked out osd.11.
[root@ceph-node1 ~]#
```

2. As soon as you mark an OSD out of the cluster, Ceph will start rebalancing the cluster by migrating the PGs out of the OSDs that were made out to other OSDs inside the cluster. Your cluster state would become unhealthy for some time, but it would be good for the server data to clients. Based on the number of OSDs removed, there might be some drop in cluster performance until the recovery time is complete. Once the cluster is healthy again, it should perform as usual:

   `# ceph -s`

```
[root@ceph-node1 ~]# ceph -s
    cluster 9609b429-eee2-4e23-af31-28a24fcf5cbc
     health HEALTH_WARN 65 pgs degraded; 8 pgs recovering; 22 pgs stuck unclean;
recovery 1594/11226 objects degraded (14.199%)
     monmap e6: 4 mons at {ceph-node1=192.168.1.101:6789/0,ceph-node2=192.168.1.1
02:6789/0,ceph-node3=192.168.1.103:6789/0,ceph-node4=192.168.1.104:6789/0}, elect
ion epoch 978, quorum 0,1,2,3 ceph-node1,ceph-node2,ceph-node3,ceph-node4
     mdsmap e222: 1/1/1 up {0=ceph-node2=up:active}
     osdmap e4081: 12 osds: 12 up, 9 in
      pgmap v32727: 1628 pgs, 45 pools, 2422 MB data, 3742 objects
            8065 MB used, 127 GB / 134 GB avail
            1594/11226 objects degraded (14.199%)
                1563 active+clean
                  57 active+degraded
                   8 active+recovering+degraded
recovery io 27934 kB/s, 2 keys/s, 35 objects/s
  client io 297 kB/s wr, 0 op/s
[root@ceph-node1 ~]#
```

Here, you can see that the cluster is in recovery mode but at the same time is serving data to clients. You can observe the recovery process using the following:

```
# ceph -w
```

```
[root@ceph-node1 ~]# ceph -w
    cluster 9609b429-eee2-4e23-af31-28a24fcf5cbc
    health HEALTH_OK
    monmap e6: 4 mons at {ceph-node1=192.168.1.101:6789/0,ceph-node2=192.168.1.102:6789/0,
ceph-node3=192.168.1.103:6789/0,ceph-node4=192.168.1.104:6789/0}, election epoch 978, quoru
m 0,1,2,3 ceph-node1,ceph-node2,ceph-node3,ceph-node4
    mdsmap e222: 1/1/1 up {0=ceph-node2=up:active}
    osdmap e4081: 12 osds: 12 up, 9 in
     pgmap v32734: 1628 pgs, 45 pools, 2422 MB data, 3742 objects
            8514 MB used, 126 GB / 134 GB avail
               1628 active+clean

2015-07-26 23:01:05.012972 mon.0 [INF] pgmap v32734: 1628 pgs: 1628 active+clean; 2422 MB d
ata, 8514 MB used, 126 GB / 134 GB avail; 38045 kB/s, 35 objects/s recovering
2015-07-26 23:01:54.896226 mon.0 [INF] pgmap v32735: 1628 pgs: 1628 active+clean; 2422 MB d
ata, 8514 MB used, 126 GB / 134 GB avail
```

3. As we have marked `osd.9`, `osd.10`, and `osd.11` as out of the cluster, they will not participate in storing data, but their services are still running. Let's stop these OSDs:

```
# ssh ceph-node4 service ceph stop osd
```

```
[root@ceph-node1 ~]# ssh ceph-node4 service ceph stop osd
=== osd.11 ===
Stopping Ceph osd.11 on ceph-node4...kill 4721...kill 4721...done
=== osd.10 ===
Stopping Ceph osd.10 on ceph-node4...kill 2341...kill 2341...done
=== osd.9 ===
Stopping Ceph osd.9 on ceph-node4...kill 4319...kill 4319...done
[root@ceph-node1 ~]#
```

Once the OSDs are down, check the OSD tree; you will observe that the OSDs are down and out:

```
# Ceph osd tree
```

```
[root@ceph-node1 ~]# ceph osd tree
# id    weight  type name       up/down reweight
-1      0.12    root default
-3      0.03            host ceph-node2
3       0.009995                        osd.3   up      1
4       0.009995                        osd.4   up      1
5       0.009995                        osd.5   up      1
-4      0.03            host ceph-node3
6       0.009995                        osd.6   up      1
7       0.009995                        osd.7   up      1
8       0.009995                        osd.8   up      1
-2      0.02998         host ceph-node1
0       0.009995                        osd.0   up      1
1       0.009995                        osd.1   up      1
2       0.009995                        osd.2   up      1
-5      0.02998         host ceph-node4
9       0.009995                        osd.9   down    0
10      0.009995                        osd.10  down    0
11      0.009995                        osd.11  down    0
[root@ceph-node1 ~]#
```

4. Now that the OSDs are no longer part of the Ceph cluster, let's remove them from the CRUSH map:

```
# ceph osd crush remove osd.9
# ceph osd crush remove osd.10
# ceph osd crush remove osd.11
```

```
[root@ceph-node1 ~]# ceph osd crush remove osd.9
removed item id 9 name 'osd.9' from crush map
[root@ceph-node1 ~]# ceph osd crush remove osd.10
removed item id 10 name 'osd.10' from crush map
[root@ceph-node1 ~]# ceph osd crush remove osd.11
removed item id 11 name 'osd.11' from crush map
[root@ceph-node1 ~]#
```

5. As soon as the OSDs are removed from the CRUSH map, the Ceph cluster becomes healthy. You should also observe the OSD map; since we have not removed the OSDs, it will still show 12 OSDs, 9 UP and 9 IN.

6. Remove the OSD authentication keys:

```
# ceph auth del osd.9
# ceph auth del osd.10
# ceph auth del osd.11
```

```
[root@ceph-node1 ~]# ceph auth del osd.9
updated
[root@ceph-node1 ~]# ceph auth del osd.10
updated
[root@ceph-node1 ~]# ceph auth del osd.11
updated
[root@ceph-node1 ~]#
```

7. Finally, remove the OSD and check your cluster status; you should observe 9 OSDs, 9 UP, and 9 IN, and the cluster health should be OK:

```
# ceph osd rm osd.9
# ceph osd rm osd.10
# ceph osd rm osd.11
```

```
[root@ceph-node1 ~]# ceph osd rm osd.9
removed osd.9
[root@ceph-node1 ~]# ceph osd rm osd.10
removed osd.10
[root@ceph-node1 ~]# ceph osd rm osd.11
removed osd.11
[root@ceph-node1 ~]#
```

8. To keep your cluster clean, perform some housekeeping; as we have removed all the OSDs from the CRUSH map, ceph-node4 does not hold any item. Remove ceph-node4 from the CRUSH map; this will remove all the traces of this node from the Ceph cluster:

```
# ceph osd crush remove ceph-node4
# ceph -s
```

```
[root@ceph-node1 ~]# ceph -s
    cluster 9609b429-eee2-4e23-af31-28a24fcf5cbc
     health HEALTH_OK
     monmap e6: 4 mons at {ceph-node1=192.168.1.101:6789/0,ceph-node2=192.168.1.102:6789/0,
ceph-node3=192.168.1.103:6789/0,ceph-node4=192.168.1.104:6789/0}, election epoch 980, quoru
m 0,1,2,3 ceph-node1,ceph-node2,ceph-node3,ceph-node4
     mdsmap e222: 1/1/1 up {0=ceph-node2=up:active}
     osdmap e4095: 9 osds: 9 up, 9 in
      pgmap v32801: 1628 pgs, 45 pools, 2422 MB data, 3742 objects
            8185 MB used, 126 GB / 134 GB avail
                 1628 active+clean
[root@ceph-node1 ~]#
```

Removing Ceph MON

Removing a Ceph monitor is generally not a very frequently required task. When you remove monitors from a cluster, consider that Ceph monitors use the PAXOS algorithm to establish consensus about the master cluster map. You must have a sufficient number of monitors to establish a quorum for consensus on the cluster map. In this recipe, we will learn how to remove the `ceph-node4` monitor from the Ceph cluster.

How to do it...

1. Check the monitor status:

   ```
   # ceph mon stat
   ```

   ```
   [root@ceph-node1 ~]# ceph mon stat
   e6: 4 mons at {ceph-node1=192.168.1.101:6789/0,ceph-node2=192.168.1.102:6789/0,ceph-node3=192.168.1.103:6789/0,c
   eph-node4=192.168.1.104:6789/0}, election epoch 996, quorum 0,1,2,3 ceph-node1,ceph-node2,ceph-node3,ceph-node4
   [root@ceph-node1 ~]#
   ```

2. To remove the Ceph monitor `ceph-node4`, execute the following command from `ceph-node1`:

   ```
   # ceph-deploy mon destroy ceph-node4
   ```

   ```
   [root@ceph-node1 ceph]# ceph-deploy mon destroy ceph-node4
   [ceph_deploy.conf][DEBUG ] found configuration file at: /root/.cephdeploy.conf
   [ceph_deploy.cli][INFO  ] Invoked (1.5.25): /bin/ceph-deploy mon destroy ceph-node4
   [ceph_deploy.mon][DEBUG ] Removing mon from ceph-node4
   [ceph-node4][DEBUG ] connected to host: ceph-node4
   [ceph-node4][DEBUG ] detect platform information from remote host
   [ceph-node4][DEBUG ] detect machine type
   [ceph-node4][DEBUG ] get remote short hostname
   [ceph-node4][INFO  ] Running command: ceph --cluster=ceph -n mon. -k /var/lib/ceph/mon/ceph-ceph-node4/keyring mon
   remove ceph-node4
   [ceph-node4][WARNIN] removed mon.ceph-node4 at 192.168.1.104:6789/0, there are now 3 monitors
   [ceph-node4][INFO  ] polling the daemon to verify it stopped
   [ceph-node4][INFO  ] Running command: service ceph status mon.ceph-node4
   [ceph-node4][INFO  ] Running command: mkdir -p /var/lib/ceph/mon-removed
   [ceph-node4][DEBUG ] move old monitor data
   [root@ceph-node1 ceph]#
   ```

3. Check to see that your monitors have left the quorum:

   ```
   # ceph quorum_status --format json-pretty
   ```

   ```
   [root@ceph-node1 ceph]# ceph quorum_status --format json-pretty

   { "election_epoch": 998,
     "quorum": [
           0,
           1,
           2],
     "quorum_names": [
           "ceph-node1",
           "ceph-node2",
           "ceph-node3"],
     "quorum_leader_name": "ceph-node1",
     "monmap": { "epoch": 7,
           "fsid": "9609b429-eee2-4e23-af31-28a24fcf5cbc",
           "modified": "2015-07-27 21:22:38.523853",
           "created": "0.000000",
           "mons": [
                 { "rank": 0,
                   "name": "ceph-node1",
                   "addr": "192.168.1.101:6789\/0"},
                 { "rank": 1,
                   "name": "ceph-node2",
                   "addr": "192.168.1.102:6789\/0"},
                 { "rank": 2,
                   "name": "ceph-node3",
                   "addr": "192.168.1.103:6789\/0"}]}}
   [root@ceph-node1 ceph]#
   ```

4. Finally, check the monitor status; the cluster should have three monitors:

   ```
   # ceph mon stat
   ```

   ```
   [root@ceph-node1 ceph]# ceph mon stat
   e7: 3 mons at {ceph-node1=192.168.1.101:6789/0,ceph-node2=192.168.1.102:6789/0,ceph-node3=192.168.1.103:6789/0},
   election epoch 998, quorum 0,1,2 ceph-node1,ceph-node2,ceph-node3
   [root@ceph-node1 ceph]#
   ```

Replacing a failed disk in the Ceph cluster

A Ceph cluster can be made up of 10 to several thousand physical disks that provide storage capacity to the cluster. As the number of physical disks increases for your Ceph cluster, the frequency of disk failures also increases. Hence, replacing a failed disk drive might become a repetitive task for a Ceph storage administrator. In this recipe, we will learn about the disk replacement process for a Ceph cluster.

How to do it...

1. Let's verify cluster health; since this cluster does not have any failed disk status, it would be HEALTH_OK:

   # ceph status

   ```
   [root@ceph-node1 ceph]# ceph -s
       cluster 9609b429-eee2-4e23-af31-28a24fcf5cbc
       health HEALTH_OK
       monmap e7: 3 mons at {ceph-node1=192.168.1.101:6789/0,ceph-node2=192.168.1.102:6789/0,ceph-node3
   =192.168.1.103:6789/0}, election epoch 998, quorum 0,1,2 ceph-node1,ceph-node2,ceph-node3
       mdsmap e232: 1/1/1 up {0=ceph-node2=up:active}
       osdmap e4118: 9 osds: 9 up, 9 in
       pgmap v33667: 1628 pgs, 45 pools, 2422 MB data, 3742 objects
             7718 MB used, 127 GB / 134 GB avail
                  1628 active+clean
   [root@ceph-node1 ceph]#
   ```

2. Since we are demonstrating this exercise on virtual machines, we need to forcefully fail a disk by bringing ceph-node1 down, detaching a disk, and powering up the VM. Execute the following commands from your HOST machine:

   # VBoxManage controlvm ceph-node1 poweroff

   # VBoxManage storageattach ceph-node1 --storagectl "SATA" --port 1 --device 0 --type hdd --medium none

   # VBoxManage startvm ceph-node1

   The following screenshot will be your output:

   ```
   teeri:ceph-cookbook ksingh$ VBoxManage  controlvm ceph-node1 poweroff
   0%...10%...20%...30%...40%...50%...60%...70%...80%...90%...100%
   teeri:ceph-cookbook ksingh$
   teeri:ceph-cookbook ksingh$ VBoxManage storageattach ceph-node1 --storagectl "SATA" --port 1 --device 0 --type hdd --medium none
   teeri:ceph-cookbook ksingh$ VBoxManage startvm ceph-node1
   Waiting for VM "ceph-node1" to power on...
   VM "ceph-node1" has been successfully started.
   teeri:ceph-cookbook ksingh$
   ```

3. Now, ceph-node1 contains a failed disk, osd.0, which should be replaced:

   # ceph osd tree

   ```
   [root@ceph-node1 ~]# ceph osd tree
   # id    weight  type name       up/down reweight
   -1      0.08998 root default
   -3      0.03            host ceph-node2
   3       0.009995                        osd.3   up      1
   4       0.009995                        osd.4   up      1
   5       0.009995                        osd.5   up      1
   -4      0.03            host ceph-node3
   6       0.009995                        osd.6   up      1
   7       0.009995                        osd.7   up      1
   8       0.009995                        osd.8   up      1
   -2      0.02998         host ceph-node1
   0       0.009995                        osd.0   down    1
   1       0.009995                        osd.1   up      1
   2       0.009995                        osd.2   up      1
   [root@ceph-node1 ~]#
   ```

You will also notice that osd.0 is DOWN, however, it's still marked as IN. As long as its status is marked IN, the Ceph cluster will not trigger data recovery for this drive. By default, the Ceph cluster takes 300 seconds to mark a down disk as OUT and then triggers data recovery. The reason for this timeout is to avoid unnecessary data movements due to short-term outages, for example, Server reboot. One can increase or even decrease this timeout value if they prefer.

4. You should wait 300 seconds to trigger data recovery, or else you can manually mark the failed OSD as OUT:

```
# ceph osd out osd.0
```

5. As soon as the OSD is marked OUT, the Ceph cluster will initiate a recovery operation for the PGs that were hosted on the failed disk. You can watch the recovery operation using the following command:

```
# ceph status
```

6. Let's now remove the failed disk OSD from the Ceph CRUSH map:

```
# ceph osd crush rm osd.0
```

7. Delete the Ceph authentication keys for the OSD:

```
# ceph auth del osd.0
```

8. Finally, remove the OSD from the Ceph cluster:

```
# ceph osd rm osd.0
```

```
[root@ceph-node1 ~]# ceph osd crush rm osd.0
removed item id 0 name 'osd.0' from crush map
[root@ceph-node1 ~]#
[root@ceph-node1 ~]# ceph auth del osd.0
updated
[root@ceph-node1 ~]# ceph osd rm osd.0
removed osd.0
[root@ceph-node1 ~]#
```

9. Since one of your OSDs is unavailable, the cluster health will not be OK, and the cluster will be performing recovery. Nothing to worry about here; this is a normal Ceph operation. Once the recovery operation is complete, your cluster will attain HEALTH_OK:

```
# ceph -s
```

```
# ceph osd stat
```

```
[root@ceph-node1 ~]# ceph -s
    cluster 9609b429-eee2-4e23-af31-28a24fcf5cbc
     health HEALTH_OK
     monmap e7: 3 mons at {ceph-node1=192.168.1.101:6789/0,ceph-node2=192.168.1.102:6789/0,
ceph-node3=192.168.1.103:6789/0}, election epoch 1028, quorum 0,1,2 ceph-node1,ceph-node2,c
eph-node3
     mdsmap e246: 1/1/1 up {0=ceph-node2=up:active}
     osdmap e4164: 8 osds: 8 up, 8 in
      pgmap v33855: 1628 pgs, 45 pools, 2422 MB data, 3742 objects
            7918 MB used, 112 GB / 119 GB avail
                1628 active+clean
[root@ceph-node1 ~]#
[root@ceph-node1 ~]# ceph osd stat
     osdmap e4164: 8 osds: 8 up, 8 in
[root@ceph-node1 ~]#
```

10. At this point, you should physically replace the failed disk with the new disk on your Ceph node. These days, almost all the servers and server OS support disk hot swapping, so you would not require any downtime for disk replacement.

11. Since we are simulating this on a virtual machine, we need to power off the VM, add a new disk, and restart the VM. Once the disk is inserted, make a note of its OS device ID:

```
# VBoxManage controlvm ceph-node1 poweroff
# VBoxManage storageattach ceph-node1 --storagectl "SATA" --port 1
--device 0 --type hdd --medium ceph-node1_disk2.vdi
# VBoxManage startvm ceph-node1
```

12. Now that the new disk has been added to the system, let's list the disk:

```
# ceph-deploy disk list ceph-node1
```

13. Before adding the disk to the Ceph cluster, perform disk zap:

```
# ceph-deploy disk zap ceph-node1:sdb
```

14. Finally, create an OSD on the disk, and Ceph will add it as osd.0:

```
# ceph-deploy --overwrite-conf osd create ceph-node1:sdb
```

15. Once the OSD is added to the Ceph cluster, Ceph will perform a backfilling operation and will start moving PGs from secondary OSDs to the new OSD. The recovery operation might take a while, but after it, your Ceph cluster will be HEALTHY_OK again:

```
# ceph -s
# ceph osd stat
```

```
[root@ceph-node1 ceph]# ceph -s
    cluster 9609b429-eee2-4e23-af31-28a24fcf5cbc
     health HEALTH_OK
     monmap e7: 3 mons at {ceph-node1=192.168.1.101:6789/0,ceph-node2=192.168.1.102:6789/0,
ceph-node3=192.168.1.103:6789/0}, election epoch 1032, quorum 0,1,2 ceph-node1,ceph-node2,c
eph-node3
     mdsmap e248: 1/1/1 up {0=ceph-node2=up:active}
     osdmap e4191: 9 osds: 9 up, 9 in
      pgmap v33983: 1628 pgs, 45 pools, 2422 MB data, 3742 objects
            8160 MB used, 126 GB / 134 GB avail
                 1628 active+clean
[root@ceph-node1 ceph]#
[root@ceph-node1 ceph]# ceph osd stat
     osdmap e4191: 9 osds: 9 up, 9 in
[root@ceph-node1 ceph]#
```

Upgrading your Ceph cluster

One of several reasons for the greatness of Ceph is that almost all the operations on a Ceph cluster can be performed online, which means that your Ceph cluster is in production and serving clients, and you can perform administrative tasks on the cluster without downtime. One of these operations is upgrading the Ceph cluster version.

Since the first chapter, we have been using the Giant release of Ceph, which was intentional so that we could demonstrate upgrading the Ceph cluster version from Giant to Hammer. As per best practice, you should follow the recommended upgrade sequence for Ceph, which is in the following order:

- ▸ The ceph-deploy tool
- ▸ The Ceph monitor daemons
- ▸ The Ceph OSD daemons
- ▸ The Ceph metadata servers
- ▸ The Ceph Object Gateways

As a general rule, it's recommended that you upgrade all the daemons of a specific type (for example, all ceph-mon daemons, all ceph-osd daemons, and so on) to ensure that they are all on the same release.

Once you upgrade a Ceph daemon, you cannot downgrade it.

Each release of Ceph may have additional steps; it's very much recommended to refer to the release-specific sections at `http://docs.ceph.com/docs/master/release-notes/` to identify release-specific procedures for upgrading the Ceph cluster.

How to do it...

In this recipe, we will upgrade our Ceph cluster, which is running on the Giant release (0.84.2), to the latest stable Hammer release.

1. Before starting the upgrade process, let's check the current versions of `ceph-deploy`, Ceph monitor, OSD, MDS, and the `ceph-rgw` daemon:

   ```
   # ceph-deploy --version
   # for i in 1 2 3 ; do ssh ceph-node$i service ceph status; done | grep -i running
   ```

   ```
   [root@ceph-node1 ~]# ceph-deploy --version
   1.5.25
   [root@ceph-node1 ~]#
   [root@ceph-node1 ~]# for i in 1 2 3 ; do ssh ceph-node$i service ceph status; done | grep -i running
   mon.ceph-node1: running {"version":"0.87.2"}
   osd.0: running {"version":"0.87.2"}
   osd.1: running {"version":"0.87.2"}
   osd.2: running {"version":"0.87.2"}
   mon.ceph-node1: running {"version":"0.87.2"}
   osd.0: running {"version":"0.87.2"}
   osd.1: running {"version":"0.87.2"}
   osd.2: running {"version":"0.87.2"}
   mon.ceph-node2: running {"version":"0.87.2"}
   osd.3: running {"version":"0.87.2"}
   osd.4: running {"version":"0.87.2"}
   osd.5: running {"version":"0.87.2"}
   mds.ceph-node2: running {"version":"0.87.2"}
   mon.ceph-node3: running {"version":"0.87.2"}
   osd.6: running {"version":"0.87.2"}
   osd.7: running {"version":"0.87.2"}
   osd.8: running {"version":"0.87.2"}
   [root@ceph-node1 ~]#
   ```

2. Update `ceph-deploy` to its latest version:

   ```
   # yum update -y ceph-deploy
   # ceph-deploy --version
   ```

3. Update the Ceph `yum` repositories to the targeted Hammer release. Update `baseurl` in `/etc/yum.repos.d/ceph.repo` for Hammer, shown as follows:

```
[root@ceph-node1 ~]# cat /etc/yum.repos.d/ceph.repo
[Ceph]
name=Ceph packages for $basearch
baseurl=http://ceph.com/rpm-hammer/el7/$basearch
enabled=1
gpgcheck=1
type=rpm-md
gpgkey=https://ceph.com/git/?p=ceph.git;a=blob_plain;f=keys/release.asc
priority=1

[Ceph-noarch]
name=Ceph noarch packages
baseurl=http://ceph.com/rpm-hammer/el7/noarch
enabled=1
gpgcheck=1
type=rpm-md
gpgkey=https://ceph.com/git/?p=ceph.git;a=blob_plain;f=keys/release.asc
priority=1

[ceph-source]
name=Ceph source packages
baseurl=http://ceph.com/rpm-hammer/el7/SRPMS
enabled=1
gpgcheck=1
type=rpm-md
gpgkey=https://ceph.com/git/?p=ceph.git;a=blob_plain;f=keys/release.asc
priority=1

[root@ceph-node1 ~]#
```

4. Copy the Ceph `yum` repositories to other Ceph nodes:

   ```
   # scp /etc/yum.repos.d/ceph.repo ceph-node2:/etc/yum.repos.d/ceph.repo
   ```

   ```
   # scp /etc/yum.repos.d/ceph.repo ceph-node3:/etc/yum.repos.d/ceph.repo
   ```

```
[root@ceph-node1 ~]# scp /etc/yum.repos.d/ceph.repo ceph-node2:/etc/yum.repos.d/ceph.repo
ceph.repo                                                      100%  611    0.6KB/s   00:00
[root@ceph-node1 ~]# scp /etc/yum.repos.d/ceph.repo ceph-node3:/etc/yum.repos.d/ceph.repo
ceph.repo                                                      100%  611    0.6KB/s   00:00
[root@ceph-node1 ~]#
```

Since our test cluster setup has MON, OSD, and MDS daemons running on the same machine, upgrading the Ceph software binaries to the Hammer release will result in the upgrade of MON, OSD, and MDS daemons in one step. However, in the production deployment of Ceph, upgrading should take place one by one. Otherwise, you might face problems.

> In a production environment, you should always follow the Ceph upgrade sequence, as mentioned at the beginning of this recipe, to avoid problems.

5. Upgrade Ceph from Giant (0.87.2) to the stable Hammer (0.94.2) release:

   ```
   # ceph-deploy install --release hammer ceph-node1 ceph-node2
     ceph-node3
   ```

6. Restart the Ceph monitor daemons on the Ceph monitor nodes one by one so that the monitor does not loose quorum:

   ```
   # service ceph restart mon
   ```

7. Restart the Ceph OSD daemons on each Ceph OSD node one by one:

   ```
   # service ceph restart osd
   ```

8. Restart the Ceph MDS daemon on the Ceph MDS node:

   ```
   # service ceph restart mds
   ```

9. Finally, once all the services have been successfully restarted, check the Ceph version:

   ```
   # ceph -v
   ```

   ```
   # for i in 1 2 3 ; do ssh ceph-node$i service ceph status; done |
     grep -i running
   ```

```
[root@ceph-node1 ~]# for i in 1 2 3 ; do ssh ceph-node$i service ceph status; done | grep -i running
mon.ceph-node1: running {"version":"0.94.2"}
osd.0: running {"version":"0.94.2"}
osd.1: running {"version":"0.94.2"}
osd.2: running {"version":"0.94.2"}
mon.ceph-node1: running {"version":"0.94.2"}
osd.0: running {"version":"0.94.2"}
osd.1: running {"version":"0.94.2"}
osd.2: running {"version":"0.94.2"}
mon.ceph-node2: running {"version":"0.94.2"}
osd.3: running {"version":"0.94.2"}
osd.4: running {"version":"0.94.2"}
osd.5: running {"version":"0.94.2"}
mds.ceph-node2: running {"version":"0.94.2"}
mon.ceph-node3: running {"version":"0.94.2"}
osd.6: running {"version":"0.94.2"}
osd.7: running {"version":"0.94.2"}
osd.8: running {"version":"0.94.2"}
[root@ceph-node1 ~]#
```

Maintaining a Ceph cluster

Being a Ceph storage admin, maintaining your Ceph cluster would be one of your top priorities. Ceph is a distributed system that is designed to grow from tens of OSDs to several thousands of them. One of the key things required to maintain a Ceph cluster is to manage its OSDs. In this recipe, we will cover Ceph sub commands for OSDs and PGs that will help you during cluster maintenance and troubleshooting.

How to do it...

To understand the need for these commands better, let's assume a scenario where you want to add a new node to your production Ceph cluster. One way is to simply add the new node with several disks to the Ceph cluster, and the cluster will start backfilling and shuffling the data on to the new node. This is fine for a test cluster.

However, the situation becomes very critical when it comes to the production setup, where you should use some of the `ceph osd` sub commands/flags, which are mentioned as follows, before adding a new node to the cluster, such as `noin`, `nobackfill`, and so on. This is done so that your cluster does not immediately start the backfilling process when the new node comes in. You can then unset these flags during non-peak hours, and the cluster will take its time to rebalance:

1. The usages of these flags are as simple as set and unset. For example, to set a flag, use the following command lines:

   ```
   # ceph osd set <flag_name>
   # ceph osd set noout
   # ceph osd set nodown
   # ceph osd set norecover
   ```

2. Now, to unset the same flags, use the following command lines:

   ```
   # ceph osd unset <flag_name>
   # ceph osd unset noout
   # ceph osd unset nodown
   # ceph osd set norecover
   ```

How it works...

We will now learn what these flags are and why they are used.

   ▶ `noout`: This forces the Ceph cluster to not mark any OSD as *out* of the cluster, irrespective of its status. It makes sure all the OSDs remain inside the cluster.

   ▶ `nodown`: This forces the Ceph cluster to not mark any OSD *down*, irrespective of its status. It makes sure all the OSDs remain UP and none of them DOWN.

   ▶ `noup`: This forces the Ceph cluster to not mark any down OSD as UP. So, any OSD that is marked DOWN can only come UP after this flag is unset. This also applies to new OSDs that are joining the cluster.

   ▶ `noin`: This forces the Ceph cluster to not allow any new OSD to join the cluster. This is quite useful if you are adding several OSDs at once and don't want them to join the cluster automatically.

- ▸ `norecover`: This forces the Ceph cluster to not perform cluster recovery.
- ▸ `nobackfill`: This forces the Ceph cluster to not perform backfilling. This is quite useful when you are adding several OSDs at once and don't want Ceph to perform automatic data placement on the new node.
- ▸ `norebalance`: This forces the Ceph cluster to not perform cluster rebalancing.
- ▸ `noscrub`: This forces Ceph to not perform OSD scrubbing.
- ▸ `nodeep-scrub`: This forces Ceph to not perform OSD deep scrubbing.
- ▸ `notieragent`: This disables the cache pool tiering agent.

In addition to these flags, you can also use the following commands to repair OSDs and PGs:

- ▸ `ceph osd repair`: This performs repairing on a specified OSD.
- ▸ `ceph pg repair`: This performs repairing on a specified PG. Use this command with caution; based on your cluster state, this command can impact user data if not used carefully.
- ▸ `ceph pg scrub`: This performs scrubbing on a specified PG.
- ▸ `ceph deep-scrub`: This performs deep-scrubbing on specified PGs.

The Ceph CLI is quite powerful for end-to-end cluster management. You can get more information at `http://ceph.com/docs/master/man/8/ceph/`.

7
Ceph under the Hood

In this chapter, we will cover the following recipes:

- ▸ Ceph scalability and high availability
- ▸ Understanding the CRUSH mechanism
- ▸ CRUSH map internals
- ▸ Ceph cluster map
- ▸ High availability monitors
- ▸ Ceph authentication and authorization
- ▸ Ceph dynamic cluster management
- ▸ Ceph placement group
- ▸ Placement group states
- ▸ Creating Ceph pools on specific OSDs

Introduction

In this chapter, we take a deep dive into the internal workings of Ceph by understanding its features such as scalability, high availability, authentication, and authorization. We will also cover CRUSH map, which is one of the most important parts of the Ceph cluster. Finally, we will go through dynamic cluster management and the custom CRUSH map settings for Ceph pools.

Ceph scalability and high availability

To understand Ceph scalability and high availability, let's first talk about the architecture of traditional storage systems. Under this architecture, to store or retrieve data, clients talk to a centralized component known as a controller or gateway. These storage controllers act as a single point of contact for a client's request. The following diagram illustrates this situation:

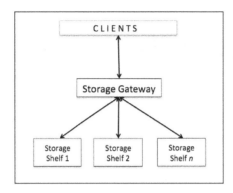

This storage gateway, which acts as a single point of entry to storage systems, also becomes the single point of failure. This also imposes a limit on both performance and scalability while introducing a single point of failure, such that if the centralized component goes down, the whole system goes down too.

Ceph does not follow this traditional storage architecture; it has been totally reinvented for the next-generation of storage. Ceph eliminates the centralized gateway by enabling the clients to interact with the Ceph OSD daemons directly. The following diagram illustrates how clients connect to the Ceph cluster:

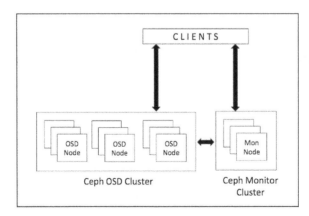

The Ceph OSD daemons create objects and their replicas on other Ceph Nodes to ensure data safety and high availability. Ceph also uses a cluster of monitors to ensure high availability, and to eliminate centralization, Ceph uses an algorithm called **CRUSH**, which stands for **Controlled Replication Under Scalable Hashing**. With the help of CRUSH, client on demand calculates where the data should be written to or read from. In the following recipe, we will examine the details of the Ceph CRUSH algorithm.

Understanding the CRUSH mechanism

When it comes to data storage and management, Ceph uses the CRUSH algorithm, which is the intelligent data distribution mechanism of Ceph. As we discussed in the last recipe, traditional storage systems use a central metadata/index table to know where the user's data is stored. Ceph, on the other hand, uses the CRUSH algorithm to deterministically compute where the data should be written to or read from. Instead of storing metadata, CRUSH computes metadata on demand, thus removing the need for a centralized server/gateway or broker. It empowers Ceph clients to compute metadata, also known as CRUSH lookup, and communicates with OSDs directly.

For a read-and-write operation to Ceph clusters, clients first contact a Ceph monitor and retrieve a copy of the cluster map, which is inclusive of 5 maps, namely the monitor, OSD, MDS, and CRUSH and PG maps; we will cover these maps later in this chapter. These cluster maps help clients know the state and configuration of the Ceph cluster. Next, the data is converted to objects using an object name and pool names/IDs. This object is then hashed with the number of PGs to generate a final PG within the required Ceph pool. This calculated PG then goes through a CRUSH lookup function to determine the primary, secondary, and tertiary OSD locations to store or retrieve data.

Once the client gets the exact OSD ID, it contacts the OSDs directly and stores the data. All of these compute operations are performed by the clients; hence, they do not affect the cluster performance. The following diagram illustrates the entire process:

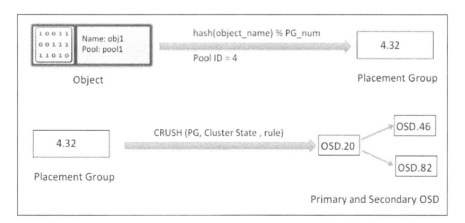

CRUSH map internals

To know what is inside a crush map, and for easy editing we need to extract and decompile it to convert it into a human-readable form. The following diagram illustrates this process:

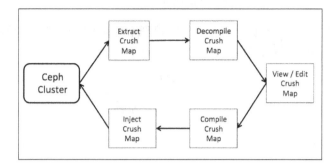

The change to the Ceph cluster by the CRUSH map is dynamic, that is, once the new crush map is injected into the Ceph cluster, all the changes will come into effect immediately, on the fly.

How to do it...

We will now take a look at the CRUSH map of our Ceph cluster:

1. Extract the CRUSH map from any of the monitor nodes:

   ```
   # ceph osd getcrushmap -o crushmap_compiled_file
   ```

2. Once you have the CRUSH map, decompile it to convert it into a human-readable/editable form:

   ```
   # crushtool -d crushmap_compiled_file -o
     crushmap_decompiled_file
   ```

   At this point, the output file, `crushmap_decompiled_file`, can be viewed/edited in your favorite editor. In the next recipe, we will learn how to perform changes to the CRUSH map.

3. Once the changes are done, you should compile these changes:

   ```
   # crushtool -c crushmap_decompiled_file -o newcrushmap
   ```

4. Finally, inject the newly compiled crush map into the Ceph cluster:

   ```
   # ceph osd setcrushmap -i newcrushmap
   ```

How it works...

Now that we know how to edit the Ceph CRUSH map, let's understand what's inside the CRUSH map. A CRUSH map file contains four main sections; they are as follows:

- **Devices**: This section of the CRUSH map keeps a list of all the OSD devices in your cluster. The OSD is a physical disk corresponding to the `ceph-osd` daemon. To map the PG to the OSD device, CRUSH requires a list of OSD devices. This list of devices appears in the beginning of the CRUSH map to declare the device in the CRUSH map. The following is the sample device list:

```
# devices
device 0 osd.0
device 1 osd.1
device 2 osd.2
device 3 osd.3
device 4 osd.4
device 5 osd.5
device 6 osd.6
device 7 osd.7
device 8 osd.8
```

- **Bucket types**: This defines the types of buckets used in your CRUSH hierarchy. Buckets consist of a hierarchical aggregation of physical locations (for example, rows, racks, chassis, hosts, and so on) and their assigned weights. They facilitate a hierarchy of `nodes` and `leaves`, where the `node` bucket represents physical location and can aggregate other nodes and leaves buckets under the hierarchy. The `leaf` bucket represents the `ceph-osd` daemon and its underlying physical device. The following table lists the default bucket types:

Number	Bucket	Description
0	**OSD**	An OSD daemon (for example, `osd.1`, `osd.2`, and so on).
1	**Host**	A host name containing one or more OSDs.
2	**Rack**	A computer rack containing one or more hosts.
3	**Row**	A row in a series of racks.
4	**Room**	A room containing racks and rows of hosts.
5	**Data Center**	A physical data center containing rooms.
6	**Root**	This is the beginning of the bucket hierarchy.

CRUSH also supports custom bucket type creation, these default bucket types can be deleted and new types can be introduced as per your needs.

▶ **Bucket instances**: Once you define bucket types, you must declare bucket instances for your hosts. A bucket instance requires the bucket type, a unique name (string), a unique ID expressed as a negative integer, a weight relative to the total capacity of its item, a bucket algorithm (straw, by default), and the hash (0, by default, reflecting the CRUSH Hash rjenkins1). A bucket may have one or more items, and these items may consist of other buckets or OSDs. The item should have a weight that reflects the relative weight of the item. The general syntax of a bucket type looks like the following:

```
[bucket-type] [bucket-name] {
  id [a unique negative numeric ID]
  weight [the relative capacity the item]
  alg [ the bucket type: uniform | list | tree | straw |
    straw2]
  hash [the hash type: 0 by default]
  item [item-name] weight [weight]
}
```

We will now briefly cover the parameters used by the CRUSH bucket instance:

- ❏ bucket-type: It's the type of bucket, where we must specify the OSD's location in the CRUSH hierarchy.

- ❏ bucket-name: A unique bucket name.

- ❏ id: The unique ID, expressed as a negative integer.

- ❏ weight: Ceph writes data evenly across the cluster disks, which helps in performance and better data distribution. This forces all the disks to participate in the cluster and make sure that all cluster disks are equally utilized, irrespective of their capacity. To do so, Ceph uses a weighting mechanism. CRUSH allocates weights to each OSD. The higher the weight of an OSD, the more physical storage capacity it will have. A weight is the relative difference between device capacities. We recommend using 1.00 as the relative weight for a 1 TB storage device. Similarly, a weight of 0.5 would represent approximately 500 GB, and a weight of 3.00 would represent approximately 3 TB.

- ❏ alg: Ceph supports multiple algorithm bucket types for your selection. These algorithms differ from each other on the basis of performance and reorganizational efficiency. Let's briefly cover these bucket types:

  - ❏ **Uniform**: The uniform bucket can be used if the storage devices have exactly the same weight. For non-uniform weights, this bucket type should not be used. The addition or removal of devices in this bucket type requires the complete reshuffling of data, which makes this bucket type less efficient.

- ❑ **List**: List buckets aggregate their contents as linked lists and can contain storage devices with arbitrary weights. In the case of cluster expansion, new storage devices can be added to the head of a linked list with minimum data migration. However, storage device removal requires a significant amount of data movement. So, this bucket type is suitable for scenarios under which the addition of new devices to the cluster is extremely rare or non-existent. In addition, list buckets are efficient for small sets of items, but they may not be appropriate for large sets.

- ❑ **Tree**: Tree buckets store their items in a binary tree. It is more efficient than list buckets because a bucket contains a larger set of items. Tree buckets are structured as a weighted binary search tree with items at the leaves. Each interior node knows the total weight of its left and right subtrees and is labeled according to a fixed strategy. Tree buckets are an all-around boon, providing excellent performance and decent reorganization efficiency.

- ❑ **Straw**: To select an item using List and Tree buckets, a limited number of hash values need to be calculated and compared by weight. They use a divide and conquer strategy, which gives precedence to certain items (for example, those at the beginning of a list). This improves the performance of the replica placement process but introduces moderate reorganization when bucket contents change due to addition, removal, or re-weighting.

  The straw bucket type allows all items to compete fairly against each other for replica placement. In a scenario where removal is expected and reorganization efficiency is critical, straw buckets provide optimal migration behavior between subtrees. This bucket type allows all items to fairly "compete" against each other for replica placement through a process analogous to a draw of straws.

- ❑ **Straw2**: This is an improved straw bucket that correctly avoids any data movement between items A and B, when neither A's nor B's weights are changed. In other words, if we adjust the weight of item C by adding a new device to it, or by removing it completely, the data movement will take place to or from C, never between other items in the bucket. Thus, the straw2 bucket algorithm reduces the amount of data migration required when changes are made to the cluster.

- ❑ `hash`: Each bucket uses a hash algorithm. Currently, Ceph supports rjenkins1. Enter 0 as your hash setting to select rjenkins1.

- ❑ `item`: A bucket may have one or more items. These items may consist of node buckets or leaves. Items may have a weight that reflects the relative weight of the item.

The following screenshot illustrates the CRUSH bucket instance. Here, we have three host bucket instances. These host bucket instances consist of OSDs buckets:

```
# buckets
host ceph-node2 {
        id -3                   # do not change unnecessarily
        # weight 0.030
        alg straw
        hash 0  # rjenkins1
        item osd.3 weight 0.010
        item osd.4 weight 0.010
        item osd.5 weight 0.010
}
host ceph-node3 {
        id -4                   # do not change unnecessarily
        # weight 0.030
        alg straw
        hash 0  # rjenkins1
        item osd.6 weight 0.010
        item osd.7 weight 0.010
        item osd.8 weight 0.010
}
host ceph-node1 {
        id -2                   # do not change unnecessarily
        # weight 0.030
        alg straw
        hash 0  # rjenkins1
        item osd.1 weight 0.010
        item osd.2 weight 0.010
        item osd.0 weight 0.010
}
```

▶ **Rules**: The CRUSH maps contain CRUSH rules that determine the data placement for pools. As the name suggests, these are the rules that define the pool properties and the way data gets stored in the pools. They define the replication and placement policy that allows CRUSH to store objects in a Ceph cluster. The default CRUSH map contains a rule for default pools, that is, `rbd`. The general syntax of a CRUSH rule looks like this:

```
rule <rulename> {
    ruleset <ruleset>
        type [ replicated | erasure ]
        min_size <min-size>
        max_size <max-size>
        step take <bucket-type>
        step [choose|chooseleaf] [firstn] <num>
          <bucket-type>
        step emit
}
```

We will now briefly cover these parameters used by the CRUSH rule:

- ❑ `ruleset`: An integer value; it classifies a rule as belonging to a set of rules.

- ❑ `type`: A string value; it's the type of pool that is either replicated or erasure coded.

- ❑ `min_size`: An integer value; if a pool makes fewer replicas than this number, CRUSH will not select this rule.

- ❑ `max_size`: An integer value; if a pool makes more replicas than this number, CRUSH will not select this rule.

- ❑ `step take`: This takes a bucket name and begins iterating down the tree.

- ❑ `step choose firstn {num} type {bucket-type}`: This selects the number (*N*) of buckets of a given type, where the number (*N*) is usually the number of replicas in the pool (that is, pool size):

  - ❑ If `num == 0`, select *N* buckets

  - ❑ If `num > 0 && < N`, select *num* buckets

  - ❑ If `num < 0`, select *N - num* buckets

  Example: `step choose firstn 1 type row`

  In this example, `num=1`, and let's suppose the pool size is 3, then CRUSH will evaluate this condition as `1 > 0 && < 3`. Hence, it will select 1 row type bucket.

- ❑ `step chooseleaf firstn {num} type {bucket-type}`: This first selects a set of buckets of a bucket type, and then chooses the leaf node from the subtree of each bucket in the set of buckets. The number of buckets in the set (*N*) is usually the number of replicas in the pool:

- ❑ If `num == 0`, selects *N* buckets

- ❑ If `num > 0 && < N`, select *num* buckets

- ❑ If `num < 0`, select *N - num* buckets

  Example: `step chooseleaf firstn 0 type row`

  In this example, `num=0`, and let's suppose the pool size is 3, then CRUSH will evaluate this condition as `0 == 0`, and then select a row type bucket set, such that the set contains 3 buckets. Then it will choose the leaf node from the subtree of each bucket. In this way, CRUSH will select 3 leaf nodes.

- ❑ `step emit`: This first outputs the current value and empties the stack. This is typically used at the end of a rule but may also be used to form different trees in the same rule.

Ceph cluster map

Ceph monitors are responsible for monitoring the health of the entire cluster as well as maintaining the cluster membership state, state of peer nodes, and cluster configuration information. The Ceph monitor performs these tasks by maintaining a master copy of the cluster map. The cluster map includes Monitor maps, OSD maps, the PG map, the CRUSH map, and the MDS map. All these maps are collectively known as cluster maps. Let's take a quick look at the functionality of each map:

- **Monitor map**: It holds end-to-end information about the monitor node, which includes the Ceph cluster id, monitor hostname, and IP address with the port number. It also stores the current epoch for map creation and last changed time too. You can check your cluster's monitor map by executing the following:

```
# ceph mon dump
```

- **OSD map**: It stores some common fields, such as cluster ID, epoch for OSD map creation and last changed, and information related to pools, such as pool names, pool ID, type, replication level, and PGs. It also stores OSD information such as count, state, weight, last clean interval, and OSD host information. You can check your cluster's OSD maps by executing the following:

```
# ceph osd dump
```

- **PG map**: It holds the PG version, time stamp, last OSD map epoch, full ratio, and near full ratio information. It also keeps track of each PG ID, object count, state, state stamp, up and acting OSD sets, and finally, the scrub details. To check your cluster PG map, execute the following:

```
# ceph pg dump
```

- **CRUSH map**: It holds information on your clusters devices, buckets, failure domain hierarchy, and the rules defined for the failure domain when storing data. To check your cluster CRUSH map, execute the following:

```
# ceph osd crush dump
```

- **MDS map**: This stores information on the current MDS map epoch, map creation and modification time, data and metadata pool ID, cluster MDS count, and the MDS state. To check your cluster MDS map, execute the following:

```
# ceph mds dump
```

High availability monitors

The Ceph monitor does not store and serve data to clients; it serves updated cluster maps to clients as well as to other cluster nodes. Clients and other cluster nodes periodically check with monitors for the most recent copies of cluster maps. Before Ceph clients can read or write data, they must contact a Ceph monitor to obtain the most recent copy of the cluster map.

A Ceph storage cluster can operate with a single monitor, however, this introduces the risk of a single point of failure to the cluster; that is, if the monitor node goes down, Ceph clients cannot read or write data. To overcome this, a typical Ceph cluster consists of a cluster of Ceph monitors. A multi-monitored Ceph architecture develops quorum and provides consensus for distributed decision-making in clusters by using the Paxos algorithm. The monitor count in your cluster should be an odd number; the bare minimum requirement is one monitor node, and the recommended count is three. Since a monitor operates in quorum, more than half of the total monitor nodes should always be available to prevent split-brain problems. Out of all the cluster monitors, one of them operates as the leader. The other monitor nodes are entitled to become leaders if the leader monitor is unavailable. A production cluster must have at least three monitor nodes to provide high availability.

Ceph authentication and authorization

In this recipe, we will cover the authentication and authorization mechanism used by Ceph. Users are either individuals or system actors such as applications, which use Ceph clients to interact with the Ceph Storage Cluster daemons. The following diagram illustrates this flow:

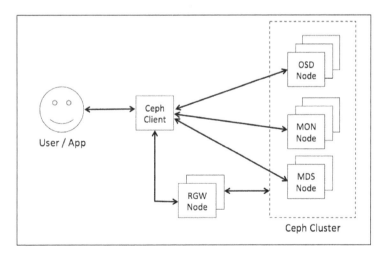

Ceph provides two authentication modes. They are as follows:

- ▶ **None**: With this mode, any user can access the Ceph cluster without authentication. This mode is disabled by default. Cryptographic authentication, which includes encrypting and decrypting user keys, has some computational costs. You can disable the Ceph authentication if you are very sure that your network infrastructure is secure, the clients/Ceph cluster nodes have established trust, and you want to save some computation by disabling authentication. However, this is not recommended, and you might be at risk of a man-in-the-middle attack. Still, if you are interested in disabling the Ceph authentication, you can do it by adding the following parameters in the global section of your Ceph configuration file on all the nodes, followed by the Ceph service restart:

```
auth cluster required = none
auth service required = none
auth client required = none
```

- ▶ **Cephx**: To identify users and protect against man-in-the-middle attacks, Ceph provides its Cephx authentication system to authenticate users and daemons. The Cephx protocol works similar to Kerberos to some extent and allows clients to access the Ceph cluster. It's worth knowing that the Cephx protocol does not do data encryption. In a Ceph cluster, the Cephx protocol is enabled by default. If you have disabled Cephx by adding the preceding auth options to your cluster configuration file, then you can enable Cephx in two ways. One is to simply remove all auth entries from the cluster configuration file, which are none, or you can explicitly enable Cephx by adding the following options in the cluster configuration file and restarting the Ceph services:

```
auth cluster required = cephx
auth service required = cephx
auth client required = cephx
```

Now that we have covered the different authentication modes of Ceph, let's understand how authentication and authorization works within Ceph.

Ceph authentication

To access the Ceph cluster, an actor/user/application invokes the Ceph client to contact the cluster's monitor node. Usually, a Ceph cluster has more than one monitor, and a Ceph client can connect to any monitor node to initiate the authentication process. This multi monitor architecture of Ceph removes a single point of failure situation during the authentication process.

To use Cephx, an administrator, that is, `client.admin`, must create a user account on the Ceph cluster. To create a user account, the `client.admin` user invokes the `ceph auth get-or-create key` command. The Ceph auth subsystem generates a username and a secret key, stores this information on the Ceph monitor, and returns the user's secret key to the `client.admin` user that has invoked the user creation command. The Ceph sys-admin should share this username and secret key with the Ceph client that wants to use the Ceph storage service in a secure manner. The following diagram visualizes this entire process:

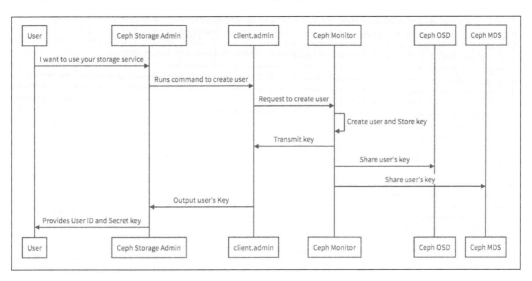

In the last recipe, we learned the process of user creation and how a user's secret keys are stored across all the cluster nodes. We will now examine how users are authenticated by Ceph and allowed access to cluster nodes.

In order to access the Ceph cluster, the client first contacts the Ceph monitor node and passes only its user name. The Cephx protocol works in such a way that both parties are able to prove to each other that they have a copy of the key without actually revealing it. This is the reason that a client only sends its user name but not its secret key.

The monitor then generates a session key for the user and encrypts it with the secret key associated with that user. Then, the monitor transmits the encrypted session key back to the client. The client then decrypts the payload with its key to retrieve the session key. This session key remains valid for that user for the current session.

Using the session key, the client requests for a ticket from the Ceph monitor. The Ceph monitor verifies the session key and then generates a ticket, encrypted with the user's secret key, and transmits this to the user. The client decrypts the ticket and uses it to sign requests to OSDs and metadata servers throughout the cluster.

The Cephx protocol authenticates ongoing communications between the client and the Ceph nodes. Each message sent between a client and Ceph nodes, subsequent to the initial authentication, is signed using a ticket that the monitors, OSDs, and metadata nodes can verify with their shared secret key. Also, Cephx tickets expire, so an attacker cannot use an expired ticket or session key to gain access to the Ceph cluster. The following diagram illustrates the entire authentication process that has been explained here:

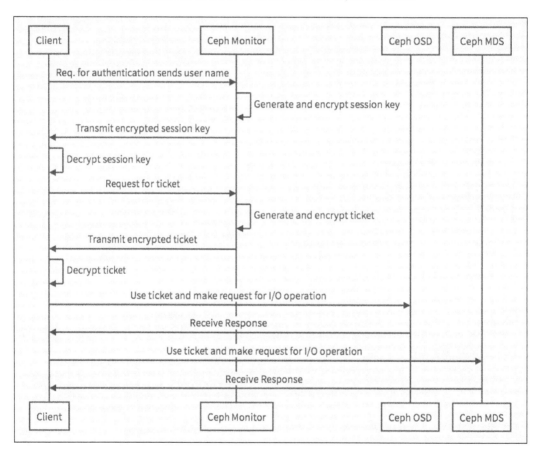

Ceph authorization

In the last recipe, we covered the authentication process used by Ceph. In this recipe, we will examine its authorization process. Once a user is authenticated, he is authorized for different types of access, activities, or roles. Ceph uses the term **capabilities**, which is abbreviated to **caps**. Capabilities are the rights a user gets that define the level of access he has to operate the cluster. The `capability` syntax looks like the following:

```
{daemon-type} 'allow {capability}' [{daemon-type} 'allow
{capability}']
```

- **Monitor caps**: Includes the r, w, x, parameters, and `allow profiles {cap}`. For example:

  mon 'allow rwx' or mon 'allow profile osd'

- **OSD caps**: Includes r, w, x, `class-read`, `class-write`, and `profile osd`. For example:

  osd 'allow rwx' or osd 'allow class-read, allow rwx pool=rbd'

- **MDS caps**: Only requires `allow`. For example:

  mds 'allow'

Let's understand each capability:

- `allow`: This implies `rw` only for MDS.
- `r`: This gives the user read access, which is required with the monitor to read CRUSH maps.
- `w`: This gives the user write access to objects.
- `x`: This gives the user the ability to call class methods, including read and write, and also, the rights to perform auth operations on monitors.

 Ceph can be extended by creating shared object classes called `Ceph Classes`. Ceph can load `.so` classes stored in the OSD class `dir`. For a class, you can create new object methods that have the ability to call native methods in the Ceph object store, for example, the objects that you have defined in your class can call native Ceph methods such as `read` and `write`.

- ► `class-read`: This is a subset of x that allows users to call class read methods.

- ► `class-write`: This is a subset of x that allows users to call class write methods.

- ► `*`: This gives users full permission (r, w, and x) on a specific pool as well as to execute admin commands.

- ► `profile osd`: This allows users to connect as an OSD to other OSDs or monitors. Used for the OSD heartbeat traffic and status reporting.

- ► `profile mds`: This allows users to connect as an MDS to other MDSs.

- ► `profile bootstrap-osd`: This allows users to bootstrap an OSD. For example, `ceph-deploy` and `ceph-disk` tools use the `client.bootstrap-osd` user, which has permission to add keys and bootstrap an OSD.

- ► `profile bootstrap-mds`: This allows the user to bootstrap the metadata server. For example, the `ceph-deploy` tool uses the `client.bootstrap-mds` user to add keys and bootstrap the metadata server.

A user can be the individual user of an application, such as cinder/nova in the case of OpenStack. Creating users allows you to control what can access your Ceph Storage Cluster, its pools, and the data within the pools. In Ceph, a user should have a type, which is always `client`, and an ID, which can be any name. So, a valid user name syntax in Ceph is `TYPE. ID`, that is, `client.<name>`, for example, `client.admin` or `client.cinder`.

How to do it...

In the following recipe, we will discuss more about Ceph user management by running some commands:

- ► To list the users in your cluster, execute the following command:

```
# ceph auth list
```

The output of this command shows that for each daemon type, Ceph creates a user with different capabilities. It also lists the `client.admin` user, which is the cluster admin user.

▶ To retrieve a specific user, for example, `client.admin`, execute the following:

`# ceph auth get client.admin`

```
[root@ceph-node1 ~]# ceph auth get client.admin
exported keyring for client.admin
[client.admin]
        key = AQAfqAhVMExcGBAAfRAg084RHNtmfK83ihee1g==
        caps mds = "allow"
        caps mon = "allow *"
        caps osd = "allow *"
[root@ceph-node1 ~]#
```

▶ Create a user, `client.hari`:

`# ceph auth get-or-create client.hari`

```
[root@ceph-node1 ~]# ceph auth get-or-create client.hari
[client.hari]
        key = AQBm5NlVZCeFHRAAhZvXXEkZn9D98HCXIu9EyQ==
[root@ceph-node1 ~]#
```

This will create the user, `client.hari`, with no capabilities, and a user with no caps is of no use.

▶ Add capabilities to the `client.hari` user:

`# ceph auth caps client.hari mon 'allow r' osd 'allow rwx pool=rbd'`

```
[root@ceph-node1 ~]# ceph auth caps client.hari mon 'allow r' osd 'allow rwx pool=rbd'
updated caps for client.hari
[root@ceph-node1 ~]#
```

▶ List the user's capabilities:

`# ceph auth get client.hari`

```
[root@ceph-node1 ~]# ceph auth get client.hari
exported keyring for client.hari
[client.hari]
        key = AQBm5NlVZCeFHRAAhZvXXEkZn9D98HCXIu9EyQ==
        caps mon = "allow r"
        caps osd = "allow rwx pool=rbd"
[root@ceph-node1 ~]#
```

Ceph dynamic cluster management

Let's have a quick recap of how clients access the Ceph cluster. To perform a write operation with the Ceph cluster, the client gets the latest copy of the cluster map from the Ceph monitor (if they do not have it already). The cluster map provides information about the Ceph cluster layout. Then the client writes/reads the object, which is stored on a Ceph pool. The pool selects OSDs based on the CRUSH ruleset for that pool. The following diagram illustrates this entire process:

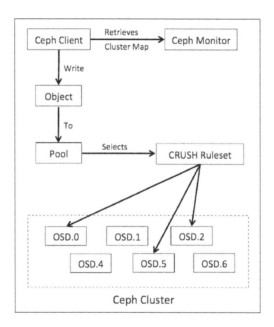

Now, let's understand the process of data storage inside the Ceph cluster. Ceph stores data in logical partitions known as pools. These pools hold multiple PGs, which in turn hold objects. Ceph is a true distributed storage system in which each object is replicated and stored across different OSDs each time. This mechanism has been explained with the help of the following diagram, in which I have tried to present how objects get stored in the Ceph cluster:

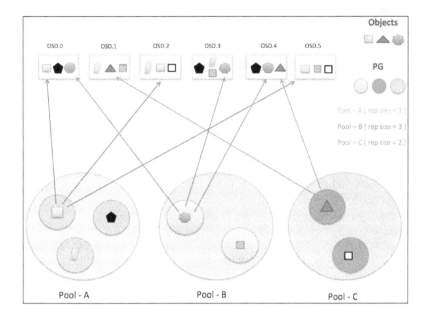

Ceph placement group

A **Placement Group** (**PG**) is a logical collection of objects that are replicated on OSDs to provide reliability in a storage system. Depending on the replication level of a Ceph pool, each PG is replicated and distributed on more than one OSD of a Ceph cluster. You can consider a PG as a logical container holding multiple objects, such that this logical container is mapped to multiple OSDs.

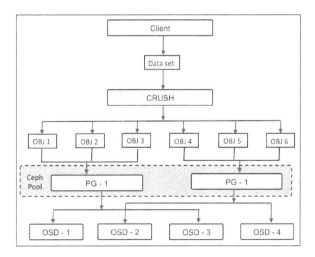

The PGs are essential for the scalability and performance of a Ceph storage system. Without PGs, it will be difficult to manage and track tens of millions of objects that are replicated and spread over hundreds of OSDs. The management of these objects without a PG will also result in a computational penalty. Instead of managing every object individually, a system has to manage the PGs with numerous objects. This makes Ceph a more manageable and less complex system.

Each PG requires some system resources, as they have to manage multiple objects. The number of PGs in a cluster should be meticulously calculated, and this is discussed later in this book. Usually, increasing the number of PGs in your cluster rebalances the OSD load. A recommended number of PGs per OSD is 50 to 100, to avoid high resource utilization on the OSD node. As the amount of data on a Ceph cluster increases, you might need to tune the cluster by adjusting the PG counts. When devices are added to or removed from a cluster, CRUSH manages the relocation of PGs in the most optimized way.

Now, we have understood that a Ceph PG stores its data on multiple OSDs for reliability and high availability. These OSDs are referred to as primary, secondary, tertiary, and so on, and they belong to a set known as the acting set for that PG. For each PG acting set, the first OSD is primary and the latter are secondary and tertiary.

How to do it...

To understand this better, let's find out the acting set for a PG from our Ceph cluster:

1. Add a temporary object with name hosts to a pool rbd:

   ```
   # rados put -p rbd hosts /etc/hosts
   ```

2. Check the PG name for object hosts:

   ```
   # ceph osd map rbd hosts
   ```

```
[root@ceph-node1 ~]# rados put -p rbd hosts /etc/hosts
[root@ceph-node1 ~]#
[root@ceph-node1 ~]# rados ls -p rbd | grep -i hosts
hosts
[root@ceph-node1 ~]# ceph osd map rbd hosts
osdmap e4376 pool 'rbd' (0) object 'hosts' -> pg 0.ea1b298e (0.8e) -> up ([8,2,4], p8) acting ([8,2,4], p8)
[root@ceph-node1 ~]#
```

If you observe the output, **Placement Group** (0.8e) has an **up set** [8,2,4] and an **acting set** [8,2,4]. So, here osd.8 is the primary OSD, and osd.2 and osd.4 are secondary and tertiary OSDs. The primary OSD is the only OSD that entertains write operations from clients. When it comes to read, by default it also comes from the primary OSD; however, we can change this behavior by setting up read affinity.

The OSD's that are up remain in the up set, as well as the acting set. Once the primary OSD is down, it is first removed from the up set and then from the acting set. The secondary OSD is then promoted to become the primary OSD. Ceph recovers PGs of the failed OSD to a new OSD and then adds it to the up and acting sets to ensure high availability. In a Ceph cluster, an OSD can be the primary OSD for some PGs, while at the same time, it can be the secondary or tertiary OSD for other PGs.

Placement group states

Ceph PGs may exhibit several states based on what's happening inside the cluster at that point in time. To know the state of a PG, you can see the output of the command `ceph status`. In this recipe, we will cover these different states of PGs and understand what each state actually means:

- **Creating**: The PG is being created. This generally happens when pools are being created or when PGs are increased for a pool.
- **Active**: All PGs are active, and requests to the PG will be processed.
- **Clean**: All objects in the PG are replicated the correct number of times.
- **Down**: A replica with necessary data is down, so the PG is offline (down).
- **Replay**: The PG is waiting for clients to replay operations after an OSD has crashed.
- **Splitting**: The PG is being split into multiple PGs. Usually, a PG attains this state when PGs are increased for an existing pool. For example, if you increase the PGs of a pool `rbd` from 64 to 128, the existing PGs will split, and some of their objects will be moved to new PGs.
- **Scrubbing**: The PG is being checked for inconsistencies.
- **Degraded**: Some objects in the PG are not replicated as many times as they are supposed to be.
- **Inconsistent**: The PG replica is not consistent. For example, there is the wrong size of object, or objects are missing from one replica after recovery is finished.
- **Peering**: The PG is undergoing the Peering process, in which it's trying to bring the OSDs that store the replicas of the PG into agreement about the state of the objects and metadata in the PG.
- **Repair**: The PG is being checked, and any inconsistencies found will be repaired (if possible).
- **Recovering**: Objects are being migrated/synchronized with replicas. When an OSD goes down, its contents may fall behind the current state of other replicas in the PGs. So, the PG goes into a recovering state and objects will be migrated/synchronized with replicas.

- **Backfill**: When a new OSD joins the cluster, CRUSH will reassign PGs from existing OSDs in the cluster to the newly added OSD. Once the backfilling is complete, the new OSD will begin serving requests when it is ready.

- **Backfill-wait**: The PG is waiting in line to start backfill.

- **Incomplete**: A PG is missing a necessary period of history from its log. This generally occurs when an OSD that contains needed information fails or is unavailable.

- **Stale**: The PG is in an unknown state—the monitors have not received an update for it since the PG mapping changed. When you start your cluster, it is common to see the stale state until the peering process completes.

- **Remapped**: When the acting set that services a PG changes, the data migrates from the old acting set to the new acting set. It may take some time for a new primary OSD to service requests. So, it may ask the old primary OSD to continue to service requests until the PG migration is complete. Once data migration completes, the mapping uses the primary OSD of the new acting set.

Creating Ceph pools on specific OSDs

A Ceph cluster typically consists of several nodes having multiple disk drives. And, these disk drives can be of mixed types. For example, your Ceph nodes might contain disks of the types SATA, NL-SAS, SAS, SSD, or even PCIe, and so on. Ceph provides you with flexibility to create pools on specific drive types. For example, you can create a high performing SSD pool from a set of SSD disks, or you can create a high capacity, low cost pool using the SATA disk drives.

In this recipe, we will understand how to create a pool named `ssd-pool` backed by SSD disks, and another pool named `sata-pool`, which is backed by SATA disks. To achieve this, we will edit CRUSH maps and make the necessary configurations.

The Ceph cluster that we deployed and have played around with in this book is hosted on virtual machines and does not have real SSD disks backing it. Hence, we will be assuming we have a few virtual disks as SSD disks for learning purposes. There will be no change if you are performing this exercise on a real SSD disk-based Ceph cluster.

For the following demonstration, let's assume that `osd.0`, `osd.3`, and `osd.6` are SSD disks, and we would be creating an SSD pool on these disks. Similarly, let's assume `osd.1`, `osd.5`, and `osd.7` are SATA disks, which would be hosting the SATA pool.

How to do it...

Let's begin the configuration:

1. Get the current CRUSH map and decompile it:

```
# ceph osd getcrushmap -o crushmapdump
# crushtool -d crushmapdump -o crushmapdump-decompiled
```

```
[root@ceph-node1 ~]# ceph osd getcrushmap -o crushmapdump
got crush map from osdmap epoch 4443
[root@ceph-node1 ~]#
[root@ceph-node1 ~]# crushtool -d crushmapdump -o crushmapdump-decompiled
[root@ceph-node1 ~]# ls -l crushmapdump-decompiled
-rw-r--r-- 1 root root 1360 Sep  1 21:41 crushmapdump-decompiled
[root@ceph-node1 ~]# _
```

2. Edit the `crushmapdump-decompiled` CRUSH map file and add the following section after the root default section:

```
root ssd {
        id -5
        alg straw
        hash 0
        item osd.0 weight 0.010
        item osd.3 weight 0.010
        item osd.6 weight 0.010
}

root sata {
        id -6
        alg straw
        hash 0
        item osd.1 weight 0.010
        item osd.4 weight 0.010
        item osd.7 weight 0.010
}
```

3. Create the CRUSH rule by adding the following rules under the rules section of the CRUSH map, and then, save and exit the file:

```
rule ssd-pool {
        ruleset 1
        type replicated
        min_size 1
        max_size 10
        step take ssd
        step chooseleaf firstn 0 type osd
        step emit
}

rule sata-pool {
        ruleset 2
        type replicated
        min_size 1
        max_size 10
        step take sata
        step chooseleaf firstn 0 type osd
        step emit
}
```

4. Compile and inject the new CRUSH map in the Ceph cluster:

```
# crushtool -c crushmapdump-decompiled -o
  crushmapdump-compiled
```

```
# ceph osd setcrushmap -i crushmapdump-compiled
```

5. Once the new CRUSH map has been applied to the Ceph cluster, check the OSD tree view for the new arrangement, and notice the ssd and sata root buckets:

```
# ceph osd tree
```

```
[root@ceph-node1 ~]# ceph osd tree
ID WEIGHT  TYPE NAME          UP/DOWN REWEIGHT PRIMARY-AFFINITY
-6 0.02998 root sata
 1 0.00999     osd.1              up  1.00000          1.00000
 4 0.00999     osd.4              up  1.00000          1.00000
 7 0.00999     osd.7              up  1.00000          1.00000
-5 0.02998 root ssd
 0 0.00999     osd.0              up  1.00000          1.00000
 3 0.00999     osd.3              up  1.00000          1.00000
 6 0.00999     osd.6              up  1.00000          1.00000
-1 0.09000 root default
-3 0.03000     host ceph-node2
 3 0.00999         osd.3          up  1.00000          1.00000
 4 0.00999         osd.4          up  1.00000          1.00000
 5 0.00999         osd.5          up  1.00000          1.00000
-4 0.03000     host ceph-node3
 6 0.00999         osd.6          up  1.00000          1.00000
 7 0.00999         osd.7          up  1.00000          1.00000
 8 0.00999         osd.8          up  1.00000          1.00000
-2 0.03000     host ceph-node1
 1 0.00999         osd.1          up  1.00000          1.00000
 2 0.00999         osd.2          up  1.00000          1.00000
 0 0.00999         osd.0          up  1.00000          1.00000
[root@ceph-node1 ~]#
```

6. Create and verify the ssd-pool.

 Since this is a small cluster hosted on virtual machines, we will create these pools with a few PGs.

1. Create the ssd-pool:

```
# ceph osd pool create ssd-pool 8 8
```

2. Verify the ssd-pool; notice that the crush_ruleset is 0, which is by default:

```
# ceph osd dump | grep -i ssd
```

```
[root@ceph-node1 ~]# ceph osd pool create ssd-pool 8 8
pool 'ssd-pool' created
[root@ceph-node1 ~]# ceph osd dump | grep -i ssd
pool 45 'ssd-pool' replicated size 3 min_size 2 crush_ruleset 0 object_hash rjenkins pg_num 8 pgp_num 8
last_change 4446 flags hashpspool stripe_width 0
[root@ceph-node1 ~]#
```

3. Let's change the `crush_ruleset` to 1 so that the new pool gets created on the SSD disks:

   # ceph osd pool set ssd-pool crush_ruleset 1

4. Verify the pool and notice the change in `crush_ruleset`:

   # ceph osd dump | grep -i ssd

```
[root@ceph-node1 ~]# ceph osd pool set ssd-pool crush_ruleset 1
set pool 45 crush_ruleset to 1
[root@ceph-node1 ~]# ceph osd dump | grep -i ssd
pool 45 'ssd-pool' replicated size 3 min_size 2 crush_ruleset 1 object_hash rjenkins pg_num 8 pgp_num 8
last_change 4448 flags hashpspool stripe_width 0
[root@ceph-node1 ~]# _
```

7. Similarly, create and verify `sata-pool`.

```
[root@ceph-node1 ~]# ceph osd pool create sata-pool 8 8
pool 'sata-pool' created
[root@ceph-node1 ~]# ceph osd dump | grep -i sata
pool 46 'sata-pool' replicated size 3 min_size 2 crush_ruleset 0 object_hash rjenkins
pg_num 8 pgp_num 8 last_change 4450 flags hashpspool stripe_width 0
[root@ceph-node1 ~]#
[root@ceph-node1 ~]# ceph osd pool set sata-pool crush_ruleset 2
set pool 46 crush_ruleset to 1
[root@ceph-node1 ~]#
[root@ceph-node1 ~]# ceph osd dump | grep -i sata
pool 46 'sata-pool' replicated size 3 min_size 2 crush_ruleset 2 object_hash rjenkins
pg_num 8 pgp_num 8 last_change 4452 flags hashpspool stripe_width 0
[root@ceph-node1 ~]#
```

8. Let's add some objects to these pools:

   1. Since these pools are new, they should not contain any objects, but let's verify this by using the `rados` list command:

      ```
      # rados -p ssd-pool ls
      # rados -p sata-pool ls
      ```

   2. We will now add an object to these pools using the rados `put` command. The syntax would be: `rados -p <pool_name> put <object_name> <file_name>`:

      ```
      # rados -p ssd-pool put dummy_object1 /etc/hosts
      # rados -p sata-pool put dummy_object1 /etc/hosts
      ```

3. Using the `rados` list command, list these pools. You should get the object names that we stored in the last step:

```
# rados -p ssd-pool ls
# rados -p sata-pool ls
```

```
[root@ceph-node1 ~]# rados -p ssd-pool ls
[root@ceph-node1 ~]# rados -p sata-pool ls
[root@ceph-node1 ~]#
[root@ceph-node1 ~]# rados -p ssd-pool put dummy_object1 /etc/hosts
[root@ceph-node1 ~]# rados -p sata-pool put dummy_object1 /etc/hosts
[root@ceph-node1 ~]#
[root@ceph-node1 ~]# rados -p ssd-pool ls
dummy_object1
[root@ceph-node1 ~]# rados -p sata-pool ls
dummy_object1
[root@ceph-node1 ~]#
```

9. Now, the interesting part of this entire section is to verify that the objects are getting stored on the correct set of OSDs:

1. For the `ssd-pool`, we have used the OSDs 0, 3, and 6. Check the `osd map` for `ssd-pool` using the syntax: `ceph osd map <pool_name> <object_name>`:

   `# ceph osd map ssd-pool dummy_object1`

2. Similarly, check the object from `sata-pool`:

   `# ceph osd map sata-pool dummy_object1`

```
[root@ceph-node1 ~]# ceph osd map ssd-pool dummy_object1
osdmap e4455 pool 'ssd-pool' (45) object 'dummy_object1' -> pg 45.71968e96 (45.6) -> up ([3,0,6], p3) acting ([3,0,6], p3)
[root@ceph-node1 ~]#
[root@ceph-node1 ~]# ceph osd map sata-pool dummy_object1
osdmap e4455 pool 'sata-pool' (46) object 'dummy_object1' -> pg 46.71968e96 (46.6) -> up ([1,7,4], p1) acting ([1,7,4], p1)
[root@ceph-node1 ~]#
```

As shown in the preceding screenshot, the object that is created on `ssd-pool` is actually stored on the OSDs set `[3,0,6]`, and the object that is created on sata-pool gets stored on the OSDs set `[1,7,4]`. This output was expected, and it verifies that the pool that we created uses the correct set of OSDs as we requested. This type of configuration can be very useful in a production setup, where you would like to create a fast pool based on SSDs only, and a medium/slower performing pool based on spinning disks.

8
Production Planning and Performance Tuning for Ceph

In this chapter, we will cover the following recipes:

- The dynamics of capacity, performance, and cost
- Choosing the hardware and software components for Ceph
- Ceph recommendation and performance tuning
- Ceph erasure coding
- Creating an erasure coded pool
- Ceph cache tiering
- Creating a pool for cache tiering
- Creating a cache tier
- Configuring a cache tier
- Testing a cache tier

Introduction

In this chapter, we will learn some very interesting concepts with regard to Ceph. It includes the Hardware/Software recommendation, performance tuning for Ceph components (that is, Ceph MON, OSD), and clients including the OS tuning. Finally, we will understand the Ceph erasure coding and cache tiering, covering different the techniques of both.

The dynamics of capacity, performance, and cost

Ceph is a software-defined storage solution that is designed to run on commodity hardware. This ability of Ceph makes it a flexible and economic solution that is tailored for your needs. Since all the intelligence of Ceph resides in its software, it requires a good set of hardware to make it an overall package that is a great storage solution.

The Ceph hardware selection requires meticulous planning based on your storage needs and the use case that you have. Organizations need optimized hardware configurations that allow them to start small and scale to several petabytes. The following diagram represents a few factors that are used to determine an optimal configuration for your Ceph cluster:

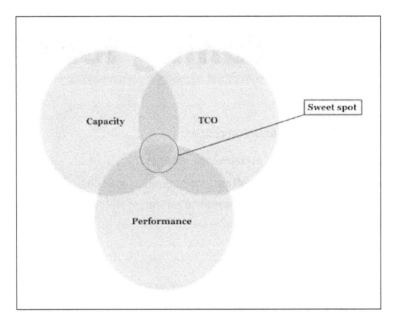

Different organizations have different storage workloads that generally require some middle-ground shared by performance, capacity, and TCO. Ceph is a unified storage, that is, it can provision File, Block, and Object storage from the same cluster. Ceph is also able to provision different types of storage pools within the same cluster that are targeted at different workloads. This ability allows an organization to tailor its storage infrastructure as per its needs. There can be multiple ways to define your storage needs; the following diagram shows one way of doing this:

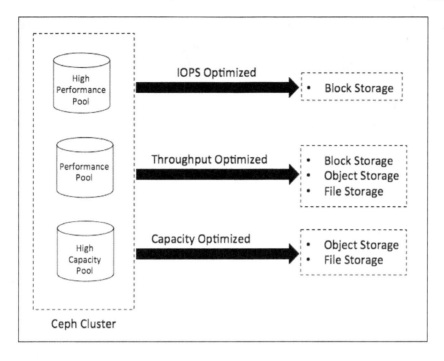

- ▸ **IOPS Optimized**: The highlight of this type of configuration is that it has the highest **IOPS (I/O operations per second)** with low **TCO (Total Cost of Ownership)** per IO. It is typically implemented using high performance nodes containing faster SSD disks, PCIe SSD, NVMe, and so on, for data storage. It is generally used for block storage, however, you can use it for other workloads that require a high IOPS.

- ▸ **Throughput Optimized:** Its highlights include the highest throughput and low cost per throughput. It is typically implemented using SSD disks and PCIe SSD for OSD journals, with a high bandwidth, physically separated dual network. It is mostly used for block storage. If your use case requires a high performance object or file storage, then you should consider this.

- ▸ **Capacity Optimized:** Its highlights include low cost per TB and low cost per rack unit of physical space in the datacenter. It is also known as economic storage, cheap storage, and archival/long-term storage, and it is typically implemented using dense servers full of spinning disks, usually 36 to 72, with 4 to 6 TB of physical disk space per server. It is generally used for low cost, large storage capacity object or filesystem storage. It is a good candidate to use erasure coding to maximize the usable capacity.

Choosing the hardware and software components for Ceph

As mentioned earlier, Ceph hardware selection requires meticulous planning based on your environment and storage needs. The type of hardware component, network infrastructure, and cluster design are some critical factors you should consider during the initial phase of Ceph storage planning. There is no golden rule for Ceph hardware selection as it depends on various factors such as budget, performance versus capacity, or both, fault tolerance level, and the use case.

Ceph is hardware agnostic; organizations are free to select any hardware of their choice based on budget, performance/capacity requirements, or use case. They have full control over their storage cluster and the underlying infrastructure. Also, one of the advantages of Ceph is that it supports heterogeneous hardware. You can mix hardware brands while creating your Ceph cluster infrastructure. For example, while building your Ceph cluster, you can mix hardware from different manufacturers such as HP, Dell, Supermicro, and so on, and even off-the-shelf hardware that can lead to significant cost savings.

You should keep in mind that hardware selection for Ceph is driven by the workload that you are planning to put on your storage cluster, the environment, and the features you will be using. In this recipe, we will learn some general practices for selecting hardware for your Ceph cluster.

Processor

The Ceph Monitor daemon maintains the cluster maps and does not serve any data to the client, hence it is light-weight and does not have very strict processor requirements. In most cases, an average single core server processor will do the job for the Ceph monitor. On the other hand, the Ceph MDS is a bit more resource hungry. It requires significantly higher CPU processing powers with quad core or more. For a small Ceph cluster or proof of concept environment, you can co-locate Ceph monitors with other Ceph components such as the OSD, Radosgw, or even the Ceph MDS. For a medium-to-large-scale environment, instead of being shared, Ceph Monitors should be hosted on dedicated machines.

A Ceph OSD daemon requires a fair amount of processing power as it serves data to clients. To estimate the CPU requirement for the Ceph OSD, it's important to know how many OSDs the server would be hosting. It's generally recommended that each OSD daemon should have a minimum of one CPU core-GHz. You can use the following formula to estimate the OSD CPU requirement:

```
((CPU sockets * CPU cores per socket * CPU clock speed in GHz) / No.
Of OSD) >=1
```

For example, a server with a single socket, 6 core, 2.5Ghz CPU should be good enough for 12 Ceph OSDs, and each OSD will get roughly 1.25Ghz of computing power: *((1*6*2.5)/12)= 1.25*.

Here are a few more examples of processors for the Ceph OSD node:

- Intel® Xeon® Processor E5-2620 v3 (2.40 GHz, 6 core)

  1 * 6 * 2.40 = 14.4 implies Good for Ceph node with up to 14 OSDs

- Intel® Xeon® Processor E5-2680 v3 (2.50 GHz, 12 core)

  1 * 12 * 2.50 = 30 implies Good for Ceph node with up to 30 OSDs

If you are planning to use the Ceph erasure coding feature, then it would be more beneficial to get a more powerful CPU, as erasure coding operations require more processing power.

> If you were planning to use the Ceph erasure coded pool, then it would be useful to get a more powerful CPU, as Ceph OSDs that host erasure-coded pools will use more CPU than Ceph OSDs that host replicated pools.

Memory

Monitor and metadata daemons need to serve their data rapidly, hence they should have enough memory for faster processing. The rule of thumb—be to have 2 GB or more memory per-daemon instance—should be good for Ceph MDS and monitor. Ceph MDS depends a lot on data caching; as they need to serve data quickly, they require plenty of RAM. The higher the RAM for Ceph MDS, the better the performance of CephFS will be.

OSDs generally require a fair amount of physical memory. For an average workload, 1 GB of memory per-OSD-daemon instance should suffice; however, from a performance point of view, 2 GB per-OSD daemon will be a good choice and having more memory also helps during recovery and for better caching. This recommendation assumes that you are using one OSD daemon for one physical disk. If you use more than one physical disk per OSD, your memory requirements will grow as well. Generally, more physical memory is good, because during cluster recovery, memory consumption increases significantly. It's worth knowing that the OSD memory consumption will increase if you consider the RAW capacity of the underlying physical disk. So, the OSD requirement for a 6 TB disk would be more than that of a 4 TB disk. You should take this decision wisely, such that memory should not become a bottleneck in your cluster's performance.

> It is usually cost-effective to over-allocate CPU and memory at an earlier stage of your cluster planning, as we can add more physical disks in a JBOD style to the same host anytime if it has enough system resources, rather than purchasing an entirely new node, which is a bit costly.

Network

Ceph is a distributed storage system and it relies heavily on the underlying network infrastructure. If you are planning your Ceph cluster to be reliable and performant, make sure that you have your network designed for it. It's recommended that all cluster nodes have two redundant separate networks for cluster and client traffic.

For a small proof of concept, or to test the Ceph cluster of a few nodes, 1Gbps network speed should go well. If you have a mid-to-large sized cluster, (a few tens of nodes), you should think of using 10Gbps or more bandwidth network. At the time of recovery/re-balancing, the network plays a vital role. If you have a good 10Gbps or more bandwidth network connection, your cluster will recover quickly, else it might take some time. So, from a performance point of view, a 10Gbps or more dual network will be a good option. A well-designed Ceph cluster makes use of two physically separated networks: one for the cluster network (internal network), and another for the client network (external network); both these networks should be physically separated right from the server to the network switch and everything in-between, as shown in the following diagram:

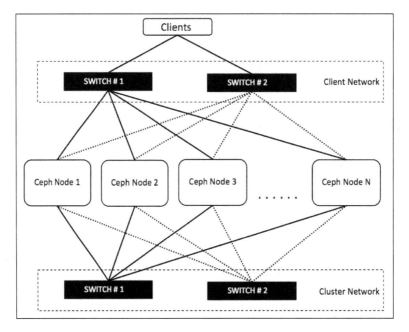

With respect to the network, another topic of debate is whether to use the Ethernet network or InfiniBand network, or more precisely a 10G network, 40G, or higher bandwidth network. It depends on several factors such as workload, size of your Ceph cluster, density and number of Ceph OSD nodes, and so on. In several deployments, I have seen customers are using both 10G and 40G networks with Ceph. In this case, their Ceph cluster ranges to several PB and a few hundreds of nodes, in which they are using the client network as 10G, and the internal cluster network as high bandwidth, low latency 40G. Nevertheless, the price of the Ethernet network is going down; based on your use case, you can decide the network type that you would like to have.

Disk

Performance and economics for the Ceph clusters both depend heavily on an effective choice of storage media. You should understand your workload and possible performance requirements before selecting storage media for your Ceph cluster. Ceph uses storage media in two ways: the OSD journal part and the OSD data part. As explained in earlier chapters, every `write` operation in Ceph is currently a two-step process. When an OSD receives a request to write an object, it first writes that object to the journal part of OSDs in the acting set, and sends a `write` acknowledgment to clients. Soon after, the journal data is synced to data partition. It's worth knowing that replication is also an important factor during `write` performances. The replication factor is usually a trade off between reliability, performance, and TCO. In this way, all the cluster performance revolves around the OSD journal and data partition.

Ceph OSD Journal partition

If your workload is performance-centric, then it's recommended to use SSDs for journals. By using an SSD, you can achieve significant throughput improvements by reducing the access time and `write` latency. To use SSDs as journals, we create multiple logical partitions on each physical SSD, such that each SSD logical partition (journal) is mapped to one OSD data partition. In this case, the OSD data partition is located on a spinning disk and has its journal on the faster SSD partition. The following diagram illustrates this configuration:

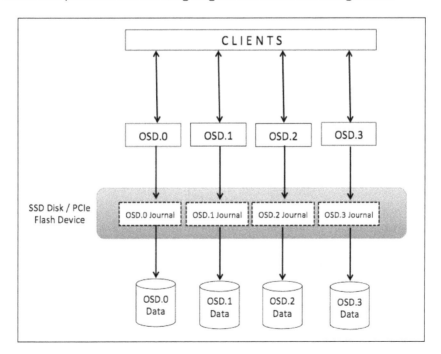

In this type of setup, you should keep in mind not to overload SSDs by storing multiple journals beyond their limits. Usually, 10 to 20GB journal sizes should be good enough for most cases, however, if you have a larger SSD, you can create a larger journal device; in this case, don't forget to increase the filestore maximum and minimum synchronization time intervals for OSD.

The two most common types of non-volatile fast storage that are used with Ceph are SATA or SAS SSDs and PCIe or NVMe SSDs. To achieve good performance out of your SATA/SAS SSDs, your SSD to OSD ratio should be 1:4, that is, one SSD shared with 4 OSD data disks. In the case of PCIe or NVMe flash devices, depending on device performance, the SSD to OSD ratio can vary from 1:12 to 1:18, that is, one flash device shared with 12 to 18 OSD data disks.

> The SSD to OSD ratio recontamination mentioned here is very general and works well in most of the cases. However, I would encourage you to test your SSD/PCIe against your specific workloads and environment, to get best out of it.

The dark side of using a single SSD for multiple journals is that if you lose your SSD hosting multiple journals, all the OSDs associated with this SSD will fail, and you might lose your data. However, you can overcome this situation by using RAID 1 for journals, but this will increase your storage cost. Also, the SSD cost per gigabyte is nearly 10 times more as compared to HDD. So, if you are building a cluster with SSDs, it will increase the cost per gigabyte for your Ceph cluster. However, if you are looking for significant performance improvements out of your Ceph cluster, it's worth investing on SSD for journals.

We have learned a lot about SSD journals and understood that they can contribute a lot to improving the `write` performance. However, if you are not concerned about extreme performance, and cost per TB is a deciding factor for you, then you should consider configuring the journal and data partition on the same hard disk drive. This means that out of your large spinning disk, you will allocate a few GBs for the OSD journal and use the remaining capacity of the same drive with the OSD data. This kind of setup might not be as performant as the SSD-journal-based one, but the TCO of price per TB of storage would be fairly less.

Ceph OSD Data partition

OSDs are the real workhorses that store all the data. In a production environment, you should use an enterprise, cloud, or archive class hard disk drive with your Ceph cluster. Typically, desktop class HDDs are not well suited to a production Ceph cluster. The reason being that in a Ceph cluster, several hundreds of rotating HDDs are installed in close proximity, and the combined rotational vibration can become a challenge with desktop class HDDs. This increases the disk failure rate and can hamper the overall performance. The enterprise class HDDs are purposely built to handle vibrations, and they themselves generate very little rotational vibration. Also, their MTBF is significantly higher than the desktop class HDDs.

Another thing to consider for the Ceph OSD data disk is its interface, that is, SATA or SAS. The NL-SAS HDDs have dual SAS 12GB/s ports, and they are generally more high performing than single ported 6GB/s SATA interface HDDs. Also, dual SAS ports provide redundancy and can also allow simultaneous reading and writing. Another aspect of SAS devices is that they have lower **unrecoverable read errors** (**URE**) as compared to SATA drives. The lower the URE, the fewer scrubbing errors and placement group repair operations.

The density of your Ceph OSD node is also an important factor for cluster performance, usable capacity, and TCO. Generally, it's better to have a larger number of smaller nodes than a few large capacity nodes, but this is always open for debate. You should select the density of your Ceph OSD node such that one node should be less than 10% of the total cluster size.

For example, in a 1PB Ceph cluster, you should avoid using 4 x 250 TB OSD nodes, in which each node constitutes 25% of the cluster capacity. Instead, you can have 13 x 80TB OSD nodes, in which each node size is less than 10% of the cluster capacity. However, this might increase your TCO and can affect several other factors of your cluster planning.

Operating System

Ceph is a software-defined system that runs on top of a Linux-based operating system. Ceph supports most of the major Linux distributions. As of now, the valid operating system choices to run a Ceph clusters are RHEL, CentOS, Fedora, Debian, Ubuntu, OpenSuse, and SLES. For the Linux kernel version, it's recommended that you deploy Ceph on newer releases of the Linux Kernel. We also recommend deploying it on release with **long-term support** (**LTS**). At the time of writing this book, the Linux Kernel v3.16.3, or a later version, is recommended and is a good starting point. It's a good idea to keep an eye on `http://docs.ceph.com/docs/master/start/os-recommendations`. According to documentation, CentOS 7 and Ubuntu 14.04 are tier-1 distributions for which comprehensive functional, regression, and stress test suites are run on a continuous basis, and with no doubts, RHEL is the best choice if you are using the enterprise Red Hat Ceph Storage product.

OSD Filesystem

The Ceph OSD daemon runs on top of a filesystem that can be XFS, EXT, or even Btrfs. However, selecting the right Filesystem for the Ceph OSD is a critical factor as OSD daemons rely heavily on the stability and performance of the underlying filesystem. Apart from stability and performance, filesystem also provides **extended attributes** (**XATTRs**) that Ceph OSD daemon's take advantage of. The XATTR provides internal information on the object state, snapshot, metadata, and ACL to the Ceph OSD daemon, which helps in data management.

That's why the underlying filesystem should provide sufficient capacity for XATTRs. Btrfs provides significantly larger `xattr` metadata, which is stored with a file. XFS has a relatively large limit (64 KB) that most deployments won't encounter, but the ext4 is too small to be usable. If you are using the ext4 filesystem for your Ceph OSD, you should always add `filestore xattr use omap = true` to the following setting to the [OSD] section of your `ceph.conf` file. The filesystem selection is quite important for a production workload, and with respect to Ceph, these filesystems differ from each other in various ways:

- **XFS:** Is a reliable, mature, and very stable filesystem, which is recommended for production usage in the Ceph clusters. However, XFS stands lower as compared to Btrfs. XFS has small performance issues in metadata scaling. Also, XFS is a journaling filesystem, that is, each time a client sends data to write to a Ceph cluster, it is first written to a journaling space and then to an XFS filesystem. This increases the overhead of writing the same data twice, and thus makes the XFS perform slower as compared to Btrfs, which does not use journals. However, due to its reliability and stability, XFS is the most popular and recommended filesystem for Ceph deployments.

- **Btrfs:** The OSD, with the Btrfs filesystem underneath, delivers the best performance as compared to XFS and the ext4 filesystem-based OSDs. One of the major advantages of using Btrfs is its support to copy-on-write and writable snapshots. With the Btrfs filesystem, Ceph uses parallel journaling, that is, Ceph writes to the OSD journal and OSD data in parallel, which is a big boost for `write` performance. It also supports transparent compression and pervasive checksums, and it incorporates multi-device management in a filesystem. It has an attractive feature of online FSCK. However, despite these new features, Btrfs is currently not production ready, but it's a good candidate for test deployment.

- **Ext4:** The fourth extended filesystem (Ext4) is also a journaling filesystem that is a production-ready filesystem for the Ceph OSD. However, it's not as popular as XFS. From a performance point of view, the ext4 filesystem is not on par with Btrfs.

 Don't get confused with Ceph journaling and filesystem journaling (XFS, EXT4); they are both different. Ceph does its journaling while writing to filesystem, and then filesystem does its journaling while writing data to underlying disks.

Ceph recommendation and performance tuning

In this recipe, we will learn some performance tuning parameters for the Ceph cluster. These cluster-wide configuration parameters are defined in the Ceph configuration file so that each time any Ceph daemon starts, it will respect the defined settings. By default, the configuration file name is `ceph.conf`, which is located in the `/etc/ceph` directory. This configuration file has a global section as well as several sections for each service type. Whenever a Ceph service type starts, it applies the configuration defined under the `[global]` section as well as the daemon specific section. A Ceph configuration file has multiple sections, as shown in the following screenshot:

```
[global]
    fsid                        = {UUID}
    public network             = 192.168.0.0/24
    cluster network            = 192.168.0.0/24
    osd pool default pg num    = 128
[mon]
[mon.alpha]
    host                       = alpha
    mon addr                   = 192.168.0.10:6789
[mds]
[mds.alpha]
    host                       = alpha
[osd]
    osd recovery max active    = 3
    osd max backfills          = 5
[osd.0]
    host                       = delta
[osd.1]
    host                       = epsilon
[client]
    rbd cache                   = true
[client.radosgw.gateway]
    host                       =  ceph-radosgw
```

We will now discuss the role of each section of the configuration file.

▶ **Global section:** The global section of the cluster configuration file begins with the `[global]` keyword. All the settings defined under this section apply to all the daemons of the Ceph cluster. The following is an example of a parameter defined under the `[global]` section:

```
public network = 192.168.0.0/24
```

▶ **Monitor section:** The settings defined under the `[mon]` section of the config file are applied to all the Ceph monitor daemons in the cluster. The parameter defined under this section overrides the parameters defined under the `[global]` section. The following is an example of a parameter usually defined under the [mon] section:

```
mon initial members = ceph-mon1
```

▶ **OSD section:** The settings defined under the `[osd]` section are applied to all the Ceph OSD daemons in the Ceph cluster. The configuration defined under this section overrides the same setting defined under the `[global]` section. The following is an example of the settings in this section:

```
osd mkfs type = xfs
```

▶ **MDS section:** The settings defined under the `[mds]` section are applied to all the Ceph MDS daemons in the Ceph cluster. The configuration defined under this section overrides the same setting defined under the `[global]` section. The following is an example of the settings in this section:

```
mds cache size = 250000
```

▶ **Client section:** The settings defined under the [client] section are applied to all the Ceph clients. The configuration defined under this section overrides the same setting defined under the `[global]` section. The following is the example of the settings in this section:

```
rbd cache size = 67108864
```

In the next recipe, we will learn some tips for performance tuning of the Ceph cluster. Performance tuning is a vast topic that requires understanding of Ceph, as well as other components of your storage stack. There is no silver bullet for performance tuning. It depends a lot on the underlying infrastructure and your environment.

Global cluster tuning

The global parameters should be defined under the `[global]` section of your Ceph cluster configuration file:

▶ `network`: It's recommended that you use two physically separated networks for your Ceph cluster, which are referred to as the public and cluster networks respectively. Earlier in this chapter, we covered the need for two different networks. Let's now understand how we can define them in a Ceph configuration.

- Public Network: Use this syntax to define the public network: `public network = {public network / netmask}`:

```
public network = 192.168.100.0/24
```

- ❑ Cluster Network: Use this syntax to define the cluster network: `cluster network = {cluster network / netmask}`:

```
cluster network = 192.168.1.0/24
```

▸ `max open files`: If this parameter is in place and the Ceph cluster starts, it sets the max open file descriptors at the OS level. This keeps OSD daemons from running out of the file descriptors. The default value of this parameter is 0; you can set it as up to a 64-bit integer:

```
max open files = 131072
```

▸ `osd pool default min size`: This is the replication level in a degraded state. It sets the minimum number of replicas for the objects in pool in order to acknowledge a `write` operation from clients. The default value is 0:

```
osd pool default min size = 1
```

▸ `osd pool default pg` and `osd pool default pgp`: Make sure that the cluster has a realistic number of placement groups. The recommended value of placement group per OSD is 100. Use this formula to calculate the PG count: `(Total number of OSD * 100)/number of replicas`

For 10 OSD and a replica size of 3, the PG count should be under (10*100)/3 = 333:

```
osd pool default pg num = 128
```
```
osd pool default pgp num = 128
```

As explained earlier, the PG and PGP number should be kept the same. The PG and PGP values vary a lot depending on the cluster size. The previously mentioned configurations should not harm your cluster, but you may want to rethink before applying these values. You should know that these parameters do not change the PG and PGP numbers for existing pools; they are applied when you create a new pool without specifying the PG and PGP values.

▸ `osd pool default min size`: This is the replication level in a degraded state, which should be set lower than the `osd pool default size` value. It sets the minimum number of replicas for an object of a pool so that it can acknowledge the `write` operation even if the cluster is degraded. If the min size does not match, Ceph will not acknowledge `write` to the client:

```
osd pool default min size = 1
```

▸ `osd pool default crush rule`: The default CRUSH ruleset to use when creating a pool:

```
osd pool default crush rule = 0
```

▸ **Disable In-Memory Logs**: Each Ceph subsystem has a logging level for its output logs, and it logs in-memory. We can set different values for each of these subsystems by setting a log file level and a memory level for debug logging on a scale of 1 to 20, where 1 is terse and 20 is verbose. The first setting is the log level, and the second setting is the memory level. You must separate them with a forward slash (/): `debug <subsystem> = <log-level>/<memory-level>`

The default logging level is good enough for your cluster, unless you see that the memory level logs are impacting your performance or memory consumption. In such a case, you can try to disable the in-memory logging. To disable the default values of in-memory logs, add the following parameters:

```
debug_lockdep = 0/0
debug_context = 0/0
debug_crush = 0/0
debug_buffer = 0/0
debug_timer = 0/0
debug_filer = 0/0
debug_objecter = 0/0
debug_rados = 0/0
debug_rbd = 0/0
debug_journaler = 0/0
debug_objectcatcher = 0/0
debug_client = 0/0
debug_osd = 0/0
debug_optracker = 0/0
debug_objclass = 0/0
debug_filestore = 0/0
debug_journal = 0/0
debug_ms = 0/0
debug_monc = 0/0
debug_tp = 0/0
debug_auth = 0/0
debug_finisher = 0/0
debug_heartbeatmap = 0/0
debug_perfcounter = 0/0
debug_asok = 0/0
debug_throttle = 0/0
debug_mon = 0/0
debug_paxos = 0/0
debug_rgw = 0/0
```

Monitor tuning

The monitor tuning parameters should be defined under the `[mon]` section of your Ceph cluster configuration file:

- ▶ `mon osd down out interval`: This is the number of seconds Ceph waits before marking a Ceph OSD Daemon "down" and "out" if it doesn't respond. This option comes in handy when your OSD nodes crash and reboot by themselves or after some short glitch in the network. You don't want your cluster to start rebalancing as soon as the problem comes, rather wait for a few minutes and see if the problem gets fixed:

  ```
  mon_osd_down_out_interval = 600
  ```

- ▶ `mon allow pool delete`: To avoid the accidental deletion of the Ceph pool, set this parameter as false. This can be useful if you have many administrators managing the Ceph cluster, and you do not want to take any risk with client data:

  ```
  mon_allow_pool_delete = false
  ```

- ▶ `mon osd min down reporters`: The Ceph OSD daemon can report to MON about its peer OSDs if they are down; by default, this value is 1. With this option, you can change the minimum number of Ceph OSD Daemons required to report a down Ceph OSD to the Ceph monitor. In a large cluster, it's recommended that you have this value larger than the default; 3 should be a good number:

  ```
  mon_osd_min_down_reporters = 3
  ```

OSD tuning

In this recipe, we will understand the general OSD tuning parameters that should be defined under the `[osd]` section of your Ceph cluster configuration file.

OSD General Settings

The following settings allow the Ceph OSD daemon to determine the filesystem type, mount options, as well as some other useful settings:

- ▶ `osd mkfs options xfs`: At the time of OSD creation, Ceph will use these xfs options to create the OSD filesystem:

  ```
  osd_mkfs_options_xfs = "-f -i size=2048"
  ```

- ▶ `osd mount options xfs`: It supplies the xfs filesystem mount options to OSD. When Ceph is mounting an OSD, it will use the following options for OSD filesystem mounting:

  ```
  osd_mount_options_xfs = "rw,noatime,inode64,logbufs=8,logbsize=256
  k,delaylog,allocsize=4M"
  ```

▶ `osd max write size`: The maximum size in megabytes an OSD can write at a time:

`osd_max_write_size = 256`

▶ `osd client message size cap`: The largest client data message in bytes that is allowed in memory:

`osd_client_message_size_cap = 1073741824`

▶ `osd map dedup`: Remove duplicate entries in the OSD map:

`osd_map_dedup = true`

▶ `osd op threads`: The number of threads to service the Ceph OSD Daemon operations. Set it to 0 to disable it. Increasing the number may increase the request-processing rate:

`osd_op_threads = 16`

▶ `osd disk threads`: The number of disk threads that are used to perform background disk-intensive OSD operations such as scrubbing and snap trimming:

`osd_disk_threads = 1`

▶ `osd disk thread ioprio class`: It is used in conjunction with `osd_disk_thread_ioprio_priority`. This tunable can change the I/O scheduling class of the disk thread, and it only works with the Linux kernel CFQ scheduler. The possible values are `idle`, `be`, or `rt`:

  ❑ `idle`: The disk thread will have lower priority than any other thread in the OSD. It is useful when you want to slow down the scrubbing on an OSD that is busy handling client requests.

  ❑ `be`: The disk threads have the same priority as other threads in the OSD.

  ❑ `rt`: The disk thread will have more priority than all the other threads. This is useful when scrubbing is much needed, and it can be prioritized at the expense of client operations.

  `osd_disk_thread_ioprio_class = idle`

▶ `osd disk thread ioprio priority`: It's used in conjunction with `osd_disk_thread_ioprio_class`. This tunable can change the I/O scheduling priority of the disk thread ranging from 0 (highest) to 7 (lowest). If all OSDs on a given host are in class `idle` and are competing for I/O and not doing much operations, this parameter can be used to lower the disk thread priority of one OSD to 7 so that another OSD with the priority 0 can potentially scrub faster. Like `osd_disk_thread_ioprio_class`, this also works with the Linux kernel CFQ scheduler:

`osd_disk_thread_ioprio_priority = 0`

OSD Journal settings

The Ceph OSD daemons support the following journal configurations:

- ▸ `osd journal size`: Ceph's default `osd journal size` value is 0; you should use the `osd_journal_size` parameter to set the journal size. The journal size should be at least twice the product of the expected drive speed and filestore max sync interval. If you are using SSD journals, it's usually good to create journals larger than 10 Gb and increase the filestore min/max sync interval:

  ```
  osd_journal_size = 20480
  ```

- ▸ `journal max write bytes`: The maximum number of bytes the journal can write at once:

  ```
  journal_max_write_bytes = 1073714824
  ```

- ▸ `journal max write entries`: The maximum number of entries the journal can write at once:

  ```
  journal_max_write_entries = 10000
  ```

- ▸ `journal queue max ops`: The maximum number of operations allowed in the journal queue at a given time:

  ```
  journal_queue_max_ops = 50000
  ```

- ▸ `journal queue max bytes`: The maximum number of bytes allowed in the journal queue at a given time:

  ```
  journal_queue_max_bytes = 10485760000
  ```

- ▸ `journal dio`: This enables direct i/o to the journal. It requires `journal block align` to be set to `true`:

  ```
  journal_dio = true
  ```

- ▸ `journal aio`: This enables using libaio for asynchronous writes to the journal. It requires `journal dio` to be set to `true`:

  ```
  journal_aio = true
  ```

- ▸ `journal block align`: This block aligns `write` operations. It's required for `dio` and `aio`.

OSD Filestore settings

These are a few filestore settings that can be configured for the Ceph OSD daemons:

- ▸ `filestore merge threshold`: This enables using libaio for asynchronous writes to the journal. It requires `journal dio` to be set to `true`:

  ```
  filestore_merge_threshold = 40
  ```

- ▸ `filestore split multiple`: The maximum number of files in a subdirectory before splitting into child directories:

  `filestore_split_multiple = 8`

- ▸ `filestore op threads`: The number of filesystem operation threads that execute in parallel:

  `filestore_op_threads = 32`

- ▸ `filestore xattr use omap`: Uses the object map for XATTRS (extended attributes). Needs to be set to `true` for the `ext4` file systems:

  `filestore_xattr_use_omap = true`

- ▸ `filestore sync interval`: In order to create a consistent commit point, the filestore needs to quiesce `write` operations and do a `syncfs()` operation, which syncs data from the journal to the data partition and thus frees the journal. A more frequently performed sync operation reduces the amount of data that is stored in a journal. In such cases, the journal becomes underutilized. Configuring less frequent syncs allows the filesystem to coalesce small writes better, and we might get improved performance. The following parameters define the minimum and maximum time period between two syncs:

  `filestore_min_sync_interval = 10`

  `filestore_max_sync_interval = 15`

- ▸ `filestore queue max ops`: The maximum number of operations that a filestore can accept before blocking new operations from joining the queue:

  `filestore_queue_max_ops = 2500`

- ▸ `filestore queue max bytes`: The maximum number of bytes in an operation:

  `filestore_queue_max_bytes = 10485760`

- ▸ `filestore queue committing max ops`: The maximum number of operations the filestore can commit:

  `filestore_queue_committing_max_ops = 5000`

- ▸ `filestore queue committing max bytes`: The maximum number of bytes the filestore can commit:

  `filestore_queue_committing_max_bytes = 10485760000`

OSD Recovery settings

These settings should be used when you want performance over recovery or vice versa. If your Ceph cluster is unhealthy and is under recovery, you might not get its usual performance, as OSDs will be busy with recovery. If you still prefer performance over recovery, you can reduce the recovery priority to keep OSDs less occupied with recovery. You can also set these values if you want a quick recovery for your cluster, helping OSDs to perform recovery faster.

- ▸ osd recovery max active: The number of active recovery requests per OSD at a given moment:

  osd_recovery_max_active = 1

- ▸ osd recovery max single start: This is used in conjunction with osd_recovery_max_active. To understand this, let's assume osd_recovery_max_single_start is equal to 1, and osd_recovery_max_active is equal to 3. In this case, it means that the OSD will start a maximum of one recovery operation at a time, out of a total of three operations active at that time:

  osd_recovery_max_single_start = 1

- ▸ osd recovery op priority: This is the priority set for the recovery operation. The lower the number, the higher the recovery priority:

  osd_recovery_op_priority = 50

- ▸ osd recovery max chunk: The maximum size of a recovered chunk of data in bytes:

  osd_recovery_max_chunk = 1048576

- ▸ osd recovery threads: The number of threads needed for recovering data:

  osd_recovery_threads = 1

OSD Backfilling settings

OSD backfilling settings allow Ceph to set backfilling operations at a lower priority than requests to read and write:

- ▸ osd max backfills: The maximum number of backfills allowed to or from a single OSD:

  osd_max_backfills = 2

- ▸ osd backfill scan min: The minimum number of objects per backfill scan:

  osd_backfill_scan_min = 8

- ▸ osd backfill scan max: The maximum number of objects per backfill scan:

  osd_backfill_scan_max = 64

OSD scrubbing settings

OSD Scrubbing is important for maintaining data integrity, but it can reduce performance. You can adjust the following settings to increase or decrease scrubbing operations:

- ▸ `osd max scrubs`: The maximum number of simultaneous scrub operations for a Ceph OSD daemon:

    `osd_max_scrubs = 1`

- ▸ `osd scrub sleep`: The time in seconds that scrubbing sleeps between two consecutive scrubs:

    `osd_scrub_sleep = .1`

- ▸ `osd scrub chunk min`: The minimum number of data chunks an OSD should perform scrubbing on:

    `osd_scrub_chunk_min = 1`

- ▸ `osd scrub chunk max`: The maximum number of data chunks an OSD should perform scrubbing on:

    `osd_scrub_chunk_max = 5`

- ▸ `osd deep scrub stride`: The `read` size in bytes while doing a deep scrub:

    `osd_deep_scrub_stride = 1048576`

- ▸ `osd scrub begin hour`: The earliest hour that scrubbing can begin. This is used in conjunction with `osd_scrub_end_hour` to define a scrubbing time window:

    `osd_scrub_begin_hour = 19`

- ▸ `osd scrub end hour`: This is the upper bound when the scrubbing can be performed. This works in conjunction with `osd_scrub_begin_hour` to define a scrubbing time window:

    `osd_scrub_end_hour = 7`

Client tuning

The client tuning parameters should be defined under the `[client]` section of your Ceph configuration file. Usually, this `[client]` section should also be present in the Ceph configuration file hosted on the client node:

- ▸ `rbd cache`: Enable caching for the **RADOS Block Device** (**RBD**):

    `rbd_cache = true`

- ▸ `rbd cache writethrough until flush`: Start out in the `write-through` mode, and switch to `writeback` after the first flush request is received:

    `rbd_cache_writethrough_until_flush = true`

- ► `rbd concurrent management ops`: The number of concurrent management operations that can be performed on `rbd`:

  `rbd_concurrent_management_ops = 10`

- ► `rbd cache size`: The `rbd` cache size in bytes:

  `rbd_cache_size = 67108864   #64M`

- ► `rbd cache max dirty`: The limit in bytes at which the cache should trigger a `writeback`. It should be less than `rbd_cache_size`:

  `rbd_cache_max_dirty = 50331648   #48M`

- ► `rbd cache target dirty`: The dirty target before the cache begins writing data to the backing store:

  `rbd_cache_target_dirty = 33554432   #32M`

- ► `rbd cache max dirty age`: The number of seconds that the dirty data is in the cache before `writeback` starts:

  `rbd_cache_max_dirty_age = 2`

- ► `rbd default format`: This uses the second `rbd` format, which is supported by librbd and the Linux kernel since version 3.11. This adds support for cloning and is more easily extensible, allowing more features in the future:

  `rbd_default_format = 2`

Operating System tuning

In the last recipe, we covered the tuning parameters for Ceph MON, OSD, and Clients. In this recipe, we will cover a few general tuning parameters, which can be applied to the Operating System.

- ► `kernel pid max`: This is a Linux kernel parameter that is responsible for the maximum number of threads and process IDs. By default, the Linux kernel has a relatively small `kernel.pid_max` value. You should configure this parameter with a higher value on Ceph nodes hosting several OSDs, typically, more than 20 OSDs. This setting helps spawn multiple threads for faster recovery and rebalancing. To use this parameter, execute the following command from the root user:

  `# echo 4194303 > /proc/sys/kernel/pid_max`

▶ `file max`: This is the maximum number of open files on a Linux system. It's generally a good idea to have a larger value for this parameter:

```
# echo 26234859 > /proc/sys/fs/file-max
```

▶ **Jumbo frames**: The Ethernet frames that are more than 1,500 bytes of payload MTU are known as jumbo frames. Enabling jumbo frames of all the network interfaces that Ceph is using for both the cluster and client network should improve the network throughput and overall network performance.

Jumbo frames should be enabled on the host as well as on the network switch side, otherwise, a mismatch in the MTU size would result in packet loss. To enable jumbo frames on the interface eth0, execute the following command:

```
# ifconfig eth0 mtu 9000
```

Similarly, you should do this for other interfaces that are participating in the Ceph networks. To make this change permanent, you should add this configuration in the interface configuration file.

▶ `Disk read_ahead`: The `read_ahead` parameter speeds up the disk `read` operation by prefetching data and loading it in random access memory. Setting up a relatively higher value for `read_ahead` will benefit clients performing sequential `read` operations.

Let's assume that disk `vda` is an RBD that is mounted on a client node. Use the following command to check its `read_ahead` value, which is default in most of the cases:

```
# cat /sys/block/vda/queue/read_ahead_kb
```

To set `read_ahead` to a higher value, that is, 8 MB for `vda` RBD, execute the following command:

```
# echo "8192" > /sys/block/vda/queue/read_ahead_kb
```

The `read_ahead` settings are used on Ceph clients that use the mounts RBD. To get a `read` performance boost, you can set it to several MB, depending on your hardware and on all your RBD devices.

▶ **Virtual memory**: Due to the heavily I/O-focused profile, swap usage can result in the entire server becoming unresponsive. A low `swappiness` value is recommended for high IO workload. Set `vm.swappiness` to zero in `/etc/sysctl.conf` to prevent this:

```
echo "vm.swappiness=0" >> /etc/sysctl.conf
```

▶ `min_free_kbytes`: This gives the minimum number of kilobytes to keep free across the system. You can keep 1 to 3% of the total system memory free with `min_free_kbytes` by running the following command:

```
# echo 262144 > /proc/sys/vm/min_free_kbytes
```

▸ `I/O Scheduler`: Linux gives us the option to select the I/O scheduler, and this can be changed without rebooting too. It provides three options for I/O schedulers, which are mentioned as follows:

▸ **Deadline**: The deadline IO scheduler replaces CFQ as the default I/O scheduler in Red Hat Enterprise Linux 7 and its derivatives, as well as in Ubuntu Trusty. The Deadline scheduler favors reads over writes via the use of separate IO queues for each. This scheduler is suitable for most use cases, but particularly for those in which `read` operations occur more often than `write` operations. Queued I/O requests are sorted into a `read` or `write` batch and then scheduled for execution in increasing LBA order. The `read` batches take precedence over the `write` batches by default, as applications are more likely to block on `read` I/O. For Ceph OSD workloads deadline, the I/O scheduler looks promising.

▸ **CFQ**: The Completely Fair Queuing (CFQ) scheduler was the default scheduler in Red Hat Enterprise Linux (4, 5, and 6) and its derivatives. The default scheduler is only for devices identified as SATA disks. The CFQ scheduler divides processes into three separate classes: real time, best effort, and idle. Processes in the real time class are always performed before processes in the best effort class, which are always performed before processes in the idle class. This means that processes in the real time class can starve both the best effort and idle processes of processor time. Processes are assigned to the best effort class by default.

▸ **Noop**: The Noop I/O scheduler implements a simple FIFO (first-in first-out) scheduling algorithm. Requests are merged at the generic block layer through a simple last-hit cache. This can be the best scheduler for CPU-bound systems using fast storage. For an SSD, the NOOP I/O scheduler can reduce I/O latency and increase throughput as well as eliminate the CPU time spent re-ordering I/O requests. This scheduler typically works well with SSDs, Virtual Machines, and even with NVMe cards. Thus, the Noop IO scheduler should be a good choice for SSD disks used for Ceph journals.

Execute the following command to check the default I/O scheduler for the disk device `sda`. The default scheduler should appear inside `[]`:

```
# cat /sys/block/sda/queue/scheduler
```

Change the default I/O scheduler for disk sda to deadline:

```
# echo deadline > /sys/block/sda/queue/scheduler
```

Change the default I/O scheduler for disk sda to noop:

```
# echo noop > /sys/block/sda/queue/scheduler
```

 You must repeat these commands to change the default schedulers to either deadline or `noop`, based on your requirements for all the disks. Also, to make this change permanent, you need to update the grub boot loader with the required elevator option.

▸ I/O Scheduler queue: The default I/O scheduler queue size is 128. The scheduler queue sorts and writes in an attempt to optimize for sequential I/O and reduce the seek time. Changing the depth of the scheduler queue to 1024 can increase the proportion of sequential I/O that disks perform and improve the overall throughput.

To check the scheduler depth for block device sda, use the following command:

```
# cat /sys/block/sda/queue/nr_requests
```

To increase the scheduler depth to 1024, use the following command:

```
# echo 1024 > /sys/block/sda/queue/nr_requests
```

Ceph erasure coding

The default data protection mechanism in Ceph is replication. It's proven and is one of the most popular methods of data protection. However, the downside of replication is that it requires double the amount of storage space to provide redundancy. For instance, if you were planning to build a storage solution with 1 PB of usable capacity with a replication factor of three, you would require 3 PB of raw storage capacity for 1 PB of usable capacity, that is, 200% or more. In this way, with the replication mechanism, cost per gigabyte of storage system increases significantly. For a small cluster, you might ignore the replication overhead, but for large environments, it becomes significant.

Since the Firefly release of Ceph, it has introduced another method for data protection known as erasure coding. This method of data protection is absolutely different from the replication method. It guarantees data protection by dividing each object into smaller chunks known as data chunks, encoding them with coding chunks, and finally storing all these chunks across the different failure zones of a Ceph cluster. The concept of erasure coding revolves around the equation $n = k + m$. This is explained next:

▸ *k*: This is the number of chunks the original object is divided into; it is also known as data chunks.

▸ *m*: This is the extra code added to the original data chunks to provide data protection; it is also known as coding chunks. For ease of understanding, you can consider it as the reliability level.

▸ *n*: This is the total number of chunks created after the erasure coding process.

Based on the preceding equation, every object in an erasure-coded Ceph pool will be stored as `k+m` chunks, and each chunk is stored in a unique OSD with an acting set. In this way, all the chunks of an object are spread across the entire Ceph cluster, providing a higher degree of reliability. Now, let's discuss some useful terms with respect to erasure coding:

- **Recovery**: At the time of recovery, we will require any k chunks out of n chunks to recover the data
- **Reliability level**: With erasure coding, Ceph can tolerate failure up to m chunks
- **Encoding Rate (r)**: This can be calculated using the formula, $r = k / n$, where r is less than 1
- **Storage required**: This is calculated using the formula $1/r$

To understand these terms better, let's consider an example. A Ceph pool is created with five OSDs based on *erasure code (3, 2)* rule. Every object that is stored inside this pool will be divided into sets of data and coding chunks as given by this formula: $n = k + m$.

Consider $5 = 3 + 2$, then $n = 5$, $k = 3$ and $m = 2$. So, every object will be divided into three data chunks, and two extra erasure coded chunks will be added to it, making a total of five chunks that will be stored and distributed on five OSDs of an erasure-coded pool in a Ceph cluster. In an event of failure, to construct the original file, we need (k chunks), three chunks out of (n chunks), and five chunks to recover it. Thus, we can sustain the failure of any (m) two OSDs as the data can be recovered using three OSDs.

- **Encoding rate (r)** = $3 / 5 = 0.6 < 1$
- **Storage required** = $1/r = 1 / 0.6 = 1.6$ times of original file.

Let's suppose that there is a data file of size 1 GB. To store this file in a Ceph cluster on an erasure coded (3, 5) pool, you will need 1.6 GB of storage space, which will provide to you file storage with the sustainability of two OSD failures.

In contrast to the replication method, if the same file is stored on a replicated pool, then in order to sustain the failure of two OSDs, Ceph will need a pool of the replica size 3, which eventually requires 3 GB of storage space to reliably store 1 GB of the file. In this way, you can reduce storage costs by approximately 40 percent by using the erasure coding feature of Ceph and getting the same reliability as with replication:

Erasure-coded pools require less storage space compared to replicated pools, however, this storage saving comes at the cost of performance because the erasure coding process divides every object into multiple smaller data chunks, and few newer coding chunks are mixed with these data chunks. Finally, all these chunks are stored across the different failure zones of a Ceph cluster. This entire mechanism requires a bit more computational power from the OSD nodes. Moreover, at the time of recovery, decoding the data chunks also requires a lot of computing. So, you might find the erasure coding mechanism of storing data somewhat slower than the replication mechanism. Erasure coding is mainly use-case dependent, and you can get the most out of erasure coding based on your data storage requirements.

Erasure code plugin

Ceph gives us options to choose the erasure code plugin while creating the erasure code profile. One can create multiple erasure code profiles, with different plugins each time. Ceph supports the following plugins for erasure coding:

- **Jerasure erasure code plugin**: The Jerasure plugin is the most generic and flexible plugin. It is also the default for Ceph erasure coded pools. The Jerasure plugin encapsulates the Jerasure library. Jerasure uses the Reed Solomon Code technique. The following diagram illustrates Jerasure code (3, 2). As explained, data is first divided into three data chunks, and an additional two coded chunks are added, and they finally get stored in the unique failure zone of the Ceph cluster:

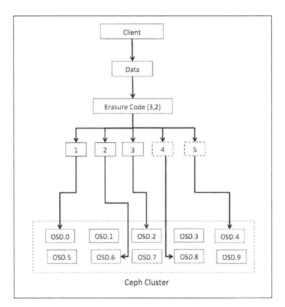

With the Jerasure plugin, when an erasure-coded object is stored on multiple OSDs, recovering from the loss of one OSD requires reading from all the others. For instance, if Jerasure is configured with $k=3$ and $m=2$, losing one OSD requires reading from all the five OSDs to repair, which is not very efficient during recovery.

- **Locally repairable erasure code plugin**: Since Jerasure erasure code (*Reed Solomon*) was not recovery efficient, it was improved by the local parity method, and the new method is known as **Locally Repairable erasure Code** (**LRC**). The Locally Repairable erasure code plugin creates local parity chunks that are able to recover using less OSD, which makes it recovery-efficient.

To understand this better, let's assume that LRC is configured with $k=8$, $m=4$, and $l=4$ (locality), it will create an additional parity chunk for every four OSDs. When a single OSD is lost, it can be recovered with only four OSDs instead of eleven, which is the case with Jerasure.

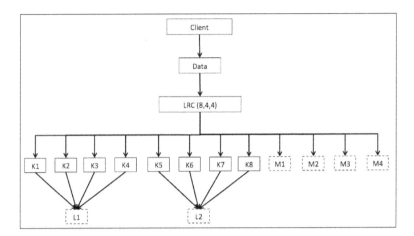

Locally Repairable Codes are designed to lower the bandwidth when recovering from the loss of a single OSD. As illustrated previously, a local parity chunk (L) is generated for every four data chunks (K). When K3 is lost, instead of recovering from all [(K+M)-K3] chunks, that is, 11 chunks, with Locally Repairable Code, it's enough to recover from the K1, K2, K4, and L1 chunks.

▸ **Shingled erasure code plugin**: The locally repairable codes are optimized for single OSD failure. For multiple OSD failure, the recovery overhead is large with LRC because it has to use global parity (M) for recovery. Let's reconsider the previous scenario and assume that multiple data chunks, K3 and K4, are lost. To recover the lost chunks using LRC, it needs to recover from K1, K2, L1 (the local parity chunk), and M1 (the global parity chunk). Thus, LRC involves overhead with multi disk failure.

To address this problem, **SHEC (Shingled Erasure Code)** has been introduced. The SHEC plugin encapsulates multiple SHEC libraries and allows Ceph to recover data more efficiently than Jerasure and Locally Repairable Codes. The goal of the SHEC method is to efficiently handle multiple disk failure. Under this method, the calculation range for local parities has been shifted, and parity the overlap with each other (like shingles on a roof) to keep enough durability.

Let's understand this by example, *SHEC (10,6,5)* where *K*=10 (data chunks), *m*=6 (parity chunks), *l*=5 (calculation range). In this case, the diagrammatic representation of SHEC looks as follows:

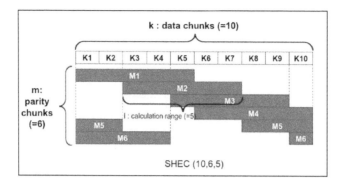

Recovery efficiency is one of the biggest features of SHEC. It minimizes the amount of data read from the disk during recovery. If chunks K6 and K9 are lost, SHEC will use the M3 and M4 parity chunks, and the K5, K7, K8, and K10 data chunks for recovery. The same has been illustrated in the following diagram:

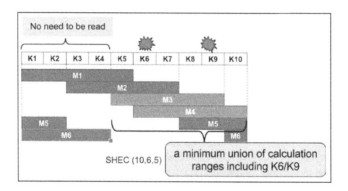

For multi disk failure, SHEC is expected to recover more efficiently than other methods. SHEC's recovery time was 18.6% faster than the Solomon code in case of a double disk failure.

ISA-I erasure code plugin: The **Intelligent Storage Acceleration (ISA)** plugin encapsulates the ISA library. ISA-I was optimized for Intel platforms using some platform-specific instructions, and thus runs only on Intel architecture. ISA can be used in either of the two forms of Reed Solomon, that is, Vandermonde or Cauchy.

Creating an erasure coded pool

Erasure code is implemented by creating a Ceph pool of the type erasure. This pool is based on an erasure code profile that defines erasure-coding characteristics. We will first create an erasure code profile, and then we will create an erasure-coded pool based on this profile.

How to do it...

1. The command mentioned in this recipe will create an erasure code profile with the name EC-profile, which will have characteristics of $k=3$ and $m=2$, which are the numbers of data and coding chunks respectively. So, every object that is stored in the erasure-coded pool will be divided into 3 (k) data chunks, and 2 (m) additional coding chunks are added to them, making a total of 5 ($k + m$) chunks. Finally, these 5 ($k + m$) chunks are spread across different OSD failure zones.

   ❏ Create the erasure code profile:

   ```
   # ceph osd erasure-code-profile set EC-profile
   rulesetfailure-domain=osd k=3 m=2
   ```

   ❏ List the profile:

   ```
   # ceph osd erasure-code-profile ls
   ```

   ❏ Get the contents of your erasure code profile:

   ```
   # ceph osd erasure-code-profile get EC-profile
   ```

```
[root@ceph-node1 ~]# ceph osd erasure-code-profile set EC-profile rulesetfailure-domain=osd k=3 m=2
[root@ceph-node1 ~]# ceph osd erasure-code-profile ls
EC-profile
default
[root@ceph-node1 ~]# ceph osd erasure-code-profile get EC-profile
directory=/usr/lib64/ceph/erasure-code
k=3
m=2
plugin=jerasure
rulesetfailure-domain=osd
technique=reed_sol_van
[root@ceph-node1 ~]# 
```

2. Create a Ceph pool of the erasure type, which is based on the erasure code profile that we created in Step 1:

   ```
   # ceph osd pool create EC-pool 16 16 erasure EC-profile
   ```

Check the status of your newly created pool; you should find that the size of the pool is 5 (k + m), that is, the erasure size 5. Hence, data will be written to five different OSDs:

```
# ceph osd dump | grep -i EC-pool
```

```
[root@ceph-node1 ~]# ceph osd pool create EC-pool 16 16 erasure EC-profile
pool 'EC-pool' created
[root@ceph-node1 ~]# ceph osd dump | grep -i EC-pool
pool 47 'EC-pool' erasure size 5 min_size 3 crush_ruleset 3 object_hash rjenkins pg_num 16 pgp_num 16
last_change 4504 flags hashpspool stripe_width 4128
[root@ceph-node1 ~]#
```

3. Let's now add some data to this newly created Ceph pool. To do this, we will create a dummy file, `hello.txt`, and add this file to the `EC-pool`.

```
[root@ceph-node1 ~]# echo "Hello Ceph" >> hello.txt
[root@ceph-node1 ~]# cat hello.txt
Hello Ceph
[root@ceph-node1 ~]# rados -p EC-pool ls
[root@ceph-node1 ~]# rados -p EC-pool put object1 hello.txt
[root@ceph-node1 ~]# rados -p EC-pool ls
object1
[root@ceph-node1 ~]#
```

4. To verify if the erasure coded pool is working correctly, we will check the OSD map for the `EC-pool` and `object1`.

```
[root@ceph-node1 ~]# ceph osd map EC-pool object1
osdmap e4601 pool 'EC-pool' (47) object 'object1' -> pg 47.bac5debc (47.c) -> up ([5,3,2,8,0], p5) acting ([5,3,2,8,0], p5)
[root@ceph-node1 ~]#
```

If you observe the above output, you will notice that `object1` is stored in the placement group `47.c`, which in turn is stored in the `EC-pool`. You will also notice that the placement group is stored on five OSDs, that is, `osd.5`, `osd.3`, `osd.2`, `osd.8`, and `osd.0`. If you go back to Step 1, you will recall that we created the erasure-coded profile of *(3,2)*. This is why `object1` is stored on five OSDs.

At this stage, we have completed the setting up of an erasure pool in a Ceph cluster. Now, we will deliberately try to break OSDs to see how the erasure pool behaves when OSDs are unavailable.

5. We will now try to bring down `OSD.5` and `OSD.3`, one by one.

 These are optional steps and you should not be performing this on your production Ceph cluster. Also, the OSD numbers might change for your cluster; replace them wherever necessary.

Bring down `osd.5` and check the OSD map for `EC-pool` and `object1`. You should notice that `osd.5` is replaced by a random number, `2147483647`, which means that `osd.5` is no longer available for this pool:

```
# ssh ceph-node2 service ceph stop osd.5
# ceph osd map EC-pool object1
```

```
[root@ceph-node1 ~]# ssh ceph-node2 service ceph stop osd.5
=== osd.5 ===
Stopping Ceph osd.5 on ceph-node2...kill 23469...kill 23469...done
[root@ceph-node1 ~]# ceph osd map EC-pool object1
osdmap e4603 pool 'EC-pool' (47) object 'object1' -> pg 47.bac5debc (47.c) -> up ([2147483647,3,2,8,0], p3) acting ([2147483647,3,2,8,0], p3)
[root@ceph-node1 ~]#
```

6. Similarly, break one more OSD, that is, `osd.3`, and notice the OSD map for the `EC-pool` and `object1`. You will notice that, like `osd.5`, `osd.3` also gets replaced by the random number, `2147483647`, which means that `osd.3` is also no longer available for this `EC-pool`:

```
# ssh ceph-node2 service ceph stop osd.3
# ceph osd map EC-pool object1
```

```
[root@ceph-node1 ~]# ssh ceph-node2 service ceph stop osd.3
=== osd.3 ===
Stopping Ceph osd.3 on ceph-node2...kill 22954...kill 22954...done
[root@ceph-node1 ~]# ceph osd map EC-pool object1
osdmap e4605 pool 'EC-pool' (47) object 'object1' -> pg 47.bac5debc (47.c) -> up ([2147483647,2147483647,2,8,0], p2) acting ([2147483647,214748
3647,2,8,0], p2)
[root@ceph-node1 ~]#
```

7. Now, the `EC-pool` is running on three OSDs, which is the minimum requirement for this setup of erasure pool. As discussed earlier, the `EC-pool` will require any three chunks out of five in order to read the data. Now, we have only three chunks left, which are on `osd.2`, `osd.8`, and `osd.0`, and we can still access the data. Let's verify the data reading:

```
# rados -p EC-pool ls
# rados -p EC-pool get object1 /tmp/object1
# cat /tmp/object1
```

```
[root@ceph-node1 ~]# rados -p EC-pool ls
object1
[root@ceph-node1 ~]# rados -p EC-pool get object1 /tmp/object1
[root@ceph-node1 ~]# cat /tmp/object1
Hello Ceph
[root@ceph-node1 ~]#
```

The Erasure code feature is greatly benefited by Ceph's robust architecture. When Ceph detects the unavailability of any failure zone, it starts its basic operation of recovery. During the recovery operation, erasure pools rebuild themselves by decoding failed chunks on to new OSDs, and after that, they make all the chunks available automatically.

8. In the last two steps mentioned, we intentionally broke `osd.5` and `osd.3`. After a while, Ceph will start recovery and will regenerate missing chunks onto different OSDs. Once the recovery operation is complete, you should check the OSD map for the `EC-pool` and `object1`. You will be amazed to see the new OSD IDs as `osd.7` and `osd.4`. And thus, an erasure pool becomes healthy without administrative input.

```
[root@ceph-node1 ~]# ceph osd stat
    osdmap e4645: 9 osds: 7 up, 7 in; 336 remapped pgs
[root@ceph-node1 ~]# ceph osd map EC-pool object1
osdmap e4645 pool 'EC-pool' (47) object 'object1' -> pg 47.bac5debc (47.c) -> up ([7,4,2,8,0], p7) acting ([7,4,2,8,0], p7)
[root@ceph-node1 ~]# 
```

Ceph cache tiering

Like erasure coding, the cache tiering feature has also been introduced in the Ceph Firefly release. A cache tier provides Ceph Clients with better I/O performance for a subset of the data stored in a cache tier. A cache tiering creates a Ceph pool on top of faster disks, typically SSDs. This cache pool should be placed in front of a regular, replicated or erasure pool such that all the client I/O operations are handled by the cache pool first; later, the data is flushed to existing data pools. The clients enjoy high performance out of the cache pool, while their data is written to regular pools transparently. The following diagram illustrates the Ceph cache tiering:

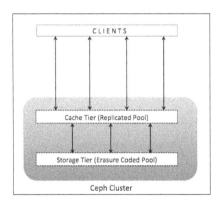

A cache tier is constructed on top of expensive, faster SSD/NVMe, thus it provides clients with better I/O performance. The cache tier is backed up by a storage tier, which is made up of HDDs with the type replicated or erasure. The entire client I/O request goes to the cache tier and gets a faster response, whether it's `read` or `write`; the faster cache tier serves the client request. Based on the policy that we have created for cache tier, it flushes all its data to the backing storage tier so that it can cache new requests from clients. All the data migration between the cache and storage tiers happens automatically and is transparent to clients. The cache tiering agent handles the migration of data between the cache tier and the storage tier. Administrators have the ability to configure how this migration takes place. There are two main scenarios.

Writeback mode

When the Ceph cache tiering is configured as a `writeback` mode, a Ceph client writes the data to the cache tier pool, that is, to the faster pool, and hence receives acknowledgement instantly. Based on the flushing/evicting policy that you have set for your cache tier, data is migrated from the cache tier to the storage tier, and eventually removed from the cache tier by a cache-tiering agent. During a `read` operation by the client, data is first transferred from the storage tier to the cache tier by the cache-tiering agent, and it is then served to clients. The data remains in the cache tier until it becomes inactive or cold. The cache tier with the `writeback` mode is ideal for mutable data such as photo or video editing, transactional data, and so on. The `writeback` mode is ideal for mutable data.

Read-only mode

When the Ceph cache tiering is configured as a `read-only` mode, it works only for the client's `read` operations. The `write` operations are not handled in this mode and they are stored in the storage tier. When any client performs `read` operations, the cache-tiering agent copies the requested data from the storage tier to the cache tier. Based on the policy that you have configured for the cache tier, stale objects are removed from the cache tier. This approach is ideal when multiple clients need to read large amounts of similar data, for example, social media content. Immutable data is a good candidate for the read-only cache tier.

Creating a pool for cache tiering

To get the best out of the cache tiering feature of Ceph, you should use faster disks such as SSDs and make a fast cache pool on top of slower/regular pools made up of HDDs. In *Chapter 8, Production Planning and Performance Tuning for Ceph*, we covered the process of creating Ceph pools on specific OSDs by modifying the CRUSH map. To set up the cache tier in your environment, you need to first modify your crush map and create a ruleset for the SSD disk. Since we have already covered this in *Chapter 8, Production Planning and Performance Tuning for Ceph* we will use the same ruleset for SSD, which is based on `osd.0`, `osd.3`, and `osd.6`. As this is a test setup, and we do not have real SSDs, we will assume the OSDs 0, 3, and 6 are SSDs and will create a cache pool on top of it, as illustrated in this diagram:

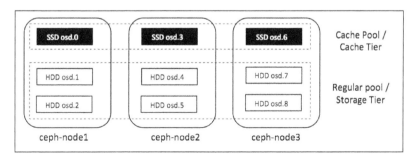

Let's check the CRUSH layout using the command, `ceph osd crush rule ls`, as shown in the following screenshot. We already have the ssd-pool CRUSH rule that we created in *Chapter 7, Ceph under the Hood*. You can get more information on this CRUSH rule by running the `ceph osd crush rule dump ssd-pool` command:

```
[root@ceph-node1 ~]# ceph osd crush rule ls
[
    "replicated_ruleset",
    "ssd-pool",
    "sata-pool",
    "EC-pool"
]

[root@ceph-node1 ~]#
```

How to do it...

1. Create a new pool with the name `cache-pool` and set `crush_ruleset` as 1 so that the new pool gets created on SSD disks:

   ```
   # ceph osd pool create cache-pool 16 16
   ```

   ```
   # ceph osd pool set cache-pool crush_ruleset 1
   ```

   ```
   [root@ceph-node1 ~]# ceph osd pool create cache-pool 16 16
   pool 'cache-pool' created
   [root@ceph-node1 ~]# ceph osd pool set cache-pool crush_ruleset 1
   set pool 48 crush_ruleset to 1
   [root@ceph-node1 ~]#
   ```

2. Make sure that your pool is created correctly, which means that it should always store all the objects on `osd.0`, `osd.3`, and `osd.6`:

   - List the `cache-pool` for contents; since it's a new pool, it should not have any content:

     ```
     # rados -p cache-pool ls
     ```

   - Add a temporary object to the `cache-pool` to make sure it's storing the object on the correct OSDs:

     ```
     # rados -p cache-pool put object1 /etc/hosts
     ```

     ```
     # rados -p cache-pool ls
     ```

   - Verify the OSD map for the `cache-pool` and `object1`; it should get stored on `osd.0`, `osd.3`, and `osd.6`:

     ```
     # ceph osd map cache-pool object1
     ```

❑ Finally, remove the object:

```
# rados -p cache-pool rm object1
```

```
[root@ceph-node1 ~]# rados -p cache-pool ls
[root@ceph-node1 ~]# rados -p cache-pool put object1 /etc/hosts
[root@ceph-node1 ~]# rados -p cache-pool ls
object1
[root@ceph-node1 ~]# ceph osd map cache-pool object1
osdmap e4767 pool 'cache-pool' (48) object 'object1' -> pg 48.bac5debc (48.c) -> up ([3,6,0], p3) acting ([3,6,0], p3)
[root@ceph-node1 ~]# rados -p cache-pool rm object1
[root@ceph-node1 ~]# rados -p cache-pool ls
[root@ceph-node1 ~]#
```

See also...

▶ Refer to the *Creating a cache tier* recipe in this chapter

Creating a cache tier

In the last recipe, we created a pool, `cache-pool`, based on SSDs. We will now use this pool as a cache tier for the erasure-coded pool, `EC-pool`, that we created earlier in this chapter:

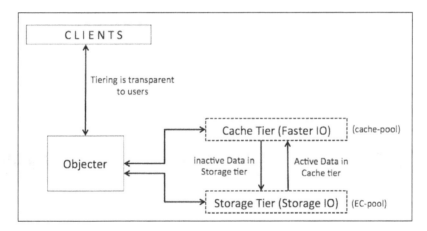

The following instructions will guide you through the creation of a cache tier with the `writeback` mode and setting the overlay with an `EC-pool`:

How to do it...

1. Create a cache tier that will associate storage-pools with cache-pools. The syntax is:
   `ceph osd tier add <storage_pool> <cache_pool>`:

   ```
   # ceph osd tier add EC-pool cache-pool
   ```

2. Set the cache mode as either `writeback` or `read-only`. In this demonstration, we will use `writeback`, and the syntax is: `ceph osd tier cachemode <cache_pool> writeback`:

```
# ceph osd tier cache-mode cache-pool writeback
```

3. To direct all the client requests from the standard pool to the cache pool, set the pool overlay using the syntax: `ceph osd tier set-overlay <storage_pool> <cache_pool>`:

```
# ceph osd tier set-overlay EC-pool cache-pool
```

```
[root@ceph-node1 ~]# ceph osd tier add EC-pool cache-pool
pool 'cache-pool' is now (or already was) a tier of 'EC-pool'
[root@ceph-node1 ~]# ceph osd tier cache-mode cache-pool writeback
set cache-mode for pool 'cache-pool' to writeback
[root@ceph-node1 ~]# ceph osd tier set-overlay EC-pool cache-pool
overlay for 'EC-pool' is now (or already was) 'cache-pool'
[root@ceph-node1 ~]#
```

4. On checking the pool details, you will notice that the `EC-pool` has `tier`, `read_tier`, and `write_tier` set as `48`, which is the pool ID for the `cache-pool`. Similarly, for `cache-pool`, the settings will be: `tier_of` set to `47` and `cache_mode` as `writeback`. All these settings imply that the cache pool is configured correctly:

```
# ceph osd dump | egrep -i "EC-pool|cache-pool"
```

```
[root@ceph-node1 ~]# ceph osd dump | egrep -i "EC-pool|cache-pool"
pool 47 'EC-pool' erasure size 5 min_size 3 crush_ruleset 3 object_hash rjenkins pg_num 16 pgp_num 16 last_change 4770
1for 4770 flags hashpspool tiers 48 read_tier 48 write_tier 48 stripe_width 4128
pool 48 'cache-pool' replicated size 3 min_size 2 crush_ruleset 1 object_hash rjenkins pg_num 16 pgp_num 16 last_change
 4770 flags hashpspool,incomplete_clones tier_of 47 cache_mode writeback stripe_width 0
[root@ceph-node1 ~]#
```

Configuring a cache tier

A cache tier has several configuration options that define the cache tier policy. This cache tier policy is required to flush data from the cache tier to the storage tier in case of a `writeback`. In the case of the read-only cache tier, it moves the data from the storage tier to the cache tier. In this recipe, I have tried to demonstrate the cache tier with the `writeback` mode. These are some settings that you should configure for your production environment, with different values based on your requirements:

How to do it...

1. For production deployment, you should use the 'bloom filters' data structure:

```
# ceph osd pool set cache-pool hit_set_type bloom
```

2. `hit_set_count` defines how much time in seconds each hit set should cover, and `hit_set_period` defines how many such hit sets are to be persisted:

```
# ceph osd pool set cache-pool hit_set_count 1
```

```
# ceph osd pool set cache-pool hit_set_period 300
```

3. `target_max_bytes` is the maximum number of bytes after the cache-tiering agent starts flushing/evicting objects from a cache pool. Whereas `target_max_objects` is the maximum number of objects after which a cache-tiering agent starts flushing/evicting objects from a cache pool:

```
# ceph osd pool set cache-pool target_max_bytes 1000000
```

```
# ceph osd pool set cache-pool target_max_objects 10000
```

```
[root@ceph-node1 ~]# ceph osd pool set cache-pool hit_set_type bloom
set pool 48 hit_set_type to bloom
[root@ceph-node1 ~]# ceph osd pool set cache-pool hit_set_count 1
set pool 48 hit_set_count to 1
[root@ceph-node1 ~]# ceph osd pool set cache-pool hit_set_period 300
set pool 48 hit_set_period to 300
[root@ceph-node1 ~]# ceph osd pool set cache-pool target_max_bytes 1000000
set pool 48 target_max_bytes to 1000000
[root@ceph-node1 ~]#
```

4. Enable `cache_min_flush_age` and `cache_min_evict_age`, which are the times in seconds that a cache-tiering agent takes to flush and evict objects from a cache tier to a storage tier:

```
# ceph osd pool set cache-pool cache_min_flush_age 300
```

```
# ceph osd pool set cache-pool cache_min_evict_age 300
```

```
[root@ceph-node1 ~]# ceph osd pool set cache-pool target_max_objects 10000
set pool 48 target_max_objects to 10000
[root@ceph-node1 ~]# ceph osd pool set cache-pool cache_min_flush_age 300
set pool 48 cache_min_flush_age to 300
[root@ceph-node1 ~]# ceph osd pool set cache-pool cache_min_evict_age 300
set pool 48 cache_min_evict_age to 300
[root@ceph-node1 ~]#
```

5. Enable `cache_target_dirty_ratio`, which is the percentage of the cache pool containing dirty (modified) objects before the cache-tiering agent flushes them to the storage tier:

```
# ceph osd pool set cache-pool cache_target_dirty_ratio .01
```

6. Enable `cache_target_full_ratio`, which is the percentage of the cache pool containing unmodified objects before the cache-tiering agent flushes them to the storage tier:

```
# ceph osd pool set cache-pool cache_target_full_ratio .02
```

Once you have completed these steps, the Ceph cache tiering setup should complete, and you can start adding workload to it:

7. Create a temporary file of 500 MB that we will use to write to the `EC-pool`, and which will eventually be written to a `cache-pool`:

```
# dd if=/dev/zero of=/tmp/file1 bs=1M count=500
```

```
[root@ceph-node1 ~]# ceph osd pool set cache-pool cache_target_dirty_ratio .01
set pool 48 cache_target_dirty_ratio to .01
[root@ceph-node1 ~]# ceph osd pool set cache-pool cache_target_full_ratio .02
set pool 48 cache_target_full_ratio to .02
[root@ceph-node1 ~]# dd if=/dev/zero of=/tmp/file1 bs=1M count=500
500+0 records in
500+0 records out
524288000 bytes (524 MB) copied, 5.81312 s, 90.2 MB/s
[root@ceph-node1 ~]#
```

Testing a cache tier

Since our cache tier is ready, during the `write` operation, clients will see what is being written to their regular pools, but actually, it's being written on cache-pools first and then based on the cache tier policy data, it will be flushed to the storage tier. This data migration is transparent to the client.

How to do it...

1. In the previous recipe, we created a 500 MB test file named `/tmp/file1`; we will now put this file in an `EC-pool`:

```
# rados -p EC-pool put object1 /tmp/file1
```

2. Since an `EC-pool` is tiered with a `cache-pool` named `file1` should not get written to the `EC-pool` in the first step, however, it will get written to the `cache-pool`. To verify this, list each pool to get the object names. Use the date command to track the time and changes:

```
# rados -p EC-pool ls
```

```
# rados -p cache-pool ls
```

```
# date
```

```
[root@ceph-node1 ~]# rados -p EC-pool put object1 /tmp/file1
[root@ceph-node1 ~]# rados -p EC-pool ls
[root@ceph-node1 ~]# rados -p cache-pool ls
object1
[root@ceph-node1 ~]#
[root@ceph-node1 ~]# date
Sun Sep 14 02:14:58 EEST 2014
[root@ceph-node1 ~]#
```

3. After 300 seconds (as we have configured `cache_min_evict_age` to `300` seconds), the cache-tiering agent will migrate `object1` from the `cache-pool` to the `EC-pool`, and `object1` will be removed from the `cache-pool`:

```
# rados -p EC-pool ls
```

```
# rados -p cache-pool ls
```

```
# date
```

```
[root@ceph-node1 ~]# date
Sun Sep 14 02:27:41 EEST 2014
[root@ceph-node1 ~]# rados -p EC-pool ls
object1
[root@ceph-node1 ~]# rados -p cache-pool ls
[root@ceph-node1 ~]#
```

If you take a closer look at Step 2 and 3, you will notice that data has migrated from the `cache-pool` to the `EC-pool` after a certain amount of time, which is totally transparent to the users.

9

The Virtual Storage Manager for Ceph

In this chapter, we will cover the following recipes:

- ▶ Understanding the VSM architecture
- ▶ Setting up the VSM environment
- ▶ Getting ready for VSM
- ▶ Installing VSM
- ▶ Creating a Ceph cluster using VSM
- ▶ Exploring the VSM dashboard
- ▶ Upgrading the Ceph cluster using VSM
- ▶ VSM roadmap
- ▶ VSM resources

Introduction

The **Virtual Storage Manager** (**VSM**) is a software originally initiated and developed by Intel for Ceph cluster management; it was later open sourced by Intel under the Apache 2.0 License. Ceph comes with the `ceph-deploy` CLI tool for cluster deployment, and it also provides a rich CLI for cluster management. VSM on the other hand provides a web-based user interface to simplify the creation and management of Ceph clusters. By using the VSM GUI Ceph cluster, the operator can monitor overall cluster health, manage cluster hardware and storage capacity, as well as attach the Ceph storage pools to the OpenStack cinder.

VSM is developed in Python using OpenStack Horizon as its base for the application framework. It has the familiar look and feel of OpenStack Horizon for both software developers and OpenStack administrators. Some of the key features of VSM include the following:

- ▶ A Web-based user interface for the easy administration of the Ceph cluster
- ▶ It better organizes and manages the server and storage devices
- ▶ It aids the Ceph cluster's deployment and scale up by adding the MON, OSD, and MDS nodes
- ▶ It aids the Ceph cluster component and capacity monitoring
- ▶ It is beneficial to the overall cluster and individual node performance monitoring
- ▶ It allows the creation of erasure coded and cache tier pools
- ▶ It assists in creating and attaching pools to the OpenStack cinder
- ▶ It brings the multi user management interface to Ceph cluster
- ▶ It allows for the upgrading of the Ceph cluster

 Currently, VSM is not able to manage the Ceph cluster, which is not created by it.

Understanding the VSM architecture

In this recipe, we will quickly go through the architecture of the Virtual Storage Manager, which consists of the following components:

The VSM Controller

VSM is a web-based application that is typically hosted on a controller machine, which is referred to as a VSM Controller node. You can use a dedicated physical or virtual server that can act as a VSM controller node. The VSM controller software is the core component of VSM that connects to the Ceph cluster through VSM agents. The VSM controller gathers all the data coming from VSM agents and monitors the Ceph cluster. For operations such as cluster creation, pool creation, and so on, the VSM controller sends instructions to VSM Agents to perform the required operation. As shown in the following diagram, Ceph administrators/ operators connect to the VSM controller node via HTTPs or APIs, and they can use VSM software. The VSM controller node also connects to the OpenStack controller to configure OpenStack to use Ceph. In addition to the web user interface service, the VSM controller also hosts MariaDB and RabbitMQ.

The VSM Agent

The VSM agent is a process that runs on all Ceph cluster nodes. The job of the VSM Agent is to send server configuration, cluster health/status information, as well as performance data to the VSM Controller. The VSM agent uses the server manifest file to identify the VSM controller node, authenticate against it, and determine server configuration.

The following diagram illustrates the interaction of different VSM components with each other as well as with OpenStack infrastructure and VSM operators:

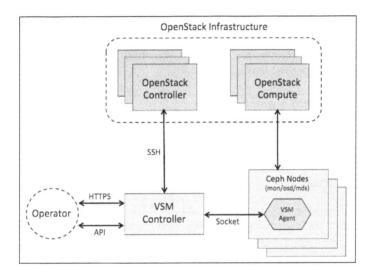

Setting up the VSM environment

In order to use VSM, you are required to build the Ceph cluster using VSM. VSM cannot control or manage the existing Ceph cluster. In this recipe, we will use Vagrant to launch four virtual machines named `vsm-controller`, `vsm-node1`, `vsm-node2`, and `vsm-node3`. The `vsm-controller` virtual machine will act as the VSM controller node and `vsm-nodes {1,2,3}` will act as VSM agent nodes running the Ceph cluster.

How to do it...

1. The Vagrantfile for launching the VSM virtual machines is available on the `ceph-cookbook` GitHub repository. Clone this repository, if you have not already done so:

   ```
   $ git clone https://github.com/ksingh7/ceph-cookbook.git
   ```

2. Vagrantfile for launching the VSM nodes is located on the `vsm` directory:

    ```
    $ cd vsm
    ```

3. Launch the virtual machines:

    ```
    $ vagrant up vsm-controller vsm-node1 vsm-node2 vsm-node3
    ```

    ```
    teeri:vsm ksingh$ vagrant up vsm-controller vsm-node1 vsm-node2 vsm-node3
    Bringing machine 'vsm-controller' up with 'virtualbox' provider...
    Bringing machine 'vsm-node1' up with 'virtualbox' provider...
    Bringing machine 'vsm-node2' up with 'virtualbox' provider...
    Bringing machine 'vsm-node3' up with 'virtualbox' provider...
    ```

4. Once the virtual machines are launched, you should have four virtual machines running with proper networking in place.

    ```
    teeri:vsm ksingh$ vagrant status
    Current machine states:

    vsm-node1                 running (virtualbox)
    vsm-node2                 running (virtualbox)
    vsm-node3                 running (virtualbox)
    vsm-controller            running (virtualbox)

    This environment represents multiple VMs. The VMs are all listed
    above with their current state. For more information about a specific
    VM, run `vagrant status NAME`.
    ```

5. To log in to these VMs, use `cephuser` as both the username and password. For a `root` login, the password is `vagrant`. Vagrant automates the networking between these VMs with the following details:

    ```
    192.168.123.100 vsm-controller
    ```

    ```
    192.168.123.101 vsm-node1
    ```

    ```
    192.168.123.102 vsm-node2
    ```

    ```
    192.168.123.103 vsm-node3
    ```

Getting ready for VSM

In the last recipe, we preconfigured virtual machines using Vagrant; they are to be used with VSM. In this recipe, we will learn about the pre-flight configuration that is needed on these VMs so that it can be used with VSM.

Please note that by using Vagrant, we have done most of this pre-flight configuration using the shell script file, `ceph-cookbook/vsm/post-deploy.sh`, present in the GIT repository that we cloned in the last recipe. You might not want to repeat these first four steps as Vagrant already performed them. We are explaining these steps here so that you can know what Vagrant did in the background.

How to do it...

1. Create the user, `cephuser`, on all the nodes that will be used for VSM deployment. For simplicity, we will set the password of this user as `cephuser`. You can always use a username of your choice. Also, provide `sudo` rights to this user:

    ```
    # useradd cephuser
    # echo 'cephuser:cephuser' | chpasswd
    # echo "cephuser ALL=(ALL)      NOPASSWD: ALL" >>
      /etc/sudoers
    ```

2. Ensure that the NTP is configured:

    ```
    # systemctl stop ntpd
    # systemctl stop ntpdate
    # ntpdate 0.centos.pool.ntp.org > /dev/null 2> /dev/null
    # systemctl start ntpdate
    # systemctl start ntpd
    ```

3. Install `tree` (Optional), `git`, and the `epel` packages:

    ```
    # yum install -y tree git epel-release
    ```

4. Add host information to the `/etc/hosts` file:

    ```
    192.168.123.100 vsm-controller
    192.168.123.101 vsm-node1
    192.168.123.102 vsm-node2
    192.168.123.103 vsm-node3
    ```

    These are some steps that we have automated using Vagrant, which uses the `post-deploy.sh` script. If you are using the specified GitHub `ceph-cookbook` repository that I have created for VSM, then you do not need to perform these four steps.

The following steps must be performed on the nodes as specified:

1. Log in to the `vsm-controller` node, and generate and share the SSH keys with other VSM nodes. During this step, you will need to input the `cephuser` password, which is `cephuser`:

```
# ssh cephuser@192.168.123.100
$ mkdir .ssh;ssh-keygen -f .ssh/id_rsa -t rsa -N ''
$ ssh-copy-id vsm-node1
$ ssh-copy-id vsm-node2
$ ssh-copy-id vsm-node3
```

2. Using Vagrant, we have attached three VirtualBox virtual disks on each `vsm-node` `{1,2,3}`, which will be used as Ceph OSD disks. We need to partition these disks manually for the Ceph OSD and Journal so that VSM can use them with Ceph. Execute the following commands on all `vsm-nodes` `{1,2,3}`:

```
$ sudo parted /dev/sdb -- mklabel gpt
$ sudo parted -a optimal /dev/sdb -- mkpart primary 10% 100%
$ sudo parted -a optimal /dev/sdb -- mkpart primary 0 10%
$ sudo parted /dev/sdc -- mklabel gpt
$ sudo parted -a optimal /dev/sdc -- mkpart primary 10% 100%
$ sudo parted -a optimal /dev/sdc -- mkpart primary 0 10%
$ sudo parted /dev/sdd -- mklabel gpt
$ sudo parted -a optimal /dev/sdd -- mkpart primary 0 10%
$ sudo parted -a optimal /dev/sdd -- mkpart primary 10% 100%
```

```
[cephuser@vsm-node1 ~]$ sudo parted /dev/sdb -- mklabel gpt
Warning: The existing disk label on /dev/sdb will be destroyed and all data on this disk will be
lost. Do you want to continue?
Yes/No? yes
Information: You may need to update /etc/fstab.

[cephuser@vsm-node1 ~]$
[cephuser@vsm-node1 ~]$ sudo parted -a optimal /dev/sdb -- mkpart primary 10% 100%
Information: You may need to update /etc/fstab.

[cephuser@vsm-node1 ~]$ sudo parted -a optimal /dev/sdb -- mkpart primary 0 10%
Warning: The resulting partition is not properly aligned for best performance.
Ignore/Cancel? Ignore
Information: You may need to update /etc/fstab.

[cephuser@vsm-node1 ~]$
```

3. Once you have created partitions on all disks, list block devices on these nodes to verify that the partitions look as shown next:

```
$ lsblk
```

```
[cephuser@vsm-node1 ~]$ lsblk
NAME             MAJ:MIN RM   SIZE RO TYPE MOUNTPOINT
sda                  8:0   0    8G  0 disk
├─sda1               8:1   0  500M  0 part /boot
└─sda2               8:2   0  7,5G  0 part
  ├─centos-swap  253:0   0  820M  0 lvm  [SWAP]
  └─centos-root  253:1   0  6,7G  0 lvm  /
sdb                 8:16   0   20G  0 disk
├─sdb1              8:17   0   18G  0 part
└─sdb2              8:18   0    2G  0 part
sdc                 8:32   0   20G  0 disk
├─sdc1              8:33   0   18G  0 part
└─sdc2              8:34   0    2G  0 part
sdd                 8:48   0   20G  0 disk
├─sdd1              8:49   0    2G  0 part
└─sdd2              8:50   0   18G  0 part
sr0                11:0   1 1024M  0 rom
[cephuser@vsm-node1 ~]$
```

4. At this stage, we have completed the prerequisites required for VSM. As an optional step, it's a good idea to take a snapshot of the virtual machine, so that it can be restored if anything goes wrong.

```
teeri:vsm ksingh$ for i in controller node1 node2 node3 ; do VBoxManage snapshot vsm-$i take good-state ; done
0%...10%...20%...30%...40%...50%...60%...70%...80%...90%...100%
0%...10%...20%...30%...40%...50%...60%...70%...80%...90%...100%
0%...10%...20%...30%...40%...50%...60%...70%...80%...90%...100%
0%...10%...20%...30%...40%...50%...60%...70%...80%...90%...100%
teeri:vsm ksingh$
```

Installing VSM

In the last recipe, we made all the preparations required for deploying VSM. In this recipe, we will learn how to automatically deploy VSM on all the nodes.

How to do it...

1. In this demonstration, we will use CentOS7 as the base operating system; let's download the VSM repository for CentOS7. Log in to the vsm-controller node as cephuser and get VSM:

   `$ wget https://github.com/01org/virtual-storage-manager/releases/download/v2.0.0/2.0.0-216_centos7.tar.gz`

 VSM is also available for the Ubuntu OS and can be downloaded from https://github.com/01org/virtual-storage-manager.

2. Extract VSM:

```
$ tar -xvf 2.0.0-216_centos7.tar.gz
$ cd 2.0.0-216
$ ls -la
```

```
[cephuser@vsm-controller 2.0.0-216]$ ll
total 500
-rw-r--r--. 1 cephuser cephuser  27471 Sep 30 09:44 CHANGELOG.md
-rw-r--r--. 1 cephuser cephuser 124686 Sep 30 09:44 CHANGELOG.pdf
-rwxr-xr-x. 1 cephuser cephuser     94 Sep 30 09:44 get_pass.sh
-rw-r--r--. 1 cephuser cephuser  29959 Sep 30 09:44 INSTALL.md
-rw-r--r--. 1 cephuser cephuser 251846 Sep 30 09:44 INSTALL.pdf
-rw-r--r--. 1 cephuser cephuser    684 Sep 30 09:44 installrc
-rw-r--r--. 1 cephuser cephuser  21758 Sep 30 09:44 install.sh
-rw-r--r--. 1 cephuser cephuser    580 Sep 30 09:44 LICENSE
drwxr-xr-x. 2 cephuser cephuser     65 Sep 30 09:44 manifest
-rw-r--r--. 1 cephuser cephuser    320 Sep 30 09:44 NOTICE
-rwxr-xr-x. 1 cephuser cephuser   1155 Sep 30 09:44 prov_node.sh
-rw-r--r--. 1 cephuser cephuser   3121 Sep 30 09:44 README.md
-rw-r--r--. 1 cephuser cephuser      3 Sep 30 09:44 RELEASE
-rw-r--r--. 1 cephuser cephuser   1176 Sep 30 09:44 rpms.lst
-rwxr-xr-x. 1 cephuser cephuser   1353 Sep 30 09:44 uninstall.sh
-rw-r--r--. 1 cephuser cephuser      5 Sep 30 09:44 VERSION
drwxr-xr-x. 3 cephuser cephuser   4096 Sep 30 09:44 vsmrepo
[cephuser@vsm-controller 2.0.0-216]$
```

3. Set the Controller node and agent node's address; add the following lines to the `installrc` file:

```
AGENT_ADDRESS_LIST="192.168.123.101 192.168.123.102
    192.168.123.103"

CONTROLLER_ADDRESS="192.168.123.100"
```

4. Verify the `installrc` file:

```
$ cat installrc | egrep -v "#|^$"
```

```
[cephuser@vsm-controller 2.0.0-216]$ cat installrc | egrep -v "#|^$"
AGENT_ADDRESS_LIST="192.168.123.101 192.168.123.102 192.168.123.103"
CONTROLLER_ADDRESS="192.168.123.100"
[cephuser@vsm-controller 2.0.0-216]$
```

5. In the `manifest` folder, create directories using the name of the management IP of the `vsm-controller` and `vsm-nodes`:

```
$ cd manifest
$ mkdir 192.168.123.100 192.168.123.101 192.168.123.102
192.168.123.103
```

6. Copy the sample cluster manifest file to `192.168.123.100/cluster.manifest`, which is the `vsm-controller` node:

```
$ cp cluster.manifest.sample 192.168.123.100/cluster.manifest
```

7. Edit the cluster manifest file that we added in the last step with the following changes:

   `$ vim 192.168.123.100/cluster.manifest`

   ```
   [management_addr]
   192.168.123.0/24

   [ceph_public_addr]
   192.168.123.0/24

   [ceph_cluster_addr]
   192.168.123.0/24
   ```

   You should know that in a production environment, it's recommended that you have separate networks for Ceph Management, Ceph Public, and Ceph Cluster traffic. Using the `cluster.manifest` file, VSM can be instructed to use these different networks for your Ceph cluster:

8. Edit the `manifest/server.manifest.sample` file and make the following changes:

   1. Add the VSM controller IP, `192.168.123.100`, under the `[vsm_controller_ip]` section.

   2. Add a disk device name for `[sata_device]` and `[journal_device]`, as shown in the following screenshot. Make sure that the `sata_device` and `journal_device` names are separated by a space:

      ```
      [7200_rpm_sata]
      #format [sata_device]  [journal_device]
      /dev/sdb1 /dev/sdb2
      /dev/sdc1 /dev/sdc2
      /dev/sdd1 /dev/sdd2
      ```

    The `server.manifest` file provides several configuration options for different types of disks. In a production environment, it's recommended that you use the correct disk type based on your hardware.

   3. If you are not using `10krpm_sas` disk OSDs and journals by disk path, comment the lines `%osd-by-path-1%    %journal-by-path-1%` from the **[10krpm_sas]** section, as shown in the following screenshot:

      ```
      [10krpm_sas]
      #format [sas_device]  [journal_device]
      #%osd-by-path-1%   %journal-by-path-1%
      #%osd-by-path-2%   %journal-by-path-2%
      #%osd-by-path-3%   %journal-by-path-3%
      #%osd-by-path-4%   %journal-by-path-4%
      #%osd-by-path-5%   %journal-by-path-5%
      #%osd-by-path-6%   %journal-by-path-6%
      #%osd-by-path-7%   %journal-by-path-7%
      ```

9. Once you have made changes to the `manifest/server.manifest.sample` file, verify all the changes:

    ```
    $ cat server.manifest.sample | egrep -v "#|^$"
    ```

    ```
    [cephuser@vsm-controller manifest]$ cat server.manifest.sample | egrep -v "#|^$"
    [vsm_controller_ip]
    192.168.123.100
    [role]
    storage
    monitor
    [auth_key]
    token-tenant
    [ssd]
    [7200_rpm_sata]
    /dev/sdb1 /dev/sdb2
    /dev/sdc1 /dev/sdc2
    /dev/sdd1 /dev/sdd2
    [10krpm_sas]
    [ssd_cached_7200rpm_sata]
    [ssd_cached_10krpm_sas]
    [cephuser@vsm-controller manifest]$
    ```

10. Copy the `manifest/server.manifest.sample` file that we edited in the previous steps to all the `vsm-nodes`, that is, `vsm-node {1,2,3}`:

    ```
    $ cp server.manifest.sample 192.168.123.101/server.manifest
    ```

    ```
    $ cp server.manifest.sample 192.168.123.102/server.manifest
    ```

    ```
    $ cp server.manifest.sample 192.168.123.103/server.manifest
    ```

11. Verify the manifest directory structure:

    ```
    $ tree
    ```

    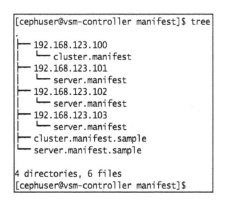

    ```
    [cephuser@vsm-controller manifest]$ tree
    .
    ├── 192.168.123.100
    │   └── cluster.manifest
    ├── 192.168.123.101
    │   └── server.manifest
    ├── 192.168.123.102
    │   └── server.manifest
    ├── 192.168.123.103
    │   └── server.manifest
    ├── cluster.manifest.sample
    └── server.manifest.sample

    4 directories, 6 files
    [cephuser@vsm-controller manifest]$
    ```

12. To begin the VSM installation, add the execute permission to the `install.sh` file:

    ```
    $ cd ..
    $ chmod +x install.sh
    ```

13. Finally, install VSM by running the `install.sh` file with the `--check-dependence-package` parameter, which downloads packages that are necessary for the VSM installation from `https//github.com/01org/vsm-dependencies`:

    ```
    $ ./install.sh -u cephuser -v 2.0 --check-dependence-package
    ```

```
[cephuser@vsm-controller 2.0.0-216]$ ./install.sh -u cephuser -v 2.0 --check-dependence-package
+ echo 'Before auto deploy the vsm, please be sure that you have set the manifest
such as manifest/192.168.100.100/server.manifest. And you have changed the file, too.'
Before auto deploy the vsm, please be sure that you have set the manifest
such as manifest/192.168.100.100/server.manifest. And you have changed the file, too.
+ sleep 5
+++ dirname ./install.sh
++ cd .
++ pwd
+ TOPDIR=/home/cephuser/2.0.0-216
```

The VSM installation will take several minutes. The installer process might require you to input the `cephuser` password for the `vsm-controller` node. In that case, please input `cephuser` as the password.

In case you encounter any errors and wish to restart the VSM installation, it is recommended that you clean your system before you retry it. Execute the `uninstall.sh` script file for a system cleanup.

You can also review the author's version of the VSM installation by checking the installation log file located in the `ceph-cookbook` repository path: `ceph-cookbook/vsm/vsm_install_log`.

14. Once the VSM installation is finished, extract the password for the user `admin` by executing `get_pass.sh` on the `vsm-controller` node:

    ```
    $ ./get_pass.sh
    ```

```
[cephuser@vsm-controller 2.0.0-216]$ ./get_pass.sh
f409fc062564b9a937d1
[cephuser@vsm-controller 2.0.0-216]$
```

15. Finally, log in to the VSM dashboard, `https://192.168.123.100/dashboard/vsm`, with the user, `admin`, and password that we extracted in the last step.

16. The `vsm-dashboard` landing page looks like this:

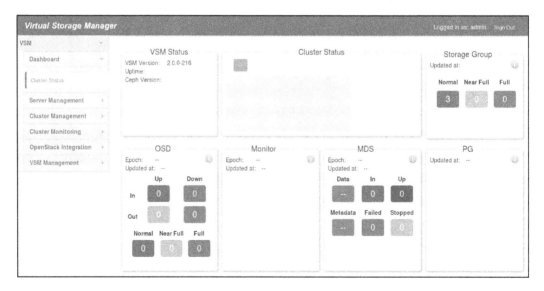

The VSM Cluster monitoring option shows some nice graphs for IPOS, Latency, Bandwidth, and CPU utilization, which gives you the big picture of what's going on in your cluster.

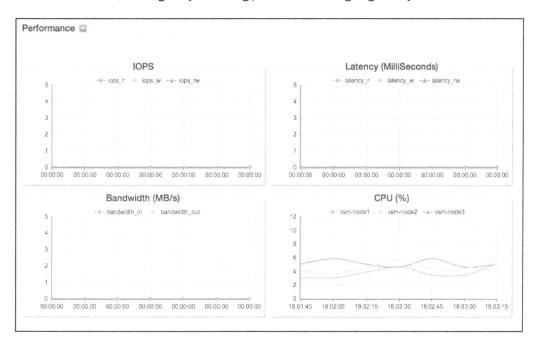

Creating a Ceph cluster using VSM

In the last recipe, we just installed VSM; we do not yet have a Ceph cluster. In this recipe, we will create the Ceph cluster using VSM so that VSM can manage this cluster later. You will find that deploying the Ceph cluster is extremely easy with VSM.

How to do it...

1. To create the Ceph cluster from the VSM dashboard, navigate to **Cluster Management** | **Create Cluster**, and then click on the **Create Cluster** button.

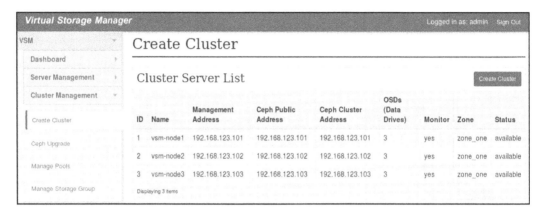

2. Select all the nodes by clicking on the checkbox next to the ID, and finally, click on the **Create Cluster** button:

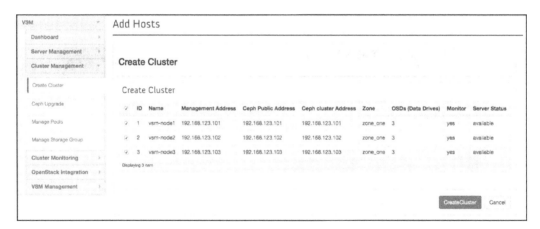

3. The Ceph cluster's creation will take a few minutes. VSM will display very briefly what it's doing in the background under the status field of the dashboard, as shown next:

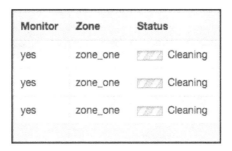

After cleaning, it will mount disks, as shown under the status field of the dashboard in the following screenshot:

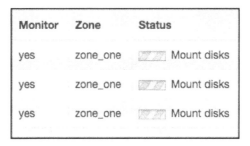

4. Once the Ceph cluster deployment is completed, VSM will display the node status as **Active**.

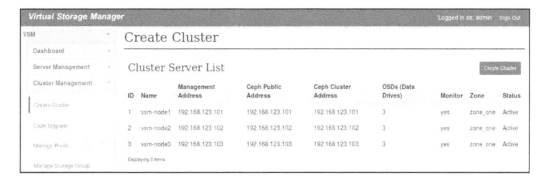

5. Finally, check the cluster status from **Dashboard | Cluster Status**.

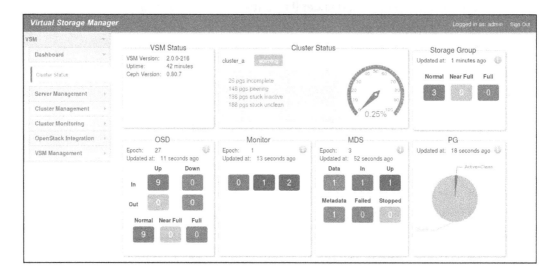

Exploring the VSM dashboard

The VSM dashboard makes most of the operations around the Ceph cluster extremely easy, whether it's deployment, server management, cluster management/monitoring, or even OpenStack integration. The VSM dashboard is very user friendly and you can explore most of its features by yourself. The VSM dashboard provides the following options:

- ▶ **Dashboard**: This provides the complete status of the system including the following:
    - ❑ **VSM Status**: This gives you the VSM version, uptime, Ceph version, and so on
    - ❑ **Cluster Summary**: This gives you the Ceph cluster status, similar to `ceph -s` output
    - ❑ **OSD Summary**
    - ❑ **Monitor Summary**
    - ❑ **MDS Summary**
    - ❑ **PG Summary**

        It also gives performance metric such as IOPS, Latency, Bandwidth and CPU utilization for all Ceph nodes

- ▶ **Server Management**: This includes the following:
    - ❑ **Manage Servers**: The functions are described as follows:
        - ❑ It provides lists of all servers with information such as management, cluster and public network addresses, Ceph version, status, and so on.
        - ❑ It provides options to add or remove servers, Ceph monitors, and start or stop servers.

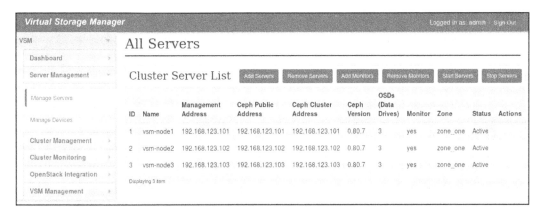

❑ **Manage Devices**: The functions are described as follows:

    ❑ This gives the list of all Ceph OSDs including their status, weight, server they are hosted on, as well as storage class.

    ❑ This allows the creation of new OSDs as well as the restarting, removing, and restoring of OSDs.

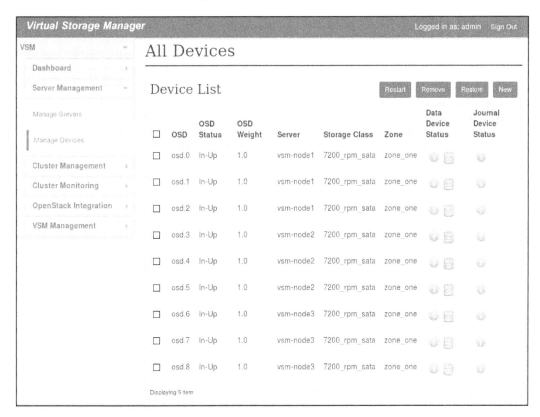

▶ **Cluster Management**

This section of the VSM dashboard provides several options to manage the Ceph cluster:

  ❑ **Create Cluster**

  ❑ **Upgrade Cluster**

  ❑ **Manage Pools**: This helps you to create replicated/erasure coded pools, add/remove cache tier, and so on

  ❑ **Manage Storage Group**: Add new storage groups

▶ **Cluster Monitoring**: This section of the VSM dashboard provides complete cluster monitoring, including all of its components:

  ❑ **Storage Group Status**

  ❑ **Pool Status**

  ❑ **OSD Status**

  ❑ **Monitor Status**

  ❑ **MDS Status**

  ❑ **PG Status**

  ❑ **RBD Status**

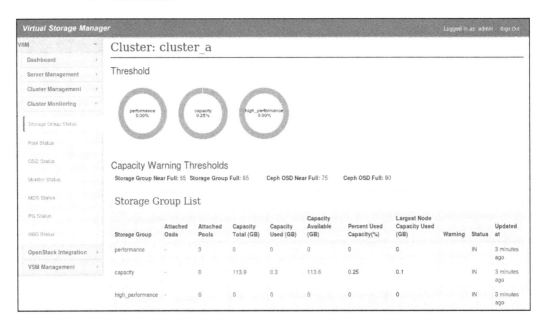

▶ **OpenStack Integration**: This section of the VSM dashboard allows us to integrate Ceph storage to OpenStack by adding OpenStack endpoints and presenting RBD pools to OpenStack:

❑ **Manage RBD Pools**: Present RBD Pools to OpenStack

❑ **OpenStack Access**: Add the OpenStack endpoint

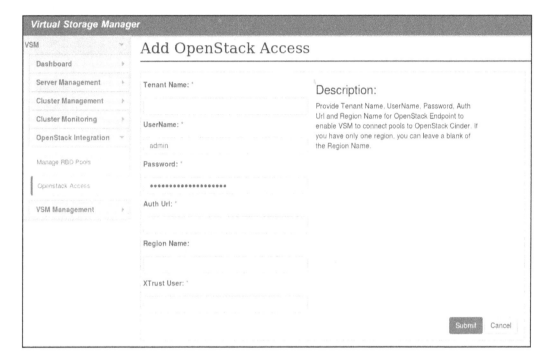

▶ **VSM Management**: This section of the VSM dashboard allows us to manage settings related to the VSM dashboard itself:

❑ **Add/Remove User**: Create or remove a user and change the password

❑ **Settings**: Various settings related to Ceph

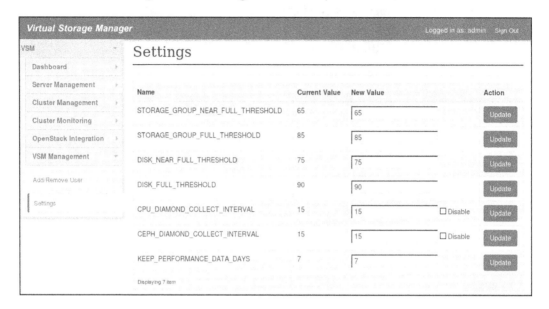

Upgrading the Ceph cluster using VSM

You are now quite familiar with VSM and know that it provides a nice dashboard that makes complicated Ceph related operations, such as Cluster creation, extremely easy. Another important aspect of VSM is that it automates the Ceph cluster upgrade process and simplifies it. In this recipe, we will use VSM to upgrade our Ceph Firefly cluster to Ceph Hammer.

How to do it...

1. Before starting the upgrade process, verify the current cluster version by navigating to **VSM | Dashboard | Cluster Status**. It should be the Ceph Firefly Version 0.80.7.

2. To upgrade the Ceph cluster, navigate to **VSM | Cluster Management | Ceph Upgrade**.

3. Provide the following details for the Ceph upgrade:

    1. **Package URL**: `http://download.ceph.com/rpm-hammer/el7/`.

    2. **Key URL**: This is added by default by VSM.

    3. **Proxy URL**: This is in case an Internet proxy is required to access the Internet. In this case, it's not required.

    4. **SSH User Name**: This refers to the `cephuser` username that we have created for VSM management.

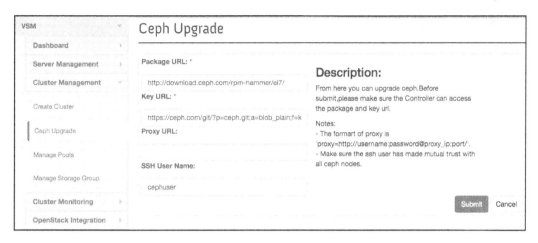

4. As soon as you provide these details to VSM and hit **Submit**, the cluster upgrade process will start, and it will take a few minutes to finish. Please be patient, and you can optionally monitor the VSM logs under `/var/log/vsm`.

5. Once the upgrade is completed, the VSM dashboard displays a message, as shown next, which confirms that your cluster has been upgraded:

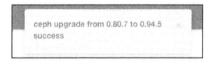

6. To verify upgrade completion, navigate to **VSM | Dashboard | Cluster Status**. The Ceph Version should now be 0.94.5, which is Ceph Hammer.

This is how VSM makes the Ceph cluster upgrade process extremely simple. Moreover, this upgrade process is completely online, that is, you do not need any scheduled maintenance break to perform the storage upgrade.

VSM roadmap

The current stable version of VSM at the time of writing this book is 2.0. This is the same version that we demonstrated in this chapter. Due to its easy-to-use, powerful, and feature-rich interface, VSM is getting quite popular in the Ceph community. The next release of VSM would be 2.1, which comes with several bug fixes and new features. Some of them are as follows:

- The new features in VSM 2.1 are
  - Reporting the server name that is running the Monitor daemon
  - Prototype—the Ceph Calamari/VSM dashboard implementation
  - Configurable mount options for filesystem
  - Identifying the physical location of a failed disk
  - Removing an unused disk path list during the addition of a new OSD
  - Displaying the disk's logical path instead of physical, while adding a new OSD
  - Attaching and managing the existing Ceph cluster
  - Monitoring the status page improvements
  - Displaying SMART information for storage devices

- The bug fixes that are required in VSM 2.1
  - The Monitors button needs to be removed in Manage Servers and it should hang when a Monitor node too has MDS daemon
  - The VSM version and uptime should be displayed even if no cluster is created
  - It accesses other options of VSM dashboard while cluster creation is ongoing.
  - The **Number of PG in each OSD is too large** warning is displayed after upgrading Ceph cluster version to Ceph Hammer.
  - The password for OpenStack access is shown in plain text
  - When it's installed with dependent packages pre-prepared, the installer will stop running and display complaints
  - If a server is down, it is not reflected in VSM

This is a very limited list of new features and bug fixes; for the latest information on VSM Roadmaps, please visit the **Virtual Storage Manager** project at `https://01.org/jira/browse/VSM`.

VSM resources

In this chapter, we covered most of the important aspects of VSM. If you were planning to use VSM in your environment, I would recommend that you check out the following resources to get more information on VSM:

- ▸ The official source code repository: `https://github.com/01org/virtual-storage-manager`.

- ▸ VSM Wiki: `https://github.com/01org/virtual-storage-manager/wiki`.

- ▸ The VSM issue, development, and roadmap tracking: `https://01.org/jira/browse/VSM`.

- ▸ The VSM mailing list: `http://vsm-discuss.33411.n7.nabble.com/`.

As you already know that VSM is an open source project, it's worth mentioning that VSM's development efforts are being led by Intel with the help of its community.

I would like to thank *Dan Ferber* and *Yaguang Wang* from *Intel*, as well as the *entire VSM community*, for delivering to us a nice piece of software for deploying and managing the Ceph cluster. To help VSM develop further, please become an active member of the community and consider giving back by making meaningful contributions.

10

More on Ceph

In this chapter, we will cover the following recipes:

- ▸ Benchmarking the Ceph cluster
- ▸ Disk performance baseline
- ▸ Baseline network performance
- ▸ Ceph RADOS bench
- ▸ RADOS load-gen
- ▸ Benchmarking the Ceph block device
- ▸ Benchmarking Ceph RBD using FIO
- ▸ Ceph admin socket
- ▸ Using the ceph tell command
- ▸ Ceph REST API
- ▸ Profiling Ceph memory
- ▸ Deploying Ceph using Ansible
- ▸ The ceph-objectstore tool

Introduction

In the previous chapters, we covered different ways to deploy, provision, and administer Ceph. In this chapter, we will cover benchmarking the Ceph cluster, which is a must-do thing before moving to production. We will also cover advanced methods of Ceph administration and troubleshooting using the admin socket, REST API, and the ceph-objectstore tool. Finally, we will learn about Ceph memory profiling as well as deploying Ceph using Ansible, which is quite an efficient way to deploy Ceph.

Benchmarking the Ceph cluster

It's very much recommended that you benchmark your Ceph cluster before using it for the production workload. Benchmarking gives you approximate results on how your cluster will perform during read, write, latency, and other workloads.

Before doing the real benchmarking, it's a good idea to establish a baseline for the expected maximum performance by measuring the performance of the hardware connected to the cluster node, such as the disk and network.

Disk performance baseline

The disk performance baseline test will be done in two steps. First, we will measure the performance of a single disk, and after that, we will measure the performance of all the disks connected to one Ceph OSD node simultaneously.

 To get realistic results, I am running the benchmarking tests described in this recipe against a Ceph cluster deployed on physical hardware. We can also run these tests on the Ceph cluster, hosted on virtual machine, but we might not get appealing results.

Single disk write performance

To get the disk read and write performance, we will use the dd command with oflag set to direct in order to bypass disk cache for realistic results.

How to do it...

1. Drop caches:

    ```
    # echo 3 > /proc/sys/vm/drop_caches
    ```

2. Use dd to write a file named deleteme of the size 10G, filled with zeros /dev/zero as the input file if to the directory where Ceph OSD is mounted, that is, /var/lib/ceph/osd/ceph-0/.

    ```
    # dd if=/dev/zero of=/var/lib/ceph/osd/ceph-0/deleteme bs=10G
    count=1 oflag=direct
    ```

Ideally, you should repeat Steps 1 and 2 a few times and take the average value. In our case, the average value for write operations comes to be 319 MB/s, as shown in the following screenshot:

```
[root@ceph-node1 ~]# dd if=/dev/zero of=/var/lib/ceph/osd/ceph-0/deleteme bs=10G count=1 oflag=direct
0+1 records in
0+1 records out
2147479552 bytes (2.1 GB) copied, 6.66535 s, 322 MB/s
[root@ceph-node1 ~]#
[root@ceph-node1 ~]# dd if=/dev/zero of=/var/lib/ceph/osd/ceph-0/deleteme bs=10G count=1 oflag=direct
0+1 records in
0+1 records out
2147479552 bytes (2.1 GB) copied, 7.09217 s, 303 MB/s
[root@ceph-node1 ~]#
[root@ceph-node1 ~]# dd if=/dev/zero of=/var/lib/ceph/osd/ceph-0/deleteme bs=10G count=1 oflag=direct
0+1 records in
0+1 records out
2147479552 bytes (2.1 GB) copied, 6.45077 s, 333 MB/s
[root@ceph-node1 ~]#
```

Multiple disk write performance

As the next step, we will run dd on all the OSD disks used by Ceph on the node, ceph-node1, to get the aggregated disk write performance out of a single node.

How to do it...

1. Get the total number of disks in use with the Ceph OSD; in my case, it's 25 disks:

   ```
   # mount | grep -i osd | wc -l
   ```

2. Drop caches:

   ```
   # echo 3 > /proc/sys/vm/drop_caches
   ```

3. The following command will execute the dd command on all the Ceph OSD disks:

   ```
   # for i in `mount | grep osd | awk '{print $3}'`; do (dd
   if=/dev/zero of=$i/deleteme bs=10G count=1 oflag=direct &) ;
   done
   ```

To get the aggregated disk write performance, take the average of all the write speed. In my case, the average comes out to be 60 MB/s.

Single disk read performance

To get the single disk read performance, we will again use the dd command.

How to do it...

1. Drop caches:

   ```
   # echo 3 > /proc/sys/vm/drop_caches
   ```

2. Use dd to read from the file, deleteme, which we created during the write test. We will read the deleteme file to /dev/null with iflag set to direct:

```
# dd if=/var/lib/ceph/osd/ceph-0/deleteme of=/dev/null bs=10G
count=1 iflag=direct
```

Ideally, you should repeat Steps 1 and 2 a few times and take the average value. In our case, the average value for read operations comes to be 178 MB/s, as shown in the following screenshot:

```
[root@ceph-node1 ~]# echo 3 > /proc/sys/vm/drop_caches
[root@ceph-node1 ~]#
[root@ceph-node1 ~]# dd if=/var/lib/ceph/osd/ceph-0/deleteme of=/dev/null bs=10G count=1 iflag=direct
0+1 records in
0+1 records out
2147479552 bytes (2.1 GB) copied, 12.0557 s, 178 MB/s
[root@ceph-node1 ~]#
[root@ceph-node1 ~]# dd if=/var/lib/ceph/osd/ceph-0/deleteme of=/dev/null bs=10G count=1 iflag=direct
0+1 records in
0+1 records out
2147479552 bytes (2.1 GB) copied, 12.0452 s, 178 MB/s
[root@ceph-node1 ~]# dd if=/var/lib/ceph/osd/ceph-0/deleteme of=/dev/null bs=10G count=1 iflag=direct
0+1 records in
0+1 records out
2147479552 bytes (2.1 GB) copied, 12.0408 s, 178 MB/s
[root@ceph-node1 ~]#
[root@ceph-node1 ~]#
```

Multiple disk read performance

Similar to the single disk read performance, we will use dd to get the aggregated multiple disk read performance.

How to do it...

1. Get the total number of disks in use with the Ceph OSD; in my case, it's 25 disks:

```
# mount | grep -i osd | wc -l
```

2. Drop caches:

```
# echo 3 > /proc/sys/vm/drop_caches
```

3. The following command will execute the dd command on all the Ceph OSD disks:

```
# for i in `mount | grep osd | awk '{print $3}'`; do (dd if=$i/
deleteme of=/dev/null bs=10G count=1 iflag=direct &); done
```

To get the aggregated disk read performance, take the average of all the read speeds. In my case, the average comes out to be 123 MB/s.

Results

Based on the tests that we performed, the results will look like this. These results vary a lot from environment to environment; the hardware that you are using and the number of disks on the OSD node can play a big part.

Operation	Per Disk	Aggregate
Read	178 MB/s	123 MB/s
Write	319 MB/s	60 MB/s

Baseline network performance

In this recipe, we will perform tests to discover the baseline performance of the network between the Ceph OSD nodes. For this, we will be using the `iperf` utility. Make sure that the `iperf` package is installed on the Ceph nodes. `iperf` is a simple, point-to-point network bandwidth tester that works on the client server model.

To start network benchmarking, execute `iperf` with the server option on the first Ceph node and with the client option on the second Ceph node.

How to do it...

1. On `Ceph-node1`, execute `iperf` with `-s` for the server, and `-p` to listen on a specific port:

    ```
    # iperf -s -p 6900
    ```

    ```
    [root@ceph-node1 ~]# iperf -s -p 6900
    ------------------------------------------------------------
    Server listening on TCP port 6900
    TCP window size: 85.3 KByte (default)
    ------------------------------------------------------------
    [  4] local 10.100.1.201 port 6900 connected with 10.100.1.202 port 39630
    [ ID] Interval       Transfer     Bandwidth
    [  4]  0.0-10.0 sec  11.5 GBytes  9.87 Gbits/sec
    ^C[root@ceph-node1 ~]#
    [root@ceph-node1 ~]#
    ```

 You can skip the `-p` option if the TPC port 5201 is open, or you can choose any other port that is open and not in use.

2. On `Ceph-node2`, execute `iperf` with the client option, -c:

```
# iperf -c ceph-node1 -p 6900
```

```
[root@ceph-node2 ~]# iperf -c ceph-node1 -p 6900
------------------------------------------------------------
Client connecting to 10.100.1.201, TCP port 6900
TCP window size: 95.8 KByte (default)
------------------------------------------------------------
[  3] local 10.100.1.202 port 39630 connected with 10.100.1.201 port 6900
[ ID] Interval        Transfer      Bandwidth
[  3]  0.0-10.0 sec   11.5 GBytes   9.87 Gbits/sec
[root@ceph-node2 ~]#
```

 You can also use the -p option with the `iperf` command to determine the number of parallel stream connections to make with the server. It will return a realistic result if you have a channel-bonding technique such as LACP.

This shows that we have a pretty nice network connectivity of ~9.80Gb/s between the Ceph nodes. Similarly, you can perform a network bandwidth check for the other nodes of your Ceph cluster. The network bandwidth really depends on the network infrastructure you are using between your Ceph nodes.

See also...

▶ Chapter 8, *Production Planning and Performance Tuning for Ceph*, where you can find more information related to Ceph networking

Ceph RADOS bench

Ceph ships with an inbuilt benchmarking tool known as the RADOS bench, which can be used to measure the performance of a Ceph cluster at the pool level. The Rados bench tool supports write, sequential read, and random read benchmarking tests, and it also allows the cleaning of temporary benchmarking data, which is quite neat.

How to do it...

Let's try to run some tests using the `rados` bench:

1. To run a 10 second write test to the pool `rbd` without cleanup, use the following command:

```
# rados bench -p rbd 10 write --no-cleanup
```

We get the following screenshot after executing the command:

```
[root@ceph-node1 ~]# rados bench -p rbd 10 write --no-cleanup
Maintaining 16 concurrent writes of 4194304 bytes for up to 10 seconds or 0 objects
Object prefix: benchmark_data_ceph-node1_3124629
  sec Cur ops   started  finished  avg MB/s  cur MB/s  last lat   avg lat
    0      0         0         0         0         0       -          0
    1     16       118       102    407.85       408 0.0584212  0.127569
    2     16       207       191   381.895       356   0.20105  0.150813
    3     16       279       263   350.581       288  0.141772  0.168736
    4     16       351       335   334.921       288   0.57108  0.181988
    5     16       420       404    323.13       276 0.0724497   0.19139
    6     16       479       463   308.601       236  0.137025  0.194498
    7     16       547       531   303.367       272  0.253194  0.206116
    8     16       615       599   299.441       272  0.172813  0.208689
    9     16       692       676   300.386       308   0.48298  0.209028
   10     16       747       731   292.345       220  0.123282  0.211807
 Total time run:         10.721111
Total writes made:      747
Write size:             4194304
Bandwidth (MB/sec):     278.702

Stddev Bandwidth:       102.44
Max bandwidth (MB/sec): 408
Min bandwidth (MB/sec): 0
Average Latency:        0.227756
Stddev Latency:         0.234691
Max latency:            1.5534
Min latency:            0.041106
[root@ceph-node1 ~]#
```

2. Similarly, to run a 10 second sequential read test on the `rbd` pool, run the following:

```
# rados bench -p rbd 10 seq
```

```
[root@ceph-node1 ~]# rados bench -p rbd 10 seq
  sec Cur ops   started  finished  avg MB/s  cur MB/s  last lat   avg lat
    0      0         0         0         0         0       -          0
    1     16       247       231   923.573       924  0.181625 0.0620505
    2     16       489       473   945.703       968 0.0366547 0.0645318
    3     16       648       632   698.411       636  0.306308 0.0814809
 Total time run:        4.223407
Total reads made:      747
Read size:             4194304
Bandwidth (MB/sec):     707.486

Average Latency:       0.0901875
Max latency:           1.03252
Min latency:           0.00977891
[root@ceph-node1 ~]#
```

It might be interesting to know, in this case, why the read test finished in a few seconds, or why it didn't execute for the specified 10 seconds. It's because the read speed is faster than the write speed, and `rados bench` had finished reading all the data generated during the write test. However, this behavior depends highly on your HW and SW infrastructure.

► Similar to running a random read test with the `rados` bench, execute the following:

```
# rados bench -p rbd 10 rand
```

How it works...

The syntax for the `rados bench` is as follows:

```
# rados bench -p <pool_name> <seconds> <write|seq|rand> -b <block
size> -t --no-cleanup
```

► `-p` or `--pool`: Specify the pool name

► `<seconds>`: Test the time in seconds

► `<write|seq|rand>`: The type of test, for example, write, sequential read, or random read

► `-b`: For the block size; by default, it's 4M

► `-t`: The number of concurrent threads; the default is 16

► `--no-cleanup`: The temporary data that is written to the pool by the RADOS bench should not be cleaned. This data will be used for read operations when they are used with sequential reads or random reads. The default is cleaned up.

As specified in the last recipe, I am running these tests against a physical Ceph cluster. You can definitely run these commands on a Ceph cluster created on virtual machines, however, you might not get satisfactory results in a virtual environment.

The Rados bench is a pretty handy tool to quickly measure the raw performance of your Ceph cluster, and you can creatively design your test cases based on write, read, and random read profiles.

RADOS load-gen

A bit similar to the rados bench, `rados load-gen` is another interesting tool provided by Ceph, which runs out-of-the-box. As the name suggests, the rados load-gen tool can be used to generate load on a Ceph cluster and can be useful to simulate high load scenarios.

How to do it...

Let's try to generate some load on our Ceph cluster with the following command:

```
# rados -p rbd load-gen \
   --num-objects 50 \
   --min-object-size 4M \
   --max-object-size 4M \
   --max-ops 16 \
   --min-op-len 4M \
   --max-op-len 4M \
   --percent 5 \
   --target-throughput 2000 \
   --run-length 60
```

How it works...

The syntax for `rados load-gen` is as follows:

```
# rados -p <pool-name> load-gen
```

 ▸   `--num-objects`: The total number of objects

 ▸   `--min-object-size`: The minimum object size in bytes

 ▸   `--max-object-size`: The maximum object size in bytes

 ▸   `--min-ops`: The minimum number of operations

 ▸   `--max-ops`: The maximum number of operations

 ▸   `--min-op-len`: The minimum operation length

 ▸   `--max-op-len`: The maximum operation length

 ▸   `--max-backlog`: The maximum backlog (in MB)

 ▸   `--percent`: The percentage of read operations

 ▸   `--target-throughput`: The target throughput (in MB)

 ▸   `--run-length`: The total run time in seconds

This command will generate load on the Ceph cluster by writing 50 objects to the `rbd` pool. Each of these objects and operation lengths are 4M in size, with 5% of the read and test runtime as 60 seconds.

```
[root@ceph-node1 ~]# rados -p rbd load-gen \
>      --num-objects 50 \
>      --min-object-size 4M \
>      --max-object-size 4M \
>      --max-ops 16 \
>      --min-op-len 4M \
>      --max-op-len 4M \
>      --percent 5 \
>      --target-throughput 2000 \
>      --run-length 60
run length 60 seconds
preparing 50 objects
load-gen will run 60 seconds
     1: throughput=0MB/sec pending data=0
READ : oid=obj-xtuVtIfS5ZQ55da off=0 len=4194304
READ : oid=obj-0NvPNB07LZlrQYa off=0 len=4194304
WRITE : oid=obj-UeV2NunBsTSrYUw off=0 len=4194304
op 17 completed, throughput=4MB/sec
READ : oid=obj-fL1p0c_7CgEtj1k off=0 len=4194304
op 18 completed, throughput=8MB/sec
```

The output has been trimmed for brevity's sake. Once the `load-gen` command finishes, it cleans all the objects it has created during the test and shows the operation throughput.

```
op 5519 completed, throughput=373MB/sec
waiting for all operations to complete
cleaning up objects
op 5522 completed, throughput=367MB/sec
op 5521 completed, throughput=367MB/sec
[root@ceph-node1 ~]#
```

There's more...

You can also monitor your cluster status for the read and write speed/operation using the `watch ceph -s` command; meanwhile, `rados load-gen` will be running, just to see how it goes.

Benchmarking the Ceph block device

The tools, `rados bench` and `rados load-gen`, which we discussed in the last recipe, are used to benchmark the Ceph cluster pool. In this recipe, we will focus on benchmarking the Ceph block device with the `rbd bench-write` tool.

Ceph rbd bench-write

The `ceph rbd` command-line interface provides an option known as `bench-write`, which is a tool to perform write benchmarking operations on the Ceph Rados Block Device.

How to do it...

To benchmark the Ceph block device, we need to create a block device and map to the Ceph client node:

1. Create a Ceph block device named `block-device1`, of size 1G, and map it:

   ```
   # rbd create block-device1 --size 10240
   ```

   ```
   # rbd info --image block-device1
   ```

   ```
   # rbd map block-device1
   ```

   ```
   # rbd showmapped
   ```

   ```
   [root@ceph-client1 ~]# rbd create block-device1 --size 10240
   [root@ceph-client1 ~]# rbd info --image block-device1
   rbd image 'block-device1':
           size 10240 MB in 2560 objects
           order 22 (4096 kB objects)
           block_name_prefix: rb.0.4cbacc.238e1f29
           format: 1
   [root@ceph-client1 ~]# rbd map block-device1
   /dev/rbd0
   [root@ceph-client1 ~]# rbd showmapped
   id pool image          snap device
   0  rbd  block-device1 -    /dev/rbd0
   [root@ceph-client1 ~]#
   ```

2. Create a filesystem on the block device and mount it:

   ```
   # mkfs.xfs /dev/rbd0
   ```

   ```
   # mkdir -p /mnt/ceph-block-device1
   ```

```
# mount /dev/rbd0 /mnt/ceph-block-device1

# df -h /mnt/ceph-block-device1
```

```
[root@ceph-client1 ~]# mkfs.xfs /dev/rbd0
log stripe unit (4194304 bytes) is too large (maximum is 256KiB)
log stripe unit adjusted to 32KiB
meta-data=/dev/rbd0              isize=256    agcount=17, agsize=162816 blks
         =                      sectsz=512   attr=2, projid32bit=1
         =                      crc=0        finobt=0
data     =                      bsize=4096   blocks=2621440, imaxpct=25
         =                      sunit=1024   swidth=1024 blks
naming   =version 2             bsize=4096   ascii-ci=0 ftype=0
log      =internal log          bsize=4096   blocks=2560, version=2
         =                      sectsz=512   sunit=8 blks, lazy-count=1
realtime =none                  extsz=4096   blocks=0, rtextents=0
[root@ceph-client1 ~]# mkdir -p /mnt/ceph-block-device1
[root@ceph-client1 ~]# mount /dev/rbd0 /mnt/ceph-block-device1
[root@ceph-client1 ~]# df -h /mnt/ceph-block-device1
Filesystem      Size  Used Avail Use% Mounted on
/dev/rbd0       10G    33M   10G   1% /mnt/ceph-block-device1
[root@ceph-client1 ~]#
```

3. To benchmark `block-device1` for 5GB of total write length, execute the following command:

```
# rbd bench-write block-device1 --io-total 5368709200
```

```
[root@ceph-client1 ~]# rbd bench-write block-device1 --io-total 5368709200
bench-write  io_size 4096 io_threads 16 bytes 5368709200 pattern seq
  SEC       OPS    OPS/SEC    BYTES/SEC
    1     67285   67304.27  275678272.46
    2    145469   72743.93  297959122.08
    3    224701   74906.90  306818647.61
    4    301802   75427.40  308950632.76
    5    372142   74432.24  304874445.83
    6    444010   75344.90  308612698.37
    7    517287   74363.64  304593457.23
    8    599236   74906.98  306818990.26
    9    672587   74178.98  303837121.67
   10    732910   72153.50  295540718.90
   11    784764   68150.81  279145733.52
   12    852044   66951.41  274232980.96
   13    918326   63817.89  261398064.96
   14    982399   61962.40  253797984.31
   15   1047148   62847.78  257424494.92
   16   1107514   64550.09  264397152.44
   17   1163126   62216.51  254838831.07
   18   1226368   61607.43  252344039.05
   19   1286892   60898.32  249439520.77
elapsed:    51 ops: 1310721 ops/sec: 25221.56  bytes/sec: 103307522.97
[root@ceph-client1 ~]#
```

As you can see, the `rbd bench-write` outputs nicely formatted results.

How it works...

The syntax for the `rbd bench-write` looks like the following:

```
# rbd bench-write <RBD image name>
```

- ▸ `--io-size`: The write size in bytes; the default is 4M
- ▸ `--io-threads`: The number of threads; the default is 16
- ▸ `--io-total`: The total bytes to write; the default is 1024M
- ▸ `--io-pattern <seq|rand>`: This is the write pattern, the default is `seq`

There's more...

You can use different options with the `rbd bench-write` tool to adjust the block size, number of threads, and io-pattern.

See also...

- ▸ *Chapter 2, Working with Ceph Block Device*, where we covered the creation of the Ceph block device in detail.

Benchmarking Ceph RBD using FIO

FIO stands for Flexible I/O; it's one of the most popular tools for generating I/O workload and benchmarking. FIO has recently added native support for RBD. FIO is highly customizable and can be used to simulate and benchmark almost all kinds of workloads. In this recipe, we will learn how FIO can be used to benchmark the Ceph RBD.

How to do it...

To benchmark the Ceph block device, we need to create a block device and map that to the Ceph client node:

1. Install the FIO package on the node where you mapped the Ceph RBD image. In our case, it's the `ceph-client1` node:

   ```
   # yum install -y fio
   ```

2. Since FIO supports RBD IOengine, we do not need to mount the RBD image as a filesystem. To benchmark RBD, we simply need to provide the RBD image name, pool, and Ceph user that will be used to connect to the Ceph cluster. Create the FIO profile with the following content:

```
[write-4M]

description="write test with block size of 4M"

ioengine=rbd

clientname=admin

pool=rbd

rbdname=block-device1

iodepth=32

runtime=120

rw=write

bs=4M
```

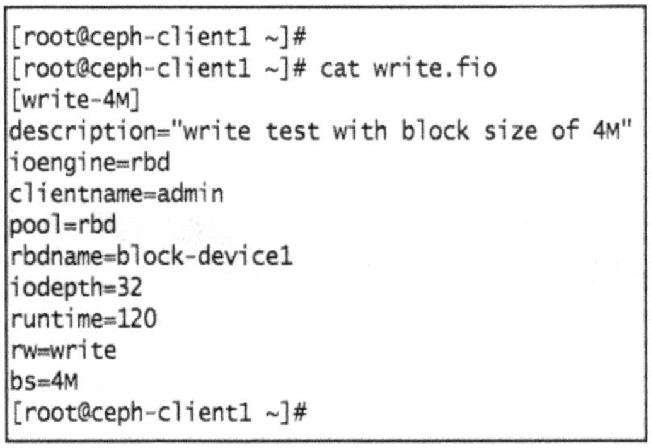

```
[root@ceph-client1 ~]#
[root@ceph-client1 ~]# cat write.fio
[write-4M]
description="write test with block size of 4M"
ioengine=rbd
clientname=admin
pool=rbd
rbdname=block-device1
iodepth=32
runtime=120
rw=write
bs=4M
[root@ceph-client1 ~]#
```

3. To start FIO benchmarking, execute by providing the FIO profile file as an argument to the FIO command:

```
# fio write.fio
```

```
[root@ceph-client1 ~]#
[root@ceph-client1 ~]# fio write.fio
write-4M: (g=0): rw=write, bs=4M-4M/4M-4M/4M-4M, ioengine=rbd, iodepth=32
fio-2.2.8
Starting 1 process
rbd engine: RBD version: 0.1.9
Jobs: 1 (f=0): [W(1)] [100.0% done] [0KB/107.7MB/0KB /s] [0/26/0 iops] [eta 00m:00s]
write-4M: (groupid=0, jobs=1): err= 0: pid=2146255: Wed Dec  9 00:54:40 2015
  Description  : ["write test with block size of 4M"]
  write: io=10240MB, bw=314736KB/s, iops=76, runt= 33316msec
    slat (usec): min=129, max=15181, avg=473.98, stdev=888.02
    clat (msec): min=102, max=2949, avg=409.87, stdev=263.06
     lat (msec): min=102, max=2949, avg=410.35, stdev=263.06
    clat percentiles (msec):
     |  1.00th=[  131],  5.00th=[  155], 10.00th=[  180], 20.00th=[  219],
     | 30.00th=[  258], 40.00th=[  310], 50.00th=[  351], 60.00th=[  392],
     | 70.00th=[  441], 80.00th=[  545], 90.00th=[  693], 95.00th=[  906],
     | 99.00th=[ 1369], 99.50th=[ 1762], 99.90th=[ 2409], 99.95th=[ 2474],
     | 99.99th=[ 2966]
    bw (KB  /s): min=74908, max=568888, per=100.00%, avg=327349.43, stdev=99611.29
    lat (msec) : 250=27.70%, 500=47.19%, 750=17.42%, 1000=4.30%, 2000=3.20%
    lat (msec) : >=2000=0.20%
  cpu          : usr=3.04%, sys=0.59%, ctx=268, majf=0, minf=52854
  IO depths    : 1=0.3%, 2=1.2%, 4=4.7%, 8=19.4%, 16=68.5%, 32=5.8%, >=64=0.0%
     submit    : 0=0.0%, 4=100.0%, 8=0.0%, 16=0.0%, 32=0.0%, 64=0.0%, >=64=0.0%
     complete  : 0=0.0%, 4=95.9%, 8=0.1%, 16=0.8%, 32=3.3%, 64=0.0%, >=64=0.0%
     issued    : total=r=0/w=2560/d=0, short=r=0/w=0/d=0, drop=r=0/w=0/d=0
     latency   : target=0, window=0, percentile=100.00%, depth=32

Run status group 0 (all jobs):
  WRITE: io=10240MB, aggrb=314736KB/s, minb=314736KB/s, maxb=314736KB/s, mint=33316msec, maxt=33316msec

Disk stats (read/write):
    dm-0: ios=0/5, merge=0/0, ticks=0/10, in_queue=10, util=0.01%, aggrios=56/5, aggrmerge=0/0, aggrticks=0/0, aggrin_queue=0, aggrutil=0.00%
    md1: ios=56/5, merge=0/0, ticks=0/0, in_queue=0, util=0.00%, aggrios=3/13, aggrmerge=24/0, aggrticks=1/6, aggrin_queue=7, aggrutil=0.01%
  sdbi: ios=7/13, merge=49/0, ticks=2/6, in_queue=8, util=0.01%
  sdbj: ios=0/13, merge=0/0, ticks=0/6, in_queue=6, util=0.01%
[root@ceph-client1 ~]#
```

4. On completion, FIO generates a lot of useful information that should be carefully observed. However, at first glance, you might be interested mostly in IOPS and the aggregated bandwidth, which are both highlighted in the previous screen shot.

See also...

▸ *Chapter 2, Working with Ceph Block Device*, where we covered the creation of the Ceph block device in detail

▸ For more information on FIO, visit `https://github.com/axboe/fio`

Ceph admin socket

Ceph components are daemons and Unix-domain sockets. Ceph allows us to use these sockets to query its daemons. The Ceph admin socket is a powerful tool to get and set the Ceph daemon configurations at runtime. With this tool, changing the daemon configuration values becomes a lot easier, rather than changing the Ceph configuration file, which requires the daemon to restart.

To do this, you should log in to the node running the Ceph daemons and execute the `ceph daemon` commands.

How to do it...

There are two ways to access the admin socket:

- Using the Ceph daemon name:

  ```
  $ sudo ceph daemon {daemon-name} {option}
  ```

- Using the absolute path of the socket file; the default location is as follows: /var/run/ceph:

  ```
  $ sudo ceph daemon {absolute path to socket file} {option}
  ```

We will now try to access the Ceph daemon using the admin socket:

1. List all the available admin socket commands for the OSD:

   ```
   # ceph daemon osd.0 help
   ```

2. Similarly, list all the available socket commands for MON:

   ```
   # ceph daemon mon.ceph-node1 help
   ```

3. Check the OSD configuration settings for osd.0:

   ```
   # ceph daemon osd.0 config show
   ```

4. Check the MON configuration settings for mon.ceph-node1:

   ```
   # ceph daemon mon.ceph-node1 config show
   ```

 The Ceph admin daemon allows you to change the daemon configuration settings at runtime. However, these changes are temporary. To permanently change the Ceph daemon configuration, update the Ceph configuration file.

5. To get the current config value for osd, use the _recover_max_chunk parameter for the osd.0 daemon:

   ```
   # ceph daemon osd.0 config get osd_recovery_max_chunk
   ```

6. To change the osd_recovery_max_chunk value for osd.0, execute the following:

   ```
   # ceph daemon osd.0 config set osd_recovery_max_chunk 1000000
   ```

```
[root@ceph-node1 ~]# ceph daemon osd.0 config get osd_recovery_max_chunk
{
    "osd_recovery_max_chunk": "8388608"
}

[root@ceph-node1 ~]#
[root@ceph-node1 ~]# ceph daemon osd.0 config set osd_recovery_max_chunk 1000000
{
    "success": "osd_recovery_max_chunk = '1000000' "
}

[root@ceph-node1 ~]#
```

Using the ceph tell command

Another efficient way to change the runtime configuration for the Ceph daemon without the overhead of logging in to that node is to use the `ceph tell` command:

How to do it...

The `ceph tell` command saves you the effort of logging into the node where the daemon is running. This command goes through the monitor node, so you can execute it from any node in the cluster:

1. To change the `osd_recovery_threads` setting from `osd.0`, execute the following:

   ```
   ceph tell osd.0 injectargs '--osd_recovery_threads=2'
   ```

2. To change the same setting for all the OSDs across the cluster, execute the following:

   ```
   ceph tell osd.* injectargs '--osd_recovery_threads=2'
   ```

3. You can also change multiple settings as a one liner:

   ```
   ceph tell osd.* injectargs '--osd_recovery_max_active=1 --osd_
   recovery_max_single_start=1 --osd_recovery_op_priority=50'
   ```

How it works...

The syntax for the `ceph tell` command is as follows:

```
ceph tell {daemon-type}.{id or *} injectargs --{config_setting_name}
{value}
```

Ceph REST API

Ceph comes with powerful REST API interface access, which allows you to administer your cluster programmatically. It can run as a WSGI application or as a standalone server, listening over the default port 5000. It provides a similar kind of functionality to that of the ceph command-line tool through an HTTP-accessible interface. Commands are submitted as HTTP GET and PUT requests, and the results can be returned in the JSON, XML, and text formats. In this recipe, I will quickly show you how to set up the Ceph REST API and interact with it.

How to do it...

1. Create a user, `client.restapi`, on the Ceph cluster with appropriate access to mon, osd, and mds:

    ```
    # ceph auth get-or-create client.restapi mds 'allow' osd
    'allow *' mon 'allow *' > /etc/ceph/ceph.client.restapi.keyring
    ```

2. Add the following section to the `ceph.conf` file:

    ```
    [client.restapi]
    log file = /var/log/ceph/ceph.restapi.log
    keyring = /etc/ceph/ceph.client.restapi.keyring
    ```

3. Execute the following command to start the `ceph-rest-api` as a standalone webserver in the background:

    ```
    # nohup ceph-rest-api > /var/log/ceph-rest-api &> /var/log/ceph-
    rest-api-error.log &
    ```

     You can also run the `ceph-rest-api` without nohup, suppressing it to background.

4. The `ceph-rest-api` should now be listening on `0.0.0.0:5000`; use `curl` to query the `ceph-rest-api` for the cluster health:

    ```
    # curl localhost:5000/api/v0.1/health
    ```

5. Similarly, check the osd and mon status via `rest-api`:

    ```
    # curl localhost:5000/api/v0.1/osd/stat
    # curl localhost:5000/api/v0.1/mon/stat
    ```

```
[root@ceph-node1 ~]# nohup ceph-rest-api > /var/log/ceph-rest-api & /var/log/ceph-rest-api-error.log &
[1] 3334321
[root@ceph-node1 ~]#
[root@ceph-node1 ~]# curl localhost:5000/api/v0.1/health
HEALTH_OK
[root@ceph-node1 ~]#
[root@ceph-node1 ~]# curl localhost:5000/api/v0.1/osd/stat
    osdmap e989: 9 osds: 9 up, 9 in
[root@ceph-node1 ~]#
[root@ceph-node1 ~]# curl localhost:5000/api/v0.1/mon/stat
e5: 3 mons at {ceph-node1=192.168.1.101:6789/0,ceph-node2=192.168.1.102:6789/0,ceph-node3=192.168.1.103:6789
/0}, election epoch 3648, quorum 0,1,2 ceph-node1,ceph-node2,ceph-node3
[root@ceph-node1 ~]#
```

6. The `ceph-rest-api` has support for most of the Ceph CLI commands. To check the list of available `ceph-rest-api` commands, execute the following:

   ```
   # curl localhost:5000/api/v0.1
   ```

   > This command will return the output in HTML; it will be good if you visit `localhost:5000/api/v0.1` from a web browser to render the HTML for easier readability.

This is a basic implementation of the `ceph-rest-api`. To use it in a production environment, it's a good idea to deploy it in more than one instance with a WSGI application wrapped with a webserver and front ended by load balancers. The `ceph-rest-api` is a scalable, light weight service that allows you to administer your Ceph cluster like a pro.

Profiling Ceph memory

Memory profiling is the process of dynamic program analysis to determine a program's memory consumption and identify ways to optimize it. In this recipe, we discuss how you can use memory profilers on the Ceph daemons for memory investigation.

How to do it...

1. Start the memory profiler on a specific daemon:

   ```
   # ceph tell osd.0 heap start_profiler
   ```

   > To auto-start profiler as soon as the ceph OSD daemon starts, set the environment variable as `CEPH_HEAP_PROFILER_INIT=true`.

2. It's a good idea to keep the profiler running for a few hours so that it can collect as much information related to memory footprint as possible. At the same time, you can also generate some load on the cluster.

3. Next, print heap statistics about the memory footprint that the profiler has collected:

```
# ceph tell osd.0 heap stats
```

```
[root@ceph-node1 ~]# ceph tell osd.0 heap start_profiler
osd.0 started profiler
[root@ceph-node1 ~]#
[root@ceph-node1 ~]# ceph tell osd.0 heap stats
osd.0 tcmalloc heap stats:-----------------------------------------------
MALLOC:      238029520 (  227.0 MiB) Bytes in use by application
MALLOC: +            0 (    0.0 MiB) Bytes in page heap freelist
MALLOC: +     13789912 (   13.2 MiB) Bytes in central cache freelist
MALLOC: +      4454720 (    4.2 MiB) Bytes in transfer cache freelist
MALLOC: +     28537112 (   27.2 MiB) Bytes in thread cache freelists
MALLOC: +      2863264 (    2.7 MiB) Bytes in malloc metadata
MALLOC:    ------------
MALLOC: =    287674528 (  274.3 MiB) Actual memory used (physical + swap)
MALLOC: +      2031616 (    1.9 MiB) Bytes released to OS (aka unmapped)
MALLOC:    ------------
MALLOC: =    289706144 (  276.3 MiB) Virtual address space used
MALLOC:
MALLOC:          13148              Spans in use
MALLOC:            424              Thread heaps in use
MALLOC:           8192              Tcmalloc page size
------------------------------------------------
Call ReleaseFreeMemory() to release freelist memory to the OS (via madvise()).
Bytes released to the OS take up virtual address space but no physical memory.
[root@ceph-node1 ~]#
```

4. You can also dump heap stats on a file that can be used later; by default, it will create the dump file as /var/log/ceph/osd.0.profile.0001.heap:

```
# ceph tell osd.0 heap dump
```

```
[root@ceph-node1 ~]# ceph tell osd.0 heap dump
osd.0 dumping heap profile now.
------------------------------------------------------
MALLOC:      238031808 (  227.0 MiB) Bytes in use by application
MALLOC: +            0 (    0.0 MiB) Bytes in page heap freelist
MALLOC: +     13589456 (   13.0 MiB) Bytes in central cache freelist
MALLOC: +      4258112 (    4.1 MiB) Bytes in transfer cache freelist
MALLOC: +     28964656 (   27.6 MiB) Bytes in thread cache freelists
MALLOC: +      2863264 (    2.7 MiB) Bytes in malloc metadata
MALLOC:    ------------
MALLOC: =    287707296 (  274.4 MiB) Actual memory used (physical + swap)
MALLOC: +      1998848 (    1.9 MiB) Bytes released to OS (aka unmapped)
MALLOC:    ------------
MALLOC: =    289706144 (  276.3 MiB) Virtual address space used
MALLOC:
MALLOC:          13152              Spans in use
MALLOC:            424              Thread heaps in use
MALLOC:           8192              Tcmalloc page size
------------------------------------------------------
Call ReleaseFreeMemory() to release freelist memory to the OS (via madvise()).
Bytes released to the OS take up virtual address space but no physical memory.
[root@ceph-node1 ~]#
```

5. To read this dump file, you will require `google-perftools`:

    `# yum install -y google-perftools`

6. To view the profiler logs:

    `# pprof --text {path-to-daemon}  {log-path/filename}`

    `# pprof --text /usr/bin/ceph-osd /var/log/ceph/osd.0.profile.0001.heap`

7. For granule comparison, generate several profile dump files for the same daemon, and use the Google profiler tool to compare it:

    `# pprof --text --base /var/log/ceph/osd.0.profile.0001.heap /usr/bin/ceph-osd /var/log/ceph/osd.0.profile.0002.heap`

8. Release memory that TCMALLOC has allocated but is not being used by Ceph:

    `# ceph tell osd.0 heap release`

9. Once you are finished, stop the profiler:

    `# ceph tell osd.0 heap stop_profiler`

The Ceph daemons process has matured much, and you might not really need memory profilers for analysis, unless you encounter a bug that's causing memory leaks. You can use the previously discussed procedure to figure out memory issues with the Ceph daemons.

Deploying Ceph using Ansible

In this book, we have discussed deploying Ceph in multiple ways, which includes using Ceph-deploy and the Virtual Storage Manager (VSM). Both of these methods require the manual installation and configuration of the Ceph cluster. However, there exist other tools and methods that can install and deploy Ceph for you in a highly automated fashion. With such tools, you no longer need to type boring commands to deploy Ceph; configuration management tools such as Ansible, Puppet, and Chef, among others, can install and configure the Ceph cluster as you like.

Getting ready

In this recipe, we will go through Ansible, which is a very simple IT automation and configuration management tool; for more information on Ansible, take a look at `http://www.ansible.com/how-ansible-works`. The Ceph ecosystem has a vibrant community around it that has developed ready-to-use Ansible modules for Ceph. We will be using these `ceph-ansible` modules (refer to `https://github.com/ceph/ceph-ansible`) to deploy the Ceph cluster using Ansible.

How to do it...

There are two ways you can deploy Ceph using the `ceph-ansible` modules:

▶ Use the `ceph-ansible` module to first launch a few virtual machines using Vagrant and VirtualBox/VMware, and then install and configure Ceph using Ansible.

▶ Use the `ceph-ansible` module to install and configure the Ceph cluster using the Ansible playbooks on bare metal machines.

In this recipe, we will be using the first method, that is, using the `ceph-ansible` module to launch the VirtualBox virtual machines, and Ansible to install and deploy the Ceph cluster.

> The `ceph-ansible` modules are community focused and mature enough for you to use to deploy Ceph in your production environment. I would like to appreciate the great work done by the `ceph-ansible` community in developing, improving, and maintaining the `ceph-ansible` modules.

1. On your VirtualBox host machine, Git clone the latest `ceph-ansible` module:

```
$ git clone https://github.com/ceph/ceph-ansible.git
$ cd ceph-ansible
```

2. `ceph-ansible` uses Vagrant. For this purpose, it comes with `Vagrantfile`, which tells Vagrant how to spin up VMs. This file requires some variables that are being defined by another file: `vagrant_variables.yml`. The `ceph-ansible` module comes with `vagrant_variables.yml.sample`, which can be used directly with minimal changes:

   ```
   $ cp vagrant_variables.yml.sample vagrant_variables.yml
   ```

3. The default configuration for Vagrant is defined in `vagrant_variables.yml`, and it's good to go. If you like, you can tweak the configuration by editing this file. Since this is a test cluster, we will reduce the number of Ceph monitors from 3 to 1 by changing the `mon_vms` variable to 1.

4. The `ceph-ansible` module forces Vagrant to use Ansible as its provisioner; for this purpose, copy the `site.yml.sample` file as `site.yml` in the same hierarchy:

   ```
   $ cp site.yml.sample site.yml
   ```

5. Finally, we will execute `vagrant up`, which will launch 4 VMs (1 Ceph monitor and 3 Ceph OSDs), and after that, it will start installing and deploying Ceph using the configuration management tool, Ansible:

   ```
   $ vagrant up
   ```

6. VM provisioning and Ceph deployment will take a few minutes; after completion, you should see something like this:

   ```
   PLAY RECAP ********************************************************************
   mon0                       : ok=82   changed=15   unreachable=0   failed=0
   osd0                       : ok=67   changed=9    unreachable=0   failed=0
   osd1                       : ok=67   changed=9    unreachable=0   failed=0
   osd2                       : ok=67   changed=9    unreachable=0   failed=0
   ```

7. After successful completion, you will end up with a running Ceph cluster, installed and configured by Ansible. Log in to the `mon0` node and check your cluster status:

   ```
   $ vagrant ssh mon0
   ```

   ```
   $ sudo ceph -s
   ```

   ```
   vagrant@ceph-mon0:~$ sudo ceph -s
       cluster 4a158d27-f750-41d5-9e7f-26ce4c9d2d45
       health HEALTH_OK
       monmap e1: 1 mons at {ceph-mon0=192.168.42.10:6789/0}
               election epoch 2, quorum 0 ceph-mon0
       mdsmap e2: 0/0/1 up
       osdmap e21: 6 osds: 6 up, 6 in
               flags sortbitwise
        pgmap v27: 320 pgs, 3 pools, 0 bytes data, 0 objects
               212 MB used, 65121 MB / 65333 MB avail
                    320 active+clean
   vagrant@ceph-mon0:~$
   ```

There's more...

This Vagrant setup can be destroyed using `vagrant destroy -f` and recreated anytime within a few minutes in an automated, smart fashion. You would have noticed how easy, quick, and seamless this Ceph deployment was compared to the manual one. For a production environment, one should really consider configuration management tools, such as Ansible, for deploying Ceph, to keep all the nodes at the same state from a configuration point of view. Also, they are very handy for managing large clusters with several tens of nodes.

The ceph-objectstore tool

One of the key features of Ceph is its self-repairing and self-healing qualities. Ceph does this by keeping multiple copies of placement groups across different OSDs and ensures very high probability that you will not lose your data. In a very rare case, you may see the failure of multiple OSDs, where one or more PG replicas are on a failed OSD, and the PG state becomes incomplete, which leads to errors in the cluster health. For granular recovery, Ceph provides a low level PG and object data recovery tool known as `ceph-objectstore-tool`.

How to do it...

The `ceph-objectstore-tool` can be a risky operation, and the command needs to be run either as root or `sudo`. Do not attempt this on a production cluster without engaging the Red Hat Ceph Storage Support, unless you are sure of what you are doing. It can cause irreversible data loss in your cluster.

1. Find incomplete PGs on your Ceph cluster. Using this command, you can get the PG ID and its acting set:

   ```
   # ceph health detail | grep incomplete
   ```

2. Using the acting set, locate the OSD host:

   ```
   # ceph osd find <osd_number>
   ```

3. Log in to the OSD node and stop the OSD that you intend to work on:

   ```
   # service ceph stop <osd_ID>
   ```

The following sections describe the OSD and placement group functions that you can use with the `ceph-objectstore-tool`:

1. To identify the objects within an OSD, execute the following. The tool will output all objects, irrespective of their placement groups:

   ```
   # ceph-objectstore-tool --data-path </path/to/osd> --journal-path
   </path/to/journal> --op list
   ```

2. To identify the objects within a placement group, execute the following:

```
# ceph-objectstore-tool --data-path </path/to/osd> --journal-path
</path/to/journal> --pgid <pgid> --op list
```

3. To list the placement groups stored on an OSD, execute the following:

```
# ceph-objectstore-tool --data-path </path/to/osd> --journal-path
</path/to/journal> --op list-pgs
```

4. If you know the object ID that you are looking for, specify it to find the PG ID:

```
# ceph-objectstore-tool --data-path </path/to/osd> --journal-path
</path/to/journal> --op list <object-id>
```

5. Retrieve information about a particular placement group:

```
# ceph-objectstore-tool --data-path </path/to/osd> --journal-path
</path/to/journal> --pgid <pg-id> --op info
```

6. Retrieve a log of operations on a placement group:

```
# ceph-objectstore-tool --data-path </path/to/osd> --journal-path
</path/to/journal> --pgid <pg-id> --op log
```

Removing a placement group is a risky operation and may cause data loss; use this feature with caution. If you have a corrupt placement group on an OSD that prevents the peering or starting of the OSD service, before removing the placement group, ensure that you have a valid copy of the placement group on another OSD. For precaution, before removing the PG, you can also take a backup of the PG by exporting it to a file:

1. To remove a placement group, execute the following command:

```
# ceph-objectstore-tool --data-path </path/to/osd> --journal-path
</path/to/journal> --pgid <pg-id> --op remove
```

2. To export a placement group to a file, execute the following:

```
# ceph-objectstore-tool --data-path </path/to/osd> --journal-path
</path/to/journal> --pgid <pg-id> --file /path/to/file --op export
```

3. To import a placement group from a file, execute the following:

```
# ceph-objectstore-tool --data-path </path/to/osd> --journal-path
</path/to/journal> --file </path/to/file> --op import
```

4. An OSD may have objects marked as "lost." To list the "lost" or "unfound" objects, execute the following:

```
# ceph-objectstore-tool --data-path </path/to/osd> --journal-path
</path/to/journal> --op list-lost
```

5. To find objects marked as lost for a single placement group, specify `pgid`:

```
# ceph-objectstore-tool --data-path </path/to/osd> --journal-path
</path/to/journal> --pgid <pgid> --op list-lost
```

6. The ceph-objectstore tool is purposely used to fix the PG's lost objects. An OSD may have objects marked "lost." To remove the "lost" setting for the lost objects of a placement group, execute the following:

```
# ceph-objectstore-tool --data-path </path/to/osd> --journal-path
</path/to/journal> --op fix-lost
```

7. To fix lost objects for a particular placement group, specify `pgid`:

```
# ceph-objectstore-tool --data-path </path/to/osd> --journal-path
</path/to/journal> --pgid <pg-id> --op fix-lost
```

8. If you know the identity of the lost object you want to fix, specify the object ID:

```
# ceph-objectstore-tool --data-path </path/to/osd> --journal-path
</path/to/journal> --op fix-lost <object-id>
```

How it works...

The syntax for the ceph-objectstore tool is: `ceph-objectstore-tool <options>`

The values for `<options>` can be as follows:

- `--data-path`: The path to the OSD
- `--journal-path`: The path to the journal
- `--op`: The operation
- `--pgid`: The Placement Group ID
- `--skip-journal-replay`: Use this when the journal is corrupted
- `--skip-mount-omap`: Use this when the `leveldb` data store is corrupted and unable to mount
- `--file`: The path to the file, used with the import/export operation

To understand this tool better, let's take an example: a pool makes two copies of an object, and PGs are located on `osd.1` and `osd.2`. At this point, if failure happens, the following sequence will occur:

1. `osd.1` goes down.
2. `osd.2` handles all the write operations in a degraded state.
3. `osd.1` comes up and peers with `osd.2` for data replication.
4. Suddenly, `osd.2` goes down before replicating all the objects to `osd.1`.
5. At this point, you have data on `osd.1`, but it's stale.

After troubleshooting, you will find that you can read the `osd.2` data from the file system, but its `osd` service is not getting started. In such a situation, one should use the `ceph-objectstore-tool` to export/retrieve data from the failed `osd`. The `ceph-objectstore-tool` provides you with enough capability to examine, modify, and retrieve object data and metadata.

 You should avoid using Linux tools such as `cp` and `rsync` for recovering data from a failed OSD, as these tools do not take all the necessary metadata into account, and the recovered object might be unusable.

Finally, we have reached the end of this chapter and the book as well. I hope your journey with the Ceph cookbook has been informative. You should have learned several concepts around Ceph that will give you enough confidence to operate the Ceph cluster in your environment. Congratulations! You have now attained the next level in Ceph.

Keep Learning, Keep Exploring, Keep Sharing...
Cheers!

Index

Symbol

-f json-pretty option 123

A

admin socket
about 279
accessing 280
Ansible
URL 286
used, for deploying Ceph 286-288
architecture, Ceph cluster
about 8
CephFS 9
Ceph Monitors (MON) 8
Ceph Object Storage Device (OSD) 9
librados 9
RADOS Block Devices (RBD) 9
RADOS Gateway interface (RGW) 9
Reliable Autonomic Distributed Object Store
    (RADOS) 9
architecture, VSM
about 242
controller 242
VSM agent 243
authentication 185-187
authorization
about 185-189
modes 186

B

baseline network performance 269, 270
Block 1
Btrfs 210

C

cache tier
about 232
configuring 236-238
creating 235, 236
pool, creating for 233, 234
read-only mode 233
writeback mode 233
testing 238, 239
Calamari
about 129
backend 130
Ceph nodes, adding 136-138
client packages, building 132, 133
documentation, URL 130
frontend 129
GitHub account, URL 130
master server, building 133-136
on IRC, URL 130
packages, URL 130
server packages, building 130-132
troubleshooting 141-143
used, for monitoring Ceph cluster 138-140

Thank you for buying
Ceph Cookbook

About Packt Publishing

Packt, pronounced 'packed', published its first book, *Mastering phpMyAdmin for Effective MySQL Management*, in April 2004, and subsequently continued to specialize in publishing highly focused books on specific technologies and solutions.

Our books and publications share the experiences of your fellow IT professionals in adapting and customizing today's systems, applications, and frameworks. Our solution-based books give you the knowledge and power to customize the software and technologies you're using to get the job done. Packt books are more specific and less general than the IT books you have seen in the past. Our unique business model allows us to bring you more focused information, giving you more of what you need to know, and less of what you don't.

Packt is a modern yet unique publishing company that focuses on producing quality, cutting-edge books for communities of developers, administrators, and newbies alike. For more information, please visit our website at www.packtpub.com.

About Packt Open Source

In 2010, Packt launched two new brands, Packt Open Source and Packt Enterprise, in order to continue its focus on specialization. This book is part of the Packt open source brand, home to books published on software built around open source licenses, and offering information to anybody from advanced developers to budding web designers. The Open Source brand also runs Packt's open source Royalty Scheme, by which Packt gives a royalty to each open source project about whose software a book is sold.

Writing for Packt

We welcome all inquiries from people who are interested in authoring. Book proposals should be sent to author@packtpub.com. If your book idea is still at an early stage and you would like to discuss it first before writing a formal book proposal, then please contact us; one of our commissioning editors will get in touch with you.

We're not just looking for published authors; if you have strong technical skills but no writing experience, our experienced editors can help you develop a writing career, or simply get some additional reward for your expertise.

Learning Ceph

ISBN: 978-1-78398-562-3   Paperback: 268 pages

A practical guide to designing, implementing, and managing your software-defined, massively scalable Ceph storage system

1. Learn how to unleash the power of Ceph and solve all your storage issues.

2. A comprehensive guide to developing and integrating Ceph with practical tutorials.

3. Get started with the essential information needed to implement a Ceph cluster.

Data Manipulation with R
Second Edition

ISBN: 978-1-78528-881-4   Paperback: 130 pages

Efficiently perform data manipulation using the split-apply-combine strategy in R

1. Perform data manipulation with add-on packages such as plyr, reshape, stringr, lubridate, and sqldf.

2. Learn about factor manipulation, string processing, and text manipulation techniques using the stringr and dplyr libraries.

3. Enhance your analytical skills in an intuitive way through step-by-step working examples.

Please check **www.PacktPub.com** for information on our titles